Eisenhower on Leadership

Ike's Enduring Lessons in Total Victory Management

Alan Axelrod

JOSSEY-BASS
A Wiley Imprint
www.josseybass.com

Published by Jossey-Bass
A Wiley Imprint
989 Market Street, San Francisco, CA 94103-1741   www.josseybass.com

Jossey-Bass books and products are available through most bookstores. To contact Jossey-Bass
directly call our Customer Care Department within the U.S. at 800-956-7739, outside the
U.S. at 317-572-3986, or fax 317-572-4002.

Jossey-Bass also publishes its books in a variety of electronic formats. Some content that
appears in print may not be available in electronic books.

Library of Congress Cataloging-in-Publication Data

Axelrod, Alan, date.
  Eisenhower on leadership: Ike's enduring lessons in total victory management / Alan Axelrod.
     p. cm.
   Includes index.
   ISBN-13: 978-0-7879-8238-6 (cloth)
   ISBN-10: 0-7879-8238-5 (cloth)
  1. Leadership.   2. Management.   3. Eisenhower, Dwight D. (Dwight David),
1890–1969—Military leadership.   4. Eisenhower, Dwight D. (Dwight David), 1890–1969—
Influence.   5. World War, 1939–1945—Campaigns.   6. Generals—United States—
Biography.   I. Title.
   UB210.A94 2006
   355.3'3041—dc22   2006006225

Printed in the United States of America
FIRST EDITION
HB Printing   10 9 8 7 6 5 4 3 2

Contents

Foreword

Peter Georgescu

Intelligence can be defined as the ability to observe seemingly nonexistent patterns. Alan Axelrod has reviewed Dwight David Eisenhower's extraordinarily brilliant deeds in preparation and action on the battlefield and deftly relates them to the business arena.

In a fascinating way, Eisenhower was a "manager" ahead of his time. His strength and style were also extraordinarily well suited for the twenty-first century. In tomorrow's world, businesses will encounter tremendous challenges. The twenty-first century will be defined by global competition and excess supply. The net result will be an explosive increase in the number of enterprises attempting to chase fewer consumers with predominantly commodity products. As a consequence, business will face ferocious price competition and an increasing casualty rate among companies big and small.

In this unforgiving economic environment, Eisenhower's core strengths shine. Clearly and rigorously articulated strategies will become imperative. And every enterprise employee must become a creative contributor, engaged in serving customers and consumers. All egos must be fed yet kept under control, and personal agendas must be sublimated to the common good of the enterprise. This is where Alan Axelrod's *Eisenhower on Leadership* takes on powerful meaning and relevance. The greatest military invasion in human history required all the twenty-first-century business skills. Unambiguous strategies, flexibility combined with decisive action, fanatical commitment to objectives, and ego management (of Patton and Montgomery, for example)—these qualities and skills, among so many others, make Eisenhower a towering leader in our own times. It is no accident that Ike, for all his position and power, had a low-profile persona. He understood the power of "we" and willingly and capably subjugated the "I" word. In page after page of this book, we see alluring results unfold. It is a masterful tale of competence and wisdom told against the backdrop of the most brilliant and fascinating war history of modern times.

Fate enabled me to appreciate a seldom publicized side of Ike Eisenhower—that of the compassionate human being. I was one of two brothers separated from their parents by the capricious events of the post–World War II era. In 1947, my father and mother, two Rumanian nationals, came to the United States to visit my father's headquarters offices in New York City. My dad ran the Ploesti oil fields for ESSO International, and had just come out of being imprisoned by the Nazis as an Allied sympathizer in Rumania during the war. While in New York, the Iron Curtain fell. The Communists, with Soviet support, took over Rumania. Instantly my father was labeled a capitalist and an imperialist, and sentenced in absentia to life imprisonment. Obviously, my parents had to remain in the United States. Back in Rumania, my grandfather, an eighty-year-old elder statesman, was arrested and eventually killed in one of the Communist gulags. My brother and I were incarcerated and placed in a hard labor camp. We worked ten-hour days, six days a week, no schooling. I was nine years old when this ugly chapter started.

Then a miracle happened. The Communists went to see my father in New York, demanding that he spy for the Soviets in return for keeping us alive. After a tortuous day and night, with help from the FBI, my parents refused and went public with the story. A scandal of global proportions exploded. My father had by now become an American citizen, and the Soviet blackmail attempt turned into a political cause célèbre. With the help of Congresswoman Francis Payne Bolton, Ike Eisenhower personally intervened in the case. The story I heard later suggested that President Eisenhower had agreed to trade a couple of Russian spies for my older brother and me, by then a fifteen-year-old.

Indeed, Ike Eisenhower's lessons in leadership took on a very special meaning in my life.

INTRODUCTION

The Soldier as CEO

Dwight David Eisenhower never led a single soldier into battle. Before World War II, he had never even heard a shot fired in anger. His only "combat wound" was the bad knee, weakened by a West Point football injury, that he twisted helping push a jeep out of the Normandy mud. Yet it was Ike Eisenhower who, as supreme Allied commander in Europe, was responsible for leading the greatest military enterprise in history. Millions of American, British and Commonwealth, Free French, and other soldiers, sailors, and airmen looked to him and answered to him in a struggle for nothing less than the salvation of the world.

Eisenhower was a desk soldier, but he always tried to move his desk as close to the action as he could. Although he was an accomplished strategist, having been educated at the Command and General Staff School and the Army War College, the strategies by which the Allies fought World War II were primarily the work of others. It was others, too, who had the job of executing the strategies, others who actually led the troops into battle. Nevertheless, most of the commanders and politicians who made the history of the war as well as the journalists and scholars who subsequently wrote it agreed: Eisenhower was at the heart of victory.

It was, in a favorite Allied phrase, *total victory*. It could be justly said that Eisenhower led that total victory, but it would be even more accurate to say that he *managed* it. For Ike Eisenhower was a new kind of military leader uniquely suited to war on an unprecedented scale, a scale that dwarfed even the "Great War" of 1914–1918. His task was not to lead men into battle but to lead those who led men into battle. As supreme Allied commander, he was the commander of the commanders. Yet nobody knew better than Eisenhower that although he had greater responsibility than any other Allied military leader, he had less absolute authority than any other high-level commander. Whereas any three-star general could order the two-star below him to do this or that, four-star (and, later, five-star) Eisenhower's "subordinates" were the top commanders of the U.S., British (and Commonwealth), and Free French armies. They answered, first and foremost, to their own political leaders as well as to their own military judgment. By consensus of the Allied heads of state, they agreed to be led by Eisenhower, yet he was ultimately answerable to them as well as to all the political leaders to whom they answered. The authority and the weight of the big decisions finally rested on Eisenhower, but those decisions could be arrived at only through a process of compromise and consensus. Although Eisenhower's leadership authority derived from the very highest international levels of government, it had no formal legal basis, and ultimately it was sustained by nothing more or less than the ongoing consent of those he led.

If Ike Eisenhower's situation was unique for a military man, it was—and remains—common enough for leaders in the civilian sphere. His position was analogous to that of a CEO or, indeed, any high-level manager in a large and complex enterprise. It was a position complexly compounded of awesome authority and what can best be described as equally awesome subordination of authority. Both a leader and a servant, he was a servant leader, expected to act as master while answering to many masters. He was, in short, a manager, in the most modern sense of the word, charged with leading, coordinating, prioritizing, judging, and cajoling others toward the common goal of total victory.

That term, *total victory*, also has a significantly modern connotation. Beginning about a quarter century after the end of World War II, Total Quality Management (TQM) became both the mantra and the Holy Grail for a growing number of managers at all levels. Although highly technical tomes have been devoted to TQM, it can be described in a nutshell as a set of systems and policies for doing the right thing, on time, all the time, in an effort to achieve both continual improvement and consistent customer satisfaction. General Eisenhower never heard of TQM, of course, but he did develop a unique approach to the unprecedented command responsibility that had been assigned to him. The purpose of his approach was to ensure that as commander of commanders—effectively the CEO of the European campaign—he and his vast command would do the right thing, on time, all the time. Ike would probably have called this nothing more or less than his "duty" or, even more simply, his "job." We might call it Total Victory Management, and it is what makes the supreme Allied commander so enduring and compelling an example of leadership for managers today.

◆   ◆   ◆

But what qualified this U.S. Army officer above all others for the job? A fair question—it was surely on the minds if not the lips of the 366 officers senior to Ike Eisenhower when General George C. Marshall, the army chief of staff, jumped him over them and into the top command slot.

In contrast to, say, George S. Patton Jr. or Douglas MacArthur, Eisenhower did not possess a distinguished military pedigree. There was nothing in his heritage that "destined" him either to a military career or military greatness. He was born on October 14, 1890, in the little town of Denison, Texas, the third of seven sons of David Jacob and Ida Elizabeth (Stover) Eisenhower. David Jacob tried to make a go of a hardware business in Denison, but, stubborn and restless, he gave up and found instead a menial and dirty job as an "engine wiper" for the Missouri, Kansas & Texas Railway at the rate of $10 a week.

Before Dwight David was a year old, the family left Denison to return to Abilene, Kansas, where they had roots in a Mennonite colony. Here David Jacob installed his wife and children in a tiny rented house near the Union Pacific tracks and found work in a creamery.

The Eisenhower boys became intimate with poverty as well as the austere Mennonite faith, but Dwight David—whom high school classmates nicknamed "Little Ike" to distinguish him from his brother Edgar, dubbed "Big Ike"—earned a reputation as a fine athlete and an indifferent student with a sunny smile and usually happy-go-lucky demeanor that concealed a quick temper liable to come over him, from time to time, like a storm. His apparent lack of interest in his studies also belied an able mind and an extraordinary memory, which eagerly devoured facts and figures as well as ideas.

After graduating from Abilene High School in 1909, Ike went to work for nearly two years at various odd jobs, including a full-time position at his father's employer, the Belle Springs Creamery, to support his brother Edgar's studies at the University of Michigan. Bored with dead-end labor in Kansas, Ike was enthralled by stories about the U.S. Naval Academy his friend and former high school classmate, Everett Edward "Swede" Hazlett Jr., now an Annapolis midshipman, told him. Ike wrote to his congressman and his senator, asking for a nomination to either Annapolis or West Point, and, after taking examinations for both academies, he secured a nomination to West Point from Senator Joseph L. Bristow. Against the wishes of his mother, who held dear the pacifist philosophy of the Mennonite faith, he enrolled in 1911 as a member of the Class of 1915, which would prove to be one of the most remarkable in the history of the institution, producing 59 generals out of 164 graduates.

In that class, Ike Eisenhower was no standout. Although he made a splash as a football player, he tore up his knee in his second year and not only had to quit playing but even faced the possibility of a disability dismissal from the academy. Fortunately, that did not come to pass, and Ike graduated just above the academic middle of the class, at 61st, and very near the bottom in discipline, at 125th out of 164.

As a brand-new second lieutenant, he was posted to Fort Sam Houston in San Antonio, Texas. There he met Mamie Geneva Doud, daughter of a wealthy Denver meat packer, who wintered with his family in an exclusive San Antonio neighborhood. Ike and

Mamie married in 1916 after a quick courtship and would have two sons: Doud Dwight, known as Ikky, who was born in 1917 and succumbed to scarlet fever just four years later, and John Sheldon Doud, born in 1922.

Like other young army officers of the era, Ike longed for a war. Advancement in the peacetime American military proceeded at a glacial pace, and only by distinguishing himself in action could a second lieutenant hope to rise through the ranks. In 1916–1917, President Woodrow Wilson ordered a large-scale "punitive expedition" against the Mexican revolutionary and social bandit Pancho Villa, whose small army had raided a New Mexico border town. Ike hoped to get in on that assignment, but was passed over, and when the United States entered World War I in April 1917, he was not sent to France, as he wanted to be, but was assigned instead to a series of Stateside training missions, including one at a tank training center. In all of these duties, he received high marks from superiors and was promoted to captain, despite his lack of combat experience. At Camp Colt, adjacent to the Gettysburg battlefield in Pennsylvania, he created on a shoestring a highly effective tank training program, an achievement for which he received the Distinguished Service Medal, the highest noncombat award the army could give. But by the time he was in line for duty overseas, the war had ended.

In 1919, after the armistice, Ike reported to Camp Meade, Maryland, as a tank officer. Here he became a close friend of another apostle of the still-emerging armored branch, George S. Patton Jr. Although Patton had fought in France and returned a decorated hero, he did not look down on Ike Eisenhower as a peacetime officer, but regarded him as a kindred spirit who shared his passion for the future of armored warfare. The pair spent long nights discussing everything from the evolving role of the tank and the nitty-gritty of mobile warfare to the mysterious nature of war and warriors. These discussions and the strong friendship with so dashing an officer as Patton had a profound influence on Eisenhower, as did his involvement in an epic public relations venture known as the 1919 transcontinental convoy. During an era when very few roads, let alone highways, existed in the United States, the army decided to stage a demonstration of long-distance overland military transport. On July 7, 1919, eighty-one assorted military vehicles embarked from Washington, D.C., on a 3,251-mile trek to San Francisco. Ike volunteered to serve with the expedition, which arrived in the City by the Bay sixty-two days after it had left the nation's capital. Completed just five days behind schedule, the expedition was counted a spectacular success. The experience impressed Eisenhower with the enormous potential of mechanized warfare, and it also impressed upon him the nation's great need for decent roads. It is no accident that thirty-seven years later, as president of the United States, Dwight David Eisenhower would sign into law the Interstate Highways Act of 1956, authorizing construction of the modern interstate highway system.

As influential as Patton was in the development of Eisenhower as an officer, it was a far less famous man, Brigadier (later Major) General Fox Conner, who served as Ike's most important mentor. Conner was Ike's commanding officer when he served in the Panama Canal Zone from 1922 to 1924. Conner instilled in Eisenhower what West Point, despite formal course work, could not: a love of military and general history. This awakened passion prepared in Ike the commanding perspective from which he viewed and interpreted the unfolding events of World War II. Thanks to the education Conner began, he was better able to appreciate, when the time came, the wants, needs, and points of view of the British and French allies as well as those of the German and Italian enemies.

Conner also had the ear of army high command and, greatly impressed with Ike Eisenhower, he successfully lobbied for his enrollment in the army's Command and General Staff School at Fort Leavenworth, Kansas—the stepping-stone for officers earmarked for senior-level staff duty. Ike's good friend Patton lent him the voluminous notebooks he had compiled when he had been a student at the school, and Patton confided to his diary that it was his notes that propelled Eisenhower, now a major, to the head of his class: first of 275 graduates in 1926.

From the Command and General Staff School Eisenhower went on to the even more prestigious Army War College. Whereas the Fort Leavenworth school trained officers to serve on the staffs of commanding generals, the War College groomed future generals, imparting the art of war at its most advanced and comprehensive level, including how armies are organized, mobilized, supplied, and used in combat. Eisenhower graduated in June 1928 and left for France to serve on the American Battle Monuments Commission. This assignment gave him two opportunities: one was to serve on the staff of the army's most senior commander, John J. Pershing, who had led the American Expeditionary Force in the Great War, and the other was to tour all the battlefields of western Europe and write a guidebook to these places. He concentrated on the sectors in which American troops had fought, but his travels encompassed the entire Western Front. These explorations and the authorial task that accompanied them gave Eisenhower an intimate familiarity with territory and terrain that would, within a matter of years, become a great battlefield yet again—*his* battlefield.

In 1929, Eisenhower returned to the United States and served in the War Department as assistant executive officer to Brigadier General George Van Horn Moseley, principal adviser to the secretary of war. He was also tapped at this time by General Pershing to edit his wartime memoirs, a task that proved largely thankless, except that it introduced him to Lieutenant Colonel George C. Marshall, Pershing's aide-de-camp and one of the army's rapidly rising stars.

In 1933, Ike Eisenhower came into the orbit of yet another key officer when he was appointed principal aide to Douglas MacArthur, U.S. Army chief of staff. From the perspective of an outsider, it was a plum job for a rising young officer, but MacArthur was notoriously difficult. A mercurial autocrat, he kept conspicuously unmilitary hours (rising late, taking long lunches, and retiring even later) and heaped mountains of work on his aides, especially Eisenhower. Ike became indispensable to MacArthur, whom he accompanied to the Philippines in 1935 to assist in the organization of the commonwealth's army. His years with MacArthur were among the most arduous and frustrating of his military career; they also kept him glued to a staff assignment when what he most wanted was to command troops in the field. Staff officers are among the most powerful people in the army, but they rarely reach the highest levels of distinction; serving "in the rear with the gear," they don't get combat medals. Nevertheless, Ike learned extraordinarily valuable lessons under MacArthur in the Philippines. He learned about the nature of power from one of the world's most powerful military figures while simultaneously gaining hard, practical experience in working successfully with a monumentally difficult, ego-driven personality. He also learned firsthand how to build an army from scratch and with the most meager of resources.

MacArthur was loath to release Lieutenant Colonel Eisenhower, who had become his strong right hand, and Manuel Quezon, president of the Philippines, felt very much the same way. But by the autumn of 1938, it became clear to Eisenhower that the attempt of the western European democracies to "appease" Adolf Hitler would ensure rather than prevent war, and to Quezon's pleas that he remain in the Philippines, Eisenhower replied, "I'm a soldier. I'm going home. We're going to go to war and I'm going to be in it." Ike asked to be relieved of duties in Manila effective as of August 1939. Quezon tried to buy him off with a handsome salary from the Philippine treasury. "Mr. President," Ike replied, "no amount of money can make me change my mind." On the day before he left, Eisenhower was guest of honor at a luncheon given by Manuel Quezon, who presented him with the distinguished Service Star of the Philippines in recognition of his "exceptional talents . . . his breadth of understanding [and] his zeal and magnetic leadership."

By the time Eisenhower returned to the United States, World War II had begun in Europe with Hitler's September 1939 invasion of Poland. Ike was thrilled to be appointed both regimental executive officer and commander of the First Battalion, Fifteenth Infantry,

Third Division, at Fort Lewis, Washington, in January 1940. He was training recruits and commanding troops—in the field—at last.

In March 1941, Ike was promoted to full colonel and in June was transferred to Fort Sam Houston, Texas, as chief of staff of the Third Army. In this capacity, promoted yet again, to the rank of temporary brigadier general, he served as one of the principal planners of the Louisiana Maneuvers, which took place in September 1941. The most ambitious war games the U.S. Army had—or has—ever staged, they involved more than half a million troops, and Eisenhower's key role in them drew the attention of army chief of staff Marshall. When the Japanese attack on Pearl Harbor propelled the United States into World War II on December 7, 1941, General Marshall summoned Eisenhower to Washington, D.C. There Marshall quickly summed up the catastrophic situation in the Pacific—the fleet at Pearl Harbor smashed, Wake Island under heavy attack, Guam fallen, the possessions of Britain and the Netherlands fallen or falling, and the Philippines under attack and about to be invaded. This summary concluded, he posed one question: "What should be our general course of action?"

It was, Ike realized, a question that defied practical answer. But after asking for a few hours to formulate a reply, he returned to Marshall's office to lay out what he believed was the only immediately viable course: do everything militarily possible, no matter how little, by establishing a base of operations in Australia. In his postwar memoir, *Crusade in Europe*, Ike recalled his rationale: "The people of China, of the Philippines, of the Dutch East Indies will be watching us. They may excuse failure but they will not excuse abandonment." Marshall agreed, and he recognized in Eisenhower an officer who was willing and able to provide realistic solutions even to apparently hopeless situations—hard answers rather than evasive excuses or alibis. Marshall named Eisenhower assistant chief of the Army Operations Division, a post in which he served through half of June 1942, having been jumped in rank, as of March 1942, to major general.

Marshall assigned Eisenhower to prepare strategy for an Allied invasion of Europe, a plan that would, however, be put on hold as the Americans yielded to British prime minister Winston Churchill's proposal to fight Germany and Italy first in North Africa, then step off from there to assault Europe by way of what Churchill called its "soft underbelly," mainland Italy and the Mediterranean coast via Sicily. That Ike's plan was temporarily shelved did not mean he was sidelined. Quite the contrary. In May, Ike was sent to London to study issues related to joint defense. On June 15, 1942, General Marshall chose him over 366 more senior officers to be commander of all U.S. troops in the European theater of operations (which included North Africa), and the following month came promotion to temporary lieutenant general.

On the eve of America's entry into World War II, Eisenhower had been so obscure an officer that he was widely misidentified in press reports of the Louisiana war games as "Lt. Col. D. D. Ersenbeing." Now, less than a year later, he was America's top commander in North Africa and Europe. As chief of staff, George C. Marshall was solely responsible for choosing a top theater commander, and what he saw in Ike Eisenhower was a unique combination of an aptitude for strategy and strategic planning, a talent for logistics and organization, and an extraordinary ability to work with others—to get along with them, to persuade them, to mediate among them, to direct them, to encourage them, and to correct them. And there was more. Ike was no small-talker or glad-hander. He was all business. Yet he possessed an infectious smile that seemed to broadcast a combination of humility, friendliness, and unassailable optimism, no matter the odds against his side. Did this reflect his true personality? Some who believed they knew him well said it most certainly did, but others, who probably knew him even better, said that Dwight D. Eisenhower was actually a difficult man with a hair-trigger temper, a man who often doubted himself, yet a man who had somehow learned to set these traits and doubts aside, to submerge them in the appearance of sunny geniality and self-confident optimism. Ultimately, the issue of whether Eisenhower the commander, the manager, and the leader was the same as Eisenhower the man matters very little. All that really matters is that he brought to bear in his command decisions and leadership style all the elements Marshall saw and recognized as indispensable in an officer given ultimate responsibility for the direction of a mission as complex as it was desperate.

◆ ◆ ◆

On November 8, 1942, Eisenhower commanded the commencement of Operation Torch, the Allied invasion of North Africa, which was successfully completed in May 1943, despite some serious errors and setbacks, for which Eisenhower willingly assumed responsibility. During the North African campaign, Ike made the difficult and controversial decision to work with the Vichy French admiral Jean-François Darlan rather than treat him as an enemy. Although the decision brought a storm of protest from some Allied officials, it received the full support of President Franklin D. Roosevelt and doubtless saved Allied lives.

Having been promoted to temporary four-star general in February 1943, Eisenhower next commanded the amphibious assault on Sicily (July 1943), followed by the invasion of the Italian mainland (September 1943). The fighting in Italy would prove heartbreakingly costly and would not end until very near the end of the war in Europe; however, on December 24, 1943, Ike had to leave others to direct the Italian campaign, as he was appointed supreme commander of Allied expeditionary forces and placed in command of Operation Overlord, the invasion of Europe via the English Channel. In January, he arrived in London to finalize plans for what the world would come to call D-Day, the largest, most dangerous, and most consequential invasion in the history of warfare.

A significant portion of this book is devoted to the many leadership decisions Ike had to make during this dauntingly complex operation, beginning with the calculated risk of launching the invasion on June 6, 1944, to take advantage of a very narrow window of acceptable weather during a period of unanticipated storms. At stake were the lives of more than 156,000 troops in the initial assault and, indeed, the very outcome of a war between the forces of democratic civilization and Nazi totalitarianism.

The success of the Normandy landings was only the beginning of what Ike himself called (in the title of his postwar memoir) the "crusade in Europe." All decisions relating to the day-to-day conduct of the campaign as well as its overall objectives either required his judgment or rested entirely with him. He had to confront not only the Allies' common enemy, Germany, but, often, elements within the Allied forces—political leaders as well as generals—whose national or personal goals differed sufficiently to create perpetual friction if not outright ruptures. The alliance that defeated the forces of Adolf Hitler was the most complex and difficult in history. While others determined political and diplomatic policy, it was Ike's responsibility to implement policy in ways that furthered rather than hindered the war effort. He had to harmonize conflicting ideologies as well as conflicting personalities. He also had to reconcile his own constitutional and personal allegiance to the United States with the requirements of the international alliance. It was a staggeringly difficult task of leadership and management.

Militarily, once the invasion beachheads had been firmly secured and the principal Allied forces had broken through the treacherous *bocage*, or hedgerow country, of Normandy, the invasion of Europe proceeded with remarkable speed. By the end of 1944, Ike faced a new problem. He called it "victory fever," a sense of invulnerability born of success, which readily led to complacence. It was victory fever that contributed to American vulnerability in the Ardennes when the Germans, supposedly beaten, launched a devastating counterattack, dubbed the Battle of the Bulge, in December. Ike's steadiness and rapid response during this crisis converted a potential Allied catastrophe into the beginning of the culminating phase of Allied total victory.

After winning the Battle of the Bulge, the Allies crossed the Rhine on March 7, 1945. Advances on all fronts resulted at last in the surrender of Germany on May 7–8, 1945, bringing the war in Europe to an end. Ike was hailed as a hero, although he also faced fierce and bitter criticism for what was only partly his decision: to allow the Soviet Red Army to capture Berlin. The political aspect of this decision was the responsibility of the Allied heads of state (who had promised Berlin to the Soviets at the Yalta conference of February 1945), but, militarily, Ike agreed: Berlin was best left to the Russians, who were closer, who had more troops, and, even more important, who were willing to lose large numbers of men in order to capture the Nazi capital. Ike's objective was never to take territory or take cities. (It was the politicians who had ordered him to liberate Paris on August 25, 1944—he wanted to pass it by.) His objective was simply to destroy the enemy army. Like Ulysses S. Grant in the Civil War, Eisenhower reasoned that it is only by killing the soldiers opposing you that you win the war. And that had little to do with capturing land or liberating towns.

By the end of 1944, Ike Eisenhower had been promoted to General of the Army, the rarely bestowed five-star rank, and in June 1945, he returned to the United States on a visit. Whatever many might have felt about Berlin, all that was demonstrated during his homecoming was the boundless gratitude of a nation. Ike was universally greeted as a hero. He announced his intention to retire from the army, but delayed retirement when, in November 1945, President Harry S. Truman named him to replace General Marshall as army chief of staff.

In February 1948, Ike did step down from active service and began work on his masterful memoir, *Crusade in Europe*. He accepted appointment as president of Columbia University, then, in December, began a three-month stint as military consultant to the nation's first secretary of defense, James Forrestal. Beginning in 1949, he served informally as chairman of the newly created Joint Chiefs of Staff, and after the Korean War began, Ike accepted, at the request of President Truman on December 18, 1950, the position of supreme commander of the North Atlantic Treaty Organization (NATO). For the next fifteen months, until he stepped down in June 1952 to begin his campaign as Republican candidate for president of the United States, General Eisenhower used his hard-won skills as a military leader and manager to forge an effective and united military organization consisting of the United States and the nations of western Europe. Throughout the long Cold War, NATO served as a defense and deterrent against Soviet aggression.

Dwight David Eisenhower was elected president on November 4, 1952, and served two terms, leading a prosperous nation that had become one of the world's two great—and mortally opposed— superpowers. After completion of his second term in January 1961, Congress ceremoniously reinstated the five-star rank he had resigned when he assumed the presidency. On March 28, 1969, the former supreme Allied commander and chief executive died at Walter Reed Army Hospital, Washington, D.C., and was buried with full military honors in Abilene, Kansas.

A Note on Sources

The major sources for Dwight D. Eisenhower's leadership insights quoted in this book are his postwar memoir, *Crusade in Europe* (Baltimore: Johns Hopkins University Press, 1997; originally published 1948), and his voluminous wartime correspondence, diary entries, memoranda, orders, and other papers, which are collected and reproduced in a five-volume series—Alfred D. Chandler Jr. (ed.), *The Papers of Dwight David Eisenhower: The War Years* (Baltimore: Johns Hopkins University Press, 1970). Quotations from other sources are cited where they occur in the text.

1

TIME OF TRIAL

Ike and America Enter the War

Although the United States was still at peace, World War II was under way in Europe when Eisenhower returned to the United States after long service as Douglas MacArthur's right-hand man in the Philippines. In January 1940, he was appointed both regimental executive officer and commander of the First Battalion, Fifteenth Infantry, Third Division, at Fort Lewis, Washington. In March 1941, he was promoted to full colonel and in June transferred to Fort Sam Houston, Texas, as chief of staff of the Third Army. Promoted yet again, to the rank of temporary brigadier general, he became one of the chief planners of the Louisiana Maneuvers, which took place in September 1941. Ike's role in this vast and crucial exercise drew the attention of George C. Marshall, the army chief of staff, and when Pearl Harbor thrust the nation into the war on December 7, 1941, Marshall summoned Ike to the War Department in Washington, D.C., and named him assistant chief of the Army War Plans Division, a post in which he served midway through June 1942, having been jumped in rank, as of March 1942, to major general.

Ike's work in the War Department during the dismal, desperate, and chaotic early months of America's involvement in the war consisted of formulating strategies for national military survival as well as for an eventual counteroffensive intended to convert defeat into victory. Assigned to prepare plans for an Allied invasion of Europe, he then had to switch to planning for the invasion of North Africa instead, because President Roosevelt agreed with Winston Churchill, the British prime minister, that the best way to approach a counteroffensive in Europe was via the Mediterranean, starting with the conquest of North Africa.

In May 1942, Marshall sent Ike to London to work on strategy and policy for joint defense, and on June 15, 1942, Marshall jumped him over 366 more senior officers to become commander of all U.S. troops in the European theater of operations (which included North Africa). After promotion to temporary lieutenant general in July 1942, Eisenhower was named to command Operation Torch, the Allied invasion of French North Africa.

Launched on November 8, 1942, Operation Torch was the first major Allied offensive of the war. Eisenhower remarked that his job, leading a diverse and often disputatious Anglo-American high command, was like "trying to arrange the blankets smoothly over several prima donnas in the same bed."

From these first, monumentally difficult phases of his World War II career emerged a leadership philosophy that is reflected in passages of Eisenhower's extraordinary postwar memoir, *Crusade in Europe*, and found within the mountains of secret cables, dispatches, official memoranda, diary notations, and personal letters he wrote from the beginning of 1940 to November 1942.

◆ ◆ ◆

Lesson 1

Compromise and Management

For those on staff work the days became ceaseless rounds of planning, directing, inspecting; compromising what had been commanded with what could be done.

—*Crusade in Europe*

The U.S. Army entered its first two offshore wars wholly unprepared. In 1898, it fought the Spanish-American War with a tiny regular army force, supplemented by militia and volunteers, and although valiant in combat, the army fell all over itself in the clumsily improvised process of shipping out to Cuba, Puerto Rico, and the Philippines. In April 1917, the United States entered World War I with a professional full-time army of just 133,000 officers and men, vastly smaller than all but the smallest armies of the smallest nations involved in the war. It is a myth that the Japanese attack on Pearl Harbor, December 7, 1941, caught the United States similarly unprepared. Ever since Hitler invaded Poland in September 1939, President Roosevelt had begun preparing the nation for war, first by gearing up production of materiel and increasing military budgets, then, on September 16, 1940, by signing the Selective Service Act, the first peacetime military draft in American history.

In January 1940, Ike returned to the United States from a long assignment in the Philippines on the staff of Douglas MacArthur. He was tasked with training and commanding troops at Fort Lewis, Washington. The draft had not yet commenced, and neither had the buildup of equipment and weapons. Ike, like other field-grade officers at this point in time, was faced with what seemed the certainty of war and the job of preparing a woefully inadequate number of underequipped troops to fight it. This was hardly a comfortable position, but, as it turned out, it provided extraordinarily valuable experience in executing the key leadership and management task of "compromising what had been commanded with what could be done."

Even at the height of the campaign in Europe, as the Allies advanced into Germany and Eisenhower commanded millions, he would find that this cardinal rule still applied. For in war, there are never enough men, never enough equipment or supplies, and what can actually be done has always to be compromised with what is commanded.

What is true of war is true as well of every complex, high-stakes enterprise. There is always the necessity of compromise. That is the very essence and art of management: a balancing of expectations and desires against resources and results. Economists call it working within the principle of scarcity. Military leaders, if they're as good as Eisenhower was, call it reality, and they are grateful for having been trained to deal with it.

◆ ◆ ◆

Lesson 2

Create Satisfaction

I determined that my answer should be short, emphatic, and based on reasoning in which I honestly believed.

—Crusade in Europe

Just days after Pearl Harbor, General George C. Marshall, the army chief of staff, summoned Ike Eisenhower to the War Department in Washington. After briefing Ike for twenty minutes on the disasters of the Pacific theater, describing what seemed at the moment a situation overwhelming in its hopelessness, Marshall stopped, then asked Eisenhower a single question: "What should be our general line of action?"

Struggling to maintain a poker face, Ike replied, "Give me a few hours."

"All right," Marshall said and, with that, dismissed Eisenhower.

Ike took the problem back to the desk that had been assigned him in the War Department's Operations Division. His first thought was, "[I]f I were to be of any service to General Marshall in the War Department, I would have to earn his confidence." This meant, he reasoned, that "the logic of this, my first answer, would have to be unimpeachable, and the answer would have to be prompt." With that, a "curious echo from long ago came to my aid."

Ike recalled something his beloved mentor, Major General Fox Conner, had said to him shortly after World War I. It was that another war was inevitable and, when the United States got into that war, it would do so with allies. "Systems of single command will have to be worked out," Conner had said to Eisenhower. "We must insist on individual and single responsibility—leaders will have to learn how to overcome nationalistic considerations in the conduct of campaigns. One man who can do it is Marshall—he is close to being a genius."

The memory of this discussion prompted Ike to conclude that whatever answer he gave to Marshall "should be short, emphatic, and based on reasoning in which I honestly believed." Why? "No oratory, plausible argument, or glittering generality would impress anyone entitled to be labeled genius by Fox Conner."

Before even tackling the daunting problem Marshall had posed, Ike thought about the true significance of the question—that it was as much Marshall's way of testing him as it was a question about the conduct of the war—and he thought about what kind of answer would satisfy Marshall—what product would satisfy this particular customer. He summoned up the most important fact he knew about Marshall: that a man Eisenhower deeply admired regarded Marshall as very nearly a genius. To pass the test Marshall had posed, Ike would have to earn the chief's confidence. Because Marshall was a genius (or very nearly so), Ike would have to earn his confidence with a short and thoroughly reasoned answer.

What he came up with was a plan to do whatever was possible, little as that might at the moment be, lest the endangered Allies in the theater give up hope and write off not only themselves but also the U.S. military: "They may excuse failure but they will not excuse abandonment."

"I agree with you," Marshall said when Eisenhower presented his report to him. "Do your best to save them."

George Marshall was famous for his laconic manner. A man of very few words, he was not given to praise. But in this exchange— a question posing the impossible and eliciting a brief, impeccably reasoned answer proposing the possible—was born the confidence that would soon move Marshall to appoint Eisenhower supreme commander of U.S. forces in North Africa and Europe and, later, motivate his nomination of Ike as commander of the Normandy invasion and supreme commander of all Allied forces in Europe.

The right answer is the one that satisfies all the needs of the person who asks the question.

◆ ◆ ◆

Lesson 3

The Sins of Leadership (According to General Marshall)

[H]e . . . gave clear indication of the types of men who in his opinion were unsuited for high position.

—Crusade in Europe

During his time in the War Department, Ike worked directly for George C. Marshall, the army chief of staff, and he dedicated himself to learning all he could from Marshall, paying particular attention to what his boss considered the cardinal sins of poor leaders.

Marshall could not tolerate "any effort to 'pass the buck,' especially to him." Ike often heard him say that he could get "a thousand men to do detailed work but too many were useless in responsible posts because they left to him the necessity of making every decision."

Although Marshall wanted "his principal assistants [to] think and act on their own conclusions within their own spheres of responsibility," he had "nothing but scorn" for the micromanager. If you "worked yourself to tatters on minor details," you could have "no ability to handle the more vital issues."

Marshall could not abide the "truculent personality—the man who confused firmness and strength with bad manners and deliberate discourtesy."

Marshall avoided those with "too great a love of the limelight."

He was "irritated" by those "who were too stupid to see that leadership in conference, even with subordinates, is as important as on the battlefield."

He "could not stand the pessimist—the individual who was always painting difficulties in the darkest colors." Marshall tried to avoid delegating responsibility to pessimists and "would never assign an officer to a responsible position unless he believed that the man was an enthusiastic supporter of the particular project and confident of its outcome."

◆ ◆ ◆

Lesson 4

Refuse to Consider Failure

[General] Marshall's . . . utter refusal to entertain any thought of failure infused the whole War Department with energy and confidence.

—Crusade in Europe

Some leaders consider themselves realists because they dare to face the possibility of failure. Following the example of George C. Marshall, however, Ike Eisenhower simply refused to entertain any thought of failure. This was not an exercise in self-delusion, but a means of preparing himself and his command for total victory. Factor out the thought of failure, and you are left with energy and confidence.

As a student of history (thanks to the tutelage of Major General Fox Conner), Eisenhower must have read the story of how Hernán Cortés, the Spanish conqueror of the Aztec empire, arrived in the New World, then bored holes in the hulls of his ships (attributing the damage to shipworm) so that he and his men could entertain no notion of returning home anytime soon—that is, they could afford no thought of failure. As a leadership tactic, banishing the very option of failure worked well for Cortés, just as it would serve Ike Eisenhower as he commanded the greatest alliance in the greatest struggle the world had ever seen.

◆ ◆ ◆

Lesson 5

Reduce and Clarify

It is a characteristic of military problems that they yield to nothing but harsh reality; things must be reduced to elemental simplicity and answers must be clear, almost obvious.

—Crusade in Europe

World War II was all about big numbers and staggeringly complex situations perpetually obscured by the fog of war. At no time was the situation more overwhelming to the Allies than it was early in the war, when Germany (and, in the Pacific, Japan) was a juggernaut and everything the Allies needed was in critically short supply. Eisenhower came into his job at the Operations Division with the conviction that it did no good to gape at the vastness and confusion of it all. "It profited nothing to wail about unpreparedness," he observed. Instead, the first task was to drill down to "harsh reality," to reduce everything to "elemental simplicity," much as one might approach a dauntingly complicated mathematical equation. Find the core, simplify the problem by identifying its elements, then formulate the answers to these.

Ike accepted the fact that many problems were complex, but he rejected the proposition that the answers to them had to be commensurately complex. If they truly addressed the elements of even the most complex problems, the right answers were almost always the simplest and most obvious. The first job of problem solving in a position of leadership is to identify the elemental reality of the situation. How do you tell when you've reached it? It looks, sounds, and feels harsher than anything swirling about and surrounding it.

◆　◆　◆

Lesson 6

Do the Hard Work

I have been here about three weeks and this noon I had my first luncheon outside of the office. Usually it is a hot-dog sandwich and a glass of milk.

—Letter to LeRoy Lutes,
December 31, 1941

To lead, Ike Eisenhower quickly discovered, is to work. After about three weeks in the War Department in Washington, he wrote to Brigadier General LeRoy Lutes, a friend who had been summoned to an assignment in the department. Eisenhower described his work routine "just to give you an inkling as to the kind of mad house you are getting into." Observing that it "is now eight o'clock New Year's Eve," Ike explained that he had a "couple hours' work ahead of me, and tomorrow will be no different from today."

Lutes's wife was in a hospital in California. "The situation with respect to your wife is a most distressing one," Ike sympathized. "I am as sorry as I can be and even more sorry that I can offer you no constructive suggestion in your problem."

Such is war; such is leadership. It entails work, and it entails sacrifice. "This letter does not sound too encouraging but it is a bald statement of fact." To commit to the work is perhaps the very first decision a leader has to make. The only way to make that decision is to base it on a "bald statement of fact," regardless of how little comfort the facts may offer.

◆ ◆ ◆

Lesson 7

Capture All Decisions

[T]he staff was able to translate every decision and agreement into appropriate action and to preserve such records as were necessary.

—Crusade in Europe

For most of his career up to World War II, Ike Eisenhower had been a staff officer, a position that put him in the middle layer of the army's command structure. Strategic decisions were made at the command level, and they were carried out by the officers and troops in the field, but it was the job of the layer in between, the staff officers, to ensure that the commands were properly translated into "action items" and to monitor the execution of those action items. Efficient staff work ensures an effective interface between the highest command levels and the personnel in the field. Faulty staff work creates delay, misunderstanding, and disaster.

Ike long regretted having been slotted as a staff officer. He wanted to lead troops. But now, elevated from assistant chief to chief of the Operations Division in the War Department, he found that his staff experience proved vital to him. Out of the innumerable conferences held in his office, Ike developed a host of decisions, "many minor but some of great significance." Ike understood that making the decisions was only a fraction of his job. Each decision "required action at some point within the Operations Division or the War Department or at some remote point where troops . . . were stationed." No manager can make decisions and then merely assume (or, worse, hope) that the appropriate actions will follow. "To insure that none [of the decisions] would be forgotten and that records for subordinates would always be available, we had resorted to an automatic recording system." Ike took this system to the next level by a "complete wiring of my war room with Dictaphones so placed to pick up every word uttered in the room." A secretary "instantly transcribed them into notes and memoranda [so that] the staff was able to translate every decision and agreement into appropriate action and to preserve such records as were necessary."

In large part, leadership is a stream of decisions, some reached alone, many in collaboration and conversation with others. It is essential to create a working environment in which all decisions are captured, put into "actionable" form, and distributed to those who must act on them. A leader's job does not end when the decisions have been made.

◆ ◆ ◆

Lesson 8

Struggle to the Same Page

We've got to quit wasting resources all over the world—and still worse—wasting time.

—Personal note, January 22, 1942

It is not easy being thrown into a world war. Exasperated after about a month and a half in the War Department, Ike scribbled a note to himself: "The struggle to secure adoption by all concerned of a common concept of strategical objectives is wearing me down." The problem was that "Everybody is too much engaged with small things of his own—or with some vague idea of larger political activity to realize what we are doing—rather *not* doing." We can practically hear Ike's anguish: "We've got to go to Europe and fight—and we've got to quit wasting resources all over the world—and still worse—wasting time."

What saved him from panic and despair? Character, doubtless, but also the understanding that the very first struggle any leader faces is to get everyone on the same page. Once everyone has agreed on common objectives and strategies, the job may remain hard as hell, but the energies of all will be focused, and success will become a realistic hope. Depending on where and when you rise to responsibility in an organization, your first leadership task may well be to pull common purpose from a welter of conflicting needs, desires, and demands. In the meantime, the cacophony can be deafening, the anguish very real.

◆ ◆ ◆

Lesson 9

Identify the Doable

[T]here are just three "musts" for the Allies this year.

—Personal note, March 10, 1942

On March 10, 1942, Ike scribbled one of the few genuinely optimistic notes he made early in the war. "Gradually," he wrote, "some
of the people with whom I have to deal are coming to agree with
me that there are just three 'musts' for the Allies this year—hold
open the line to England and support her as necessary; keep Russia
in the war as an active participant; hold the India-Middle East but-
tress between the Japs and Germans."

There was plenty to be worried about during the early months
after America's entry into World War II, but what most disturbed
Ike was the Allies' lack of focus, which caused a lot of wasteful
wheel spinning and squandering of resources. He saw his first task
as defining initial, crucial priorities that could actually be accomplished. These were the steps necessary to keep alive the Allied
prospects for ultimate victory.

When you are faced with the demands of an apparently overwhelming crisis, identify and define what must be done and can be
done to keep everyone in the game. The first choices to be made are
those that enable other choices down the road. Those critical first
choices are the essence of survival as well as the means of ultimately
converting survival into triumph.

◆ ◆ ◆

Lesson 10

Stay in the Game

*All other operations must be considered in the highly desirable
rather than in the mandatory class.*

> —Secret memorandum to George C.
> Marshall, March 25, 1942

Leadership is often about putting out fires. That can be hard enough
when a single blaze is raging, but it can be overwhelming in the midst
of multiple conflagrations. Such was World War II when the United
States was thrust into it.

"The first question that must be definitely decided," Eisenhower wrote to his boss, army chief of staff General George C. Marshall, "is the region or theater in which the first major offensive effort of the United Powers [the Allies] must take place." Ike explained that from this initial decision all others would flow. Making the decision would require the very difficult step of at least temporarily turning away from other areas that might be under threat or even under direct attack. Ike was aware, however, that concentration on one area could not come at the total neglect of others: "Another question that must be decided upon . . . is that of the vital defensive tasks we must now perform in order that, pending the time when a major offensive effort can be staged, the strategic situation will not deteriorate so badly as to render all future effort practically futile."

In this crisis of multiple conflagrations, it was necessary to decide, first, where aggressive action could best and most quickly be employed, even while ensuring that defensive steps were taken to prevent the disintegration of the overall situation into utter hopelessness.

With the basic strategic task thus laid out, Ike refined the problem: "We are principally concerned in preventing the arise of any situation that will automatically give the Axis an overwhelming tactical superiority; or one under which its productive potential becomes greater than our own." He concluded that the "loss of either England or Russia would probably give the Axis an immediate ability to nullify any of our future efforts. The loss of the Near East or of England would probably give the Axis a greater productive potential than our own." This being the case, the "immediately important tasks, aside from the protection of the American continent, are the security of England, the retention of Russia in the war as an active ally, and the defense of the Middle East."

Thus Ike gave the war effort a focus. Vast as this focus was, it ruled out attending to a lot of the other fires, most obviously Japan and the Pacific. Because the United States had been brought into the war by the Japanese surprise attack on Pearl Harbor on December 7, 1941, most Americans were eager for immediate vengeance against the Japanese. It was a natural impulse. Ike recognized, however, that Japan was not the most pressing issue. "All other operations," including any against Japan, "must be considered in the highly desirable rather than in the mandatory class." It would take great collective discipline to forsake the emotional drive for revenge in order to focus first on the "mandatory" objectives, but discipline—the disciplined application of limited resources—is precisely what management and leadership are all about. (In any event, as Ike explained, allocating some major assets to the Middle East would, indirectly, act against Japan, as "defending the Middle East . . . prevents the junction of our two most powerful enemies"—Japan and Germany—even while it "renders a definite support to the left flank of the Russian armies and keeps open an important supply line.")

Definition and focus are the principal bulwarks against the chaos of multiple fires. First decide what must be done first. Various as they may be, these initial mandatory tasks have as their common objective the preservation of the future. They make it possible to stay in the game, to buy time for the preparation of other operations. Fail to address a mandatory task right away, and you may lose the future, creating circumstances that make further operations either impossible or futile.

◆ ◆ ◆

Lesson 11

Make Now the Priority

Plans for the future could not take priority over the needs of the day.

—*Crusade in Europe*

Management leaders are by nature and definition planners, the helmsmen of an enterprise, whose job it is to see far ahead. Yet as any helmsman knows, the only job more important than seeing far ahead is seeing whatever is right in front of you. Fail in this, and distance hardly matters. Important as the future is, it does not in fact exist, whereas the needs of today are present, real, and often as hard and sharp as rocks. "Where there is no vision, the people perish" goes the proverb, but it is equally fatal to allow vision to obscure plain sight.

◆ ◆ ◆

Lesson 12

Shut Off All Business

My Father was buried today. I've shut off all business and visitors for thirty minutes—to have that much time, by myself, to think of him.

—Personal note, March 12, 1942

David Jacob Eisenhower died on March 10, 1942. "I have felt terribly," Ike wrote in his notebook on March 11. "I should like so much to be with my Mother these few days. But we're at war! And war is not soft—it has no time to indulge even the deepest and most sacred emotions." Yet Ike realized that even in the midst of war, he needed time—by himself—"to think of him." He did not allow himself much, just thirty minutes, but they were minutes absolutely his and his alone, from which all business and visitors were barred.

Even the most dedicated leader requires a compartment of private space. Its dimensions need not be defined so much by quantity as by quality. A brief interval of genuinely personal time is of greater value than an extended "working" vacation. "War is not soft." Ike understood that better than most. It affords "no time to indulge even the deepest and most sacred emotions." Yet he also understood that *some* time had to be found for those emotions, and he insisted on giving himself thirty minutes that would otherwise have been devoted to war. This was the unselfish gift of a wise and effective leader.

◆ ◆ ◆

Lesson 13

We Have Got to Win

We have got a fearful job to perform and everybody has got to unify to do it.

> —Letter to his brother Edgar Eisenhower,
> March 30, 1942

"We have got to win," Ike wrote to his brother, "and any individual in this country . . . that doesn't do his very best to fulfill his part of the job is an enemy."

It was a powerful statement made even more forceful by Ike's understanding of the consequences of *not* winning: "If they should win we would really learn something about slavery, forced labor and loss of individual freedom."

No enterprise should be undertaken without a desire and commitment to win. An effective leader builds and amplifies that desire and that commitment by selling the benefits of winning as well as the consequences of losing. Without this context, victory is a hollow word and winning an empty concept.

◆ ◆ ◆

Lesson 14

Streamline

Reduce equipment of all organizations in order to minimize demands on shipping.

> —Secret memorandum, April 20, 1942

Ike issued a memorandum calling for "a recommendation to the Chief of Staff" to direct the commanding generals of "the Ground Forces, Air Forces, and Services of Supply" to "restudy . . . the problem of excluding . . . all equipment not deemed absolutely essential to the execution of basic missions." The problem was not a shortage of equipment but a shortage of shipping: the means of delivering the equipment. Accordingly, Ike called for the streamlining of equipment requirements, paring supplies down to essentials and pooling additional equipment to be issued only "to meet special situations to be exploited to the utmost."

There is a natural tendency to load yourself and your organization with more equipment than may actually be necessary. Not only is this directly wasteful of resources, but to the degree that it actually impedes action—slows people down or requires additional resources for the maintenance of the excess equipment—overloading can be even more harmful.

Streamline. Determine minimum requirements and operate as close to those minimums as possible, provided that everyone has access to what he or she needs to "meet special situations" or exploit opportunities when they present themselves. The majority of complex organizations operate most efficiently by adopting some form of a "just-in-time" approach, a system that aims to deliver needed equipment when it is needed and neither before nor after. Such a system ensures that no resources are wasted handling unnecessary materials, yet no opportunities are lost for lack of necessary equipment. The just-in-time approach requires dynamic, proactive management, but it reduces overhead and increases efficiency, allowing people to focus on the task at hand rather than all the surplus equipment around them.

◆ ◆ ◆

Lesson 15

Invest in People

I try to pick bright boys who learn rapidly.

—Letter to Dabney Elliott, May 8, 1942

While Ike was laboring in the War Department, before he became supreme Allied commander, he had continually to vie with other officers to secure the best subordinate personnel. He soon discovered a dilemma. If he chose senior personnel—at the level of colonel—he was certain to obtain men of proven experience, but he was just as certain to lose them after a short time on the job. Good senior people were quickly promoted out of his department, and even when such promotions were not ordered by Ike's superiors, he had no desire to stand in the way of another officer's opportunity to rise. Therefore, as he explained to his friend Colonel Dabney Elliott, "I have gone to the practice of asking for only Majors and very junior Lt. Colonels. I think I have a chance of keeping this type of officer for a few months at least. In many cases, of course, I sacrifice the degree of experience I would like to have; but I try to pick bright boys who learn rapidly."

Ike understood that the business of war—like any other business, really—was first and foremost a people business. Victory depended on making the right investments in personnel. The obvious choice, of course, was to invest in proven value: senior officers with loads of experience. But Ike soon realized that these individuals tended to be volatile commodities, subject to almost instant evaporation through promotion. He therefore looked for subordinates at a more junior level who nevertheless showed great promise. An investment in such officers was riskier, but the potential rewards were proportionately greater because, provided the officer was a fast learner, he would become a valuable *long-term* asset.

An effective manager gives careful thought to the people he or she hires, often choosing to invest in those with more promise than experience—that is, with more future than past. The inherent risk in this approach is, on the face of things, greater, but the rewards—in terms of longevity and loyalty—typically justify the risk. It is a bad thing to discover that you have invested in someone who cannot do the job or do it well, but it is even worse to invest in someone only to have him or her take your investment to another department or a competing enterprise.

◆ ◆ ◆

Lesson 16

Wheedle

Since we are obviously not in a position to use force . . . we must depend on wheedling.

—Secret memorandum to George V.
Strong, May 16, 1942

George V. Strong, assistant chief of staff, G-2—an intelligence officer—in the War Department, wrote a letter to the State Department in which he demanded that the department essentially strong-arm the governments of South American countries to allow the United States to set up a much-needed intelligence network. Ike, who reviewed the proposed letter before it was transmitted, wholeheartedly agreed with Strong that such a network was urgently needed, but he sent the message back to him with the comment that "your letter is a bit abrupt. . . . I have made . . . changes I think soften it up a bit."

Why would a high-ranking War Department officer need to "soften up" a letter to the State Department?

Ike knew that however important rank was, reality always trumped it. "Since we are obviously not in a position to use force, in pursuit of our policy in the south Americas," he explained to Strong, "we must depend on wheedling." That meant appealing to the "only wheedlers we have," not the officers of the U.S. Army, but the diplomats in the State Department. Because we need the wheedling expertise of the diplomats, Ike advised Strong, "I think it to our advantage to keep the best relationship with them we can." And that meant doing a little preliminary wheedling in the form of softening the tone of a letter.

Inept leaders labor under the delusion that power and authority are derived from impressive titles and a perch in the corner office. Successful leaders understand that their power and authority consist of the continuously earned consent of those they lead. It is certainly fatal to make any absolute demand in the absence of absolute power or absolute authority, and, even when your authority is great, it is almost always more effective to seek, to win, even to wheedle cooperation than it is to demand it. A skilled leader establishes "best relationships" with key subordinates and other leaders through the use of a continual appeal to mutual and collective self-interest rather than by relying on some arbitrary hierarchy or command structure. "We need to do this so that we can succeed" is always a more compelling directive than "You need to do this because I am the boss."

◆ ◆ ◆

Lesson 17

Visualize

Wherever possible, diagrammatic charts rather than figures should be used.

—Secret memorandum to St. Clair
Streett, May 21, 1942

Early in the war, Ike ordered the "establishment of large statistical charts" to be posted at "selected places in the Operations Division," the War Department division he commanded. "I am particularly anxious," he explained to General Streett, who was in charge of compiling the statistics, "that these charts show in visual form, our projects for each theater, what we have actually done to date, and dates on which we can expect reinforcements." He closed the memorandum by reiterating his requirement for "diagrammatic charts" rather than charts listing mere "figures."

Throughout World War II, there was plenty of talk about the responsibility of higher command to "see the big picture." Ike took this responsibility seriously and literally. He appreciated the importance of statistics, but he wanted them in a form that would reflect the "big picture" as it continually evolved. By translating the numbers into a visual and graphic form, Ike found a means of actually seeing the evolving shape of the war and the war effort.

There is no such thing as having too much information, provided that the information you have is presented in a usable form. Ensure that all the data you need—statistics, feedback, profits, losses—contribute to a picture you can see, interpret, and use. The function of data is to *convey* reality, not to block your view of it.

◆ ◆ ◆

Lesson 18

The "Single Command" Concept

Success in [a complex military alliance] rests ultimately upon personalities; statesmen, generals, admirals, and air marshals—even populations—must develop confidence in the concept of single command and in the organization and the leader by which the single command is exercised. No binding regulation, law, or custom can apply to all its parts—only a highly developed sense of mutual confidence can solve the problem. Possibly this truth has equal applicability in peace.

—Crusade in Europe

Our society is one of "binding regulation, law, [and] custom." These are the hallmarks of any advanced society and, indeed, of any sophisticated organization. Leadership by one strong man or woman might be fine for a mom-and-pop operation, but great enterprises require regulations, laws, and customs. Put one person in charge of anything really big, and you have a cult of personality—a most dangerous situation. At least, that is what we fear.

We fear and distrust strong personal leadership on a large scale because it seems primitive, a throwback to more reckless times, and we prefer to comfort ourselves with the notion that our collective fate lies not so much with a single person as it does with a whole system, one that includes certain checks and balances. People are fallible, we think, but systems, immune to whims and passions, are reliable.

Dwight Eisenhower's single most significant leadership insight, from very early in the war, was the realization that, despite our fears of creating a cult of personality, of relying too completely on a single leader, the very greatest, most urgent, and most complex enterprises—those involving millions of people from different nations banded together for the highest stakes imaginable—are actually best led by a "single command" in which confidence is absolute. Moreover, he defined this "single command" in terms of a *personality*. A human being, an individual, this personality would be fallible, to be sure, but also powerful and authoritative precisely because of his very humanity and individuality.

The truly remarkable thing about the position of supreme Allied commander, which Ike was to hold, was that it had no basis in law, international or domestic. "Only trust and confidence," Eisenhower wrote, "can establish the authority of an allied commander in chief so firmly that he need never fear the absence of . . . legal power." He did not analyze or explain this insight, but, in writing these words, he showed that he understood it at a profound level.

Leaders and managers of civilian organizations may envy military officers, whose leadership authority (they believe) is derived from and supported by military regulations. Eisenhower knew better, of course. He was keenly aware of what military leaders call "command presence," an indefinable quality of *personality* that effective officers always project and that serves to encourage their troops, inspiring them to prompt and cheerful obedience as well as courageous initiative. Essential as command presence is to an officer commanding a company or a battalion, Ike believed it even more important in a supreme commander, who was responsible for a vast and varied alliance. Indeed, he thought it equally important in effective leadership during peace.

◆ ◆ ◆

Lesson 19

Be the Guy

The C/S [Chief of Staff] says I'm the guy. . . . Now we
really go to work.

—Personal note, June 11, 1942

On June 11, 1942, General George C. Marshall, the army chief of
staff, told Eisenhower that he had been designated commanding
general, European theater of operations, effective June 25. "I'm the
guy," Ike scribbled in his notebook. Colloquial and laconic, this
phrase says all that really needs to be said about the ultimate
responsibility of leadership: *you are the guy.* That is how others see
you, and that is how you must see yourself. The result of this understanding should be no less than an instant and enthusiastic commitment to "really go to work."

◆ ◆ ◆

Lesson 20

It All Depends on You—Still

[I]t is sometimes assumed that the influence of the individual
in war has become submerged, that the mistakes of one
responsible officer are corrected or concealed in the mass
action of a great number of associates. This is not true.

—Crusade in Europe

Anyone looking at the vast spectacle of America and Britain mobiliz-
ing for Operation Torch, the invasion of North Africa, might assume
that the "methods and machinery" of war had "become so extraordinarily complex and intricate," with high commanders surrounded

by "gargantuan staffs for control and direction," that "the influence of the individual" no longer much mattered.

Ike knew better.

"Personal characteristics," he wrote, "are more important than ever before in warfare." His explanation of why this was the case in war also applies to the role of the individual leader in any large, complex organization. In the day of Napoleon and Wellington, Ike pointed out, a single commander really could direct a major battle all on his own. In modern warfare, however, "teams and staffs" are required as the mediators "through which the modern commander absorbs information and exercises his authority." This middle layer of people "must be a beautifully interlocked, smooth-working mechanism. Ideally," Eisenhower wrote, "the whole should be practically a single mind." This being the ideal, Ike observed, the most important role of all is played by the "personalities of senior commanders and staff officers." Those whose abilities are marred by "too obvious avidity for public acclaim" or "the delusion that strength of purpose demands arrogant and even insufferable deportment" are not only *not* submerged by the vast machinery of war but tend to wreck it or, at least, to impair its "beautifully interlocked, smooth-working mechanism."

Modern organizations typically consist of teams, which have a most unfortunate tendency to give expression to the personality of the least congenial member. Instead of submerging the misfit, teams tend to bring him or her to the surface. They magnify rather than reduce individual flaws. Among the most dangerous assumptions a leader can make is that the individual counts for less than everything. The bigger and more complex the organization, the more dangerous this assumption is.

◆ ◆ ◆

Lesson 21

The Highest Type

The personnel of this division represents the highest type of governmental servant.

> —Farewell memorandum to Operations
> Division staff, June 16, 1942

Before he left Washington and the War Department's Operations Division to assume command of the European theater in June 1942, Ike issued a "personal message to say 'goodbye and thank you'" to the staff of his office. He told his staff that they represented the "highest type of governmental servant," which he defined as "the kind that quickly determines the basic elements of complicated problems, promptly finds acceptable answers, and energetically translates those answers into concrete directives." In this, Ike defined not merely the highest type of government worker, but the ideal employee of any great enterprise.

Managers who find it difficult to write job descriptions for staff members need look no further than this three-part list of requirements. You need people (1) who can distill complex problems to their elements; (2) who, having analyzed the problems, find answers to them; and (3) who then complete their work by formulating the means of implementing the solutions they propose.

◆ ◆ ◆

Lesson 22

Unquestionably Legal but Ethically Questionable

My government had entrusted me with important tasks, carrying grave responsibility.

> —Memorandum for the record,
> June 20, 1942

Ethical behavior is an investment in the long term. Most acts of questionable ethics result not from outright dishonesty but from shortsightedness: a desire for instant gain even at the risk of long-term loss.

Shortly before he left Washington and the War Department to assume command in London of the European theater, Ike was visited by Emanuel Quezon, the exiled president of the Philippines. "His purpose," Ike wrote in the memorandum, "was to tender me an honorarium for services rendered during the period I was acting as General MacArthur's Chief of Staff in Manila, where he (MacArthur) went as Military Adviser to the Philippine Government. . . . President Quezon brought with him to my office a draft of a citation which he had written to accompany the presentation [to] me of the honorarium."

Ike explained to Quezon that "while I understood this to be unquestionably legal, and that the President's motives were of the highest, the danger of misapprehension or misunderstanding on the part of some individual might operate to destroy whatever usefulness I may have to the allied cause in the present War." In this, Ike expressed a very advanced form of ethical understanding. First, he understood that legal behavior and ethical behavior are not one and the same. The fact is that ethical action is almost always legal, but legal action is not always ethical. Ethical behavior must meet a higher standard than legal behavior. Second, he expressed his unwillingness to sacrifice larger, longer-term, and more important objectives for the sake of immediate gain, no matter how tempting.

Dwight D. Eisenhower was by no means a wealthy man, and the offer of an honorarium must have held some very real appeal for him. But he saw the offer as a bad bargain, and he had the wisdom as well as strength of character to decline it—albeit with magnificent grace. Respecting Eisenhower's scruples, Quezon proposed presenting the general "in official form, the citation he had written to accompany the honorarium." Ike replied that "such a citation would be of great and more lasting value to me and my family than any amount of money his government could possibly present to me."

◆ ◆ ◆

Lesson 23

You've Got to Believe

Belief in an underlying cause is fully as important to success in war as any local esprit or discipline induced or produced by whatever kind of command or leadership action.

—*Crusade in Europe*

"That a soldier should understand why he is fighting would not seem to be an arguable point," Ike Eisenhower wrote, yet, he continued, he had heard commanders attempt to oversimplify the problem of belief by claiming that soldiers "fight for only a few simple and essentially local reasons," including pride in a unit, respect for the opinion of comrades, and blind devotion to an immediate leader. Eisenhower believed that all of these were in fact important, but he also understood that the "American soldier, in spite of wisecracking, sometimes cynical speech, is an intelligent human being who demands and deserves basic understanding of the reasons why his country took up arms and of the conflicting consequences of victory or defeat." Ike's own experience as well as his knowledge of history convinced him of this. He recalled the example of Baron von Steuben during the American Revolution, who "explained in a letter to a friend that in Europe you tell a soldier to do thus, and he does it; and that in America it is necessary also to tell him why he does it."

In any enterprise requiring the collaboration of intelligent people—and that means just about any enterprise worth doing—the "underlying cause," or motivating principle, should never remain a guarded secret or a vaguely articulated cliché. People work for money, it is true, and a fair salary may produce a fair day's labor, but it is a shared vision that makes possible the best work and the greatest achievement.

◆ ◆ ◆

Lesson 24

Demand Faith, Require Optimism

Any expression of defeatism or any failure to push ahead in confidence was instant cause for relief from duty, and all officers knew it.

—Crusade in Europe

"In the summer of 1942," Ike admitted, when the forces of the Axis were victorious on all fronts, "it took a very considerable faith, not to say optimism, to look forward to the day when the potentialities of the United States would be fully developed and the power of the three great Allies could be applied simultaneously and decisively against the European Axis."

As his armies rolled over most of Europe, Hitler made it very easy for his opponents to believe that their defeat was inevitable. Imminent defeat seemed nothing more or less than an entirely realistic assessment of the war situation. It was Eisenhower's job, first and foremost, to alter that destructive perception. For whether or not Hitler would finally defeat the Allies, Allied defeatism *certainly* could and would.

Even in the most threatening situations, as a leader you must counter defeatism, and when there is a paucity of hard facts to fight this devastating emotion, you must turn to faith: the simple, naked belief that you and your enterprise will prevail. If faith is difficult to create, you may emulate Ike and summarily outlaw "any expression of defeatism." If this sounds perilously close to nurturing self-delusion, that is because it is. But the risk of delusion is well worth taking to avoid the sure poison of defeatist thought.

◆ ◆ ◆

Lesson 25

Get, Use, Discard

The problem of having it when you want it, using it as you need it, and then getting it out of the way when you don't want it, is really something to solve.

—Letter to Leonard T. Gerow, July 16, 1942

Shortly after setting up his headquarters in England, Ike wrote to his friend General Leonard T. Gerow about the importance of "skill in handling motor transportation." In the course of the discussion, he distilled the essence of what today would be called just-in-time management—the logistical ideal of having what you want when you want it, using it as you need it, then getting rid of it when you don't want it. Static management concepts call for stockpiling. As mentioned in Lesson 14, "Streamline," Ike understood that stockpiling not only was wasteful of materiel in and of itself but also required a surplus of manpower and equipment to manage the stockpile. He vastly preferred a dynamic management approach, by which the right equipment reached the right hands only when actually needed and was gotten out of the way when it was needed no longer. This approach ensured that everyone's focus was on the task at hand, not on the equipment that was either standing idle or tardy in its arrival. Neither stockpiling nor waiting is a valid management technique.

◆ ◆ ◆

Lesson 26

Build Rapport

I am convinced . . . that if these things are properly explained to our personnel, the response will be highly gratifying.

—Letter to Russell P. "Scrappy" Hartle, July 19, 1942

Relations between the British and American allies were not always cordial. Faced with a flood of GIs coming into their country, Brits often said that there were three things wrong with the Yanks: "They're overpaid, oversexed, and over here." Shortly after his arrival in London, Ike wrote to one of his senior commanders, General Scrappy Hartle, to express his concern over problems created in Anglo-American relations by the "great difference between the pay scale of our men and of the British." Ike elaborated: "There is no need to recite again the risks we run, collectively and individually, of creating ill-feeling through, what the British will consider, lavish expenditure of money" by our troops.

It was one thing to recognize the existence of this problem, but quite another to do something about it, to devise a way to build rapport between the Americans and their British hosts. Ike proposed "sustained and vigorous campaigns to induce our officers and men to allot or deposit large portions of their pay or to buy bonds and war savings stamps," so that they would not have the loose cash on hand to spend so ostentatiously. He expressed his belief that if "these things are properly explained to our personnel, the response will be highly gratifying."

Ike's leadership in this case was especially impressive. He saw a situation—American soldiers were paid more than British soldiers—but refused to simply accept it as a given. Instead, he proposed a positive, innovative means of creating, without coercion, a favorable change in the work environment. It was a practical means of building rapport on the scale of the whole work environment, yet it would be accomplished through an appeal to the individual behavior of each and every American soldier stationed in Britain.

Effective leaders build rapport any way they can. And this begins with a calm but resolute refusal to accept any circumstance that threatens or undermines rapport.

◆   ◆   ◆

Lesson 27

The Action Imperative

We have . . . tried . . . not to be blinded by a mere passion for doing something.

—Memorandum to Harry C. Butcher,
July 22, 1942

Very early in the war, Ike, General Marshall, and other top U.S. military planners advocated Operation Sledgehammer, an invasion of France across the English Channel. Prime Minister Winston Churchill and top British military leaders opposed this as premature, Churchill advocating instead an Allied offensive in North Africa as a first step in launching a general assault in the Mediterranean area—what the prime minister called the "soft underbelly of Europe."

Despite British objections, Ike wanted very much to carry out Sledgehammer, but he was well aware that the odds were stacked against the success of the operation, and he frankly considered the possibility that his own advocacy of it might be nothing more than the result of a desire for action—*any* action: "We have sat up nights on the problem involved and have tried to open our eyes clearly to see all the difficulties and not to be blinded by a mere passion for doing something." This passion is a common affliction of leaders faced with the frustrations of a complex, difficult, and even overwhelming situation. Inaction breeds panic and feelings of failure, whereas action suggests mastery. As Ike explained to his naval aide, Harry C. Butcher, he finally decided that in this case and despite the long odds, there was a great and real value in action itself. "The British and American armies and the British and American people need to have the feeling that they are attempting something positive. We must not degenerate into a passive . . . attitude."

The Sledgehammer decision was one of the most difficult of the many difficult decisions Ike had to make. He clearly saw the dangers—the danger in the operation as well as the danger inherent in the proposition that action for its own sake is inherently worthwhile—and he decided to accept the very large risks entailed by mounting an Allied invasion at this early stage of the war. In the end, however, higher authority, Churchill and Roosevelt, overruled Sledgehammer and directed the military to plan instead Operation Torch, the Allied landings on North Africa. Ever since, military historians have speculated about what would have happened had Operation Sledgehammer been carried out. Most agree that it would have been grossly premature and, therefore, a military disaster. The really tough thing about making decisions? There is never any guarantee that the decision made will be the right one.

◆ ◆ ◆

Lesson 28

Caution Is Not Timidity; Timidity Is Not Caution

And it is well to remember that caution and timidity are not synonymous, just as boldness and rashness are not!

—*Crusade in Europe*

An effective leader uses words as scalpels, not butter knives. They are sharp and precise, their function to incise rather than smear. One must distinguish between caution, a necessity in leading any enterprise of genuine value, and timidity, a character flaw fatal to leadership.

Timid leaders are often rash. They act in panic and with little thought. Don't mistake this for genuine boldness, which is made possible by caution: the husbanding of resources that enables maximum effort, the thorough planning that creates the confidence to act in good faith with the whole heart and with every muscle.

◆ ◆ ◆

Lesson 29

Invasion Equation

The more I study the operation . . .

> —Secret report to George C. Marshall
> on planning for Operation Torch,
> August 9, 1942

One of the first things any good manager learns is the difference between cost and value. Bearing in mind that investment is a strategy and strategy is an investment, "cheap" and "expensive" are absolute concepts that address only one side of the investment-strategy equation and are, for that reason, meaningless. In contrast to them, the concept of value works both sides of the equation and is the very key to its solution.

Ike approached strategic planning as an equation. His purpose was to determine how best to invest the resources available to him to achieve the most favorable outcome with the least expenditure—that is, to achieve the greatest possible value.

"The more I study the Operation [Torch], the more I am convinced that a high proportion of armored vehicles should be in the assault," Ike wrote General George C. Marshall, the army chief of staff.

His explanation of this conclusion is a perfect example of strategic planning as equation solving. Bringing in the armored vehicles, Ike admitted, "introduces additional difficulties in the provision of suitable landing craft"—and, as both Ike and Marshall well knew, landing craft were in critically short supply. This, however, was only one side of the equation, so Ike continued: "but current reports indicate that the greatest weakness of the [Axis-allied Vichy] French at present is anti-tank equipment." Despite the added difficulty involved, the best solution to the strategic equation was to use against the enemy the kind of weapons for which he lacked adequate defense. When you know your enemy is weak in anti-tank equipment, invest whatever effort and resources are required to attack him with tanks, lots and lots of tanks. Playing to your strengths is important, but despite the risks, playing against your opponent's weaknesses is even more effective.

◆ ◆ ◆

Lesson 30

"The Best Is the Enemy of the Good"

Continuous study of the possibilities has forced us, as is always the case, to seek the best possible compromise between desirable execution of operations on the one hand and definitely limited resources on the other.

> —Secret report to George C. Marshall
> on planning for Operation Torch,
> August 9, 1942

One of the favorite sayings of George S. Patton Jr. was "The best is the enemy of the good." War, he believed, was not about perfection, but about doing the best you could do as soon as you could possibly do it. Waiting for perfect conditions meant losing present opportunities or, worse, simply losing. Ike quickly discovered the validity of this approach as he planned the Allies' offensive operations early in the war. There were grand objectives to be achieved, but limited resources to apply to them. However, each day of waiting for more resources gave the enemy another day for further conquest and consolidation.

War, like any great and complex enterprise, is dynamic. Both opportunity and risk are linked to this dynamism. They come, they go, they increase, they diminish—daily, even hourly. Perfection, in contrast, is static, literally timeless. For that very reason, the concept of perfection has no place in the flux of either war or business. Meaningful action in these realms always requires a compromise between what is desirable and what is, at the necessary moment, possible. Like his friend Patton, Ike understood that compromise was not a bad thing, but simply another dimension of the ongoing task at hand. In the real world, which is the only world that counts, compromise plays a role in every decision to act. Accept compromise. Better yet, embrace it.

◆ ◆ ◆

Lesson 31

Drop Everything

Right this minute I am going to drop everything and take a drive in the country for about three hours.

—Letter to Arthur Hurd, August 11, 1942

"You are quite right in your estimate as to the perplexities and responsibilities of this job," Ike wrote to his friend Hurd. "Right this minute I am going to drop everything and take a drive in the country for about three hours—I'm sick of this office, to which I've been confined for the past weeks with very little respite."

The job of commanding American and British forces in the invasion of North Africa was essentially a 24/7 proposition. Ike knew and accepted this. But he also knew that a tired commander was a bad commander. Fatigue distorts vision, typically giving rise to pessimism and panic—two commodities fatal to leadership. Ike knew he had a big job to do. He knew there was no substitute for hard work to do it. But he also knew what it meant to be "sick of this office," and if a three-hour drive in the country would buy another week of the ability to do the hard and necessary work, he would leave the office for those three hours.

The object of leadership is not personal martyrdom. It is the success of the enterprise. And that success depends in large part on the energetic optimism of a healthy, rested, and alert leader. Sometimes the best leadership decision you can make is to drop everything.

◆ ◆ ◆

Lesson 32

Let Them Call You Ike

I damn near decided to throw your note in the wastebasket and not answer it because of your conclusion that you couldn't call me "Ike."

—Letter to LeRoy Lutes, August 12, 1942

"But I decided that, after all, maybe you really did have better sense than to think I would get so over-powered by an additional star that I couldn't longer be on natural terms with my good friends."

Ike's elevation from major general to lieutenant general was a momentous promotion, and, as Ike pointed out in his letter to Major General LeRoy Lutes, "a particular and important feature of this job is that I am held personally responsible now for almost everything that happens, both British and American." Eisenhower could have been excused if he had decided that so exalted a figure as he had now become could no longer afford to allow himself to be called Ike. But, in fact, nothing was more important to Eisenhower—now, more than ever—than to remain on "natural terms" with friends. And that meant making sure they still called him Ike.

Be proud of the trust and responsibility vested in you, but don't make the mistake of trying to escape the gravity that keeps your feet on the ground. If they called you Ike before your third star, let them call you Ike today and tomorrow as well.

◆ ◆ ◆

Lesson 33

Beware "Academic Concurrence"

I have never had any trouble getting academic concurrences; but there are plenty of difficulties to be encountered when you bring up the question of actual operations.

—Letter to Fox Conner, August 21, 1942

Ike's beloved early mentor, retired major general Fox Conner, wrote him on July 20, 1942, that he believed the immediate task facing the Allies was to relieve pressure on the Russians in order to keep them in the war. If the Russians made a separate peace with the Nazis, all would indeed be lost. On August 21, Ike wrote back (Conner's letter having taken a month to reach him) in full agreement, pointing out, however, that although he was able to get "academic concurrences" from his colleagues, bosses, and subordinates on this very proposition, securing agreement on "actual operations" was another matter altogether.

Ike had discovered the enormous gulf that yawns between agreement in principle and agreement in fact, between assent to an idea and commitment to action. Winning agreement to a proposition should not be counted a victory until that agreement has been translated into action. Failure to acknowledge the often very substantial gap between academic concurrence and actual operation can be fatal. After all, it's a very long way down.

❖ ❖ ❖

Lesson 34

A Time to Push

I merely insist that if our beginning looks hopeful, then this is the time to push rather than slacken our efforts.

—Crusade in Europe

Early in Operation Torch, Ike was pressured to reduce the planned buildup for the operation "so as to proceed with other strategic purposes." Intent on maintaining focus and direction by sticking to what he deemed a well-conceived plan, he replied with a rationale for rejecting "possible reduction" and instead insisted on "seeking ways and means of speeding up the build-up to clean out North Africa." He believed that large-scale strategic planning should by all means continue, "but for God's sake let's get one job done at a time."

A leader must know precisely where the project stands at a given moment, and, armed with this knowledge, he must ensure that the enterprise remains focused on the agreed-on objectives. Ike put it this way: "We are just started working on a great venture. A good beginning must not be destroyed by any unwarranted assumptions."

Leadership is about shaping and directing energy, then husbanding that energy wisely and jealously to make sure that none is squandered as a result of poor focus, poor planning, or strategic whim.

◆ ◆ ◆

Lesson 35

Simplify

I believe in direct methods, possibly because I am too simple-minded to be an intriguer or to attempt to be clever.

—Letter to Fox Conner, August 21, 1942

As Ike saw it, all other things being equal, the simplest, most direct approach was always the best. If this seems self-evident, just consider how many people you encounter day to day who appear constitutionally incapable of producing direct and simple requests, directives, questions, answers, statements, or actions. One of a leader's hardest tasks is to shed habits of intrigue and cleverness and to cultivate instead a simple mind suited to direct methods.

◆ ◆ ◆

Lesson 36

Commit Everlastingly

By keeping everlastingly after all these problems, we can lick them.

—Letter to Russell P. "Scrappy" Hartle, August 25, 1942

Ike was keenly aware of the destructive potential of two serious personnel problems among the forces preparing to invade North Africa in Operation Torch. One was friction between African American and white soldiers. The other was friction between American and British soldiers. In a letter to his friend General Scrappy Hartle, he thanked the general for his "letter describing the methods you have developed for establishing harmonious relations between colored and white troops," and he enclosed his own thoughts on establishing similar harmony between American and British troops.

Ike was convinced that these were big and important problems and that they were not going to go away by themselves or anytime soon. They were rooted, after all, in long-lived, closely held prejudices that seemed to persist in direct proportion to their essential irrationality. Their ubiquity and stubbornness made Ike all the more determined to dispose of them by committing himself "everlastingly" to their solution.

Effective leaders identify tough problems that resist solution but nevertheless must be solved. Having identified those problems, they resolve to keep after them until they are licked. Surrender is not an option.

◆ ◆ ◆

Lesson 37

Identify and Promote Leaders

I am convinced that any officer who can produce a notable success in matters requiring constructive effort, particularly when they lie outside the realm of the written regulation, is possessed of the qualities of the real leader.

—Letter to Russell P. "Scrappy" Hartle,
August 25, 1942

Eager to promote productive and harmonious relations between British and American soldiers, Ike asked General Hartle to "bring to my attention, at any time, with a view to his promotion, the name of any officer that you find particularly skillful" in devising ways to create Anglo-American rapport on an individual, soldier-to-soldier basis.

Ike well knew that there was no rulebook, no army regulation that addressed this issue of inter-Allied relations. In fact, it was up to him to invent the rules, to create rapport, to make this titanic and unprecedented military alliance work and work effectively. He knew that rapport did not materialize in response to an order; rather, it required winning the heart and mind of each individual soldier. The people best able to do that were the army's managers—the officers in charge of the lower echelons—especially at the level of company commander. Ike was determined to identify the ablest of these managers, those capable not merely of executing orders and applying regulations but of producing "a notable success in matters requiring constructive effort, particularly when they lie outside the realm of the written regulation." These, Ike believed, were the real leaders in an organization, and it was urgent that they be identified and promoted into the most influential positions. In this way, Eisenhower hoped to speed the creation of an army—as well as an alliance—capable of victory.

Too many leaders are overly possessive of leadership and guard it jealously. The fact is that leadership is a rare and valuable commodity and, as such, constitutes one of the greatest assets of any organization. A real leader never holds leadership selfishly, but relentlessly searches for it throughout the organization, and, finding it, promotes it.

◆ ◆ ◆

Lesson 38

Look for Leaders

This is a long tough road we have to travel. The men that can do things are going to be sought out just as surely as the sun rises in the morning.

—Letter to Vernon E. Prichard,
August 27, 1942

It is need, urgent need, that finds leaders. Need tests and refines all who offer themselves as candidates for the job.

In a letter to friend and fellow commander Vernon E. Prichard, Ike took up the theme of leadership he had discussed in his letter to Scrappy Hartle just two days earlier. "Fake reputations," he wrote, "habits of glib and clever speech, and glittering surface performance are going to be discovered and kicked overboard." Those who remain are people capable of "solid, sound leadership," possessed of "inexhaustible nervous energy to spur on the efforts of lesser men, and iron-clad determination to face discouragement, risk and increasing work without flinching." Those who remain are the people who also possess "a darned strong tinge of imagination—I am continuously astounded by the utter lack of imaginative thinking among so many of our people that have reputations for being really good officers." Finally, those who escape being kicked overboard are those who are most dedicated and "able to forget . . . personal fortunes. I've relieved two seniors here because they got to worrying about 'injustice,' 'unfairness,' 'prestige.'"

Need will find leaders, but Ike counseled his friend Prichard to get a jump on need by starting to look right now. "While you are doing your stuff from day to day, constantly look and search among your subordinates for the ones that have these priceless qualities in greater or lesser degree. . . . [Y]ou will find greater and greater need for people upon whom you can depend to take the load off your shoulders."

If the advice seems obvious (Ike himself called his list of leadership characteristics "platitudes"), just consider how many bosses, managers, and supervisors, for fear of jeopardizing their own authority, are reluctant to identify and promote the leaders in their organization. Mistaking such fear for self-preservation is the surest way to self-destruction.

◆   ◆   ◆

Lesson 39

The Courage of True Delegation

True delegation implies the courage and readiness to back up a subordinate to the full; it is not to be confused with the slovenly practice of merely ignoring an unpleasant situation in the hope that someone else will handle it.

—Crusade in Europe

Delegation of authority defines the role of leader. That is, a leader is a person who delegates. A person who attempts to do everything himself may be a hard worker, a genius, a martyr, or a failure, but he is not a leader. This said, mere delegation does not a leader make. As Ike pointed out, ignoring a difficult problem in the hope that someone else will take care of it is neither true delegation nor genuine leadership. It is a kind of moral sloppiness practiced by incompetents who "are always quick to blame and punish the poor subordinate who, while attempting to do both his own and his commander's jobs, has taken some action that produces an unfortunate result."

True delegation requires sufficient courage to take responsibility not only for what you yourself do but also for what your delegates do.

◆ ◆ ◆

Lesson 40

Learning Means Changing

Until my experience in London I had been opposed to the use of women in uniform.

—Crusade in Europe

Ike welcomed to North Africa a contingent of Women's Army Corps personnel. At the Allied headquarters in London, he had seen them "perform magnificently" in jobs ranging from clerk to antiaircraft gunner and "had been converted." He understood that "many officers were still doubtful of women's usefulness in uniform," but he ascribed this to a failure "to note . . . the changing requirements of war." Gone forever was the "simple headquarters of a Grant or a Lee." It had been replaced by headquarters of great complexity, requiring an "army of filing clerks, stenographers, office managers" and so on, "and it was scarcely less than criminal to recruit these from needed manpower when great numbers of highly qualified women were available."

To learn is to change. Ike was willing to do both.

◆ ◆ ◆

Lesson 41

Assign a General Mission

A qualified commander should normally be assigned only a general mission . . . and then given the means to carry it out.

—*Crusade in Europe*

Ike thought it a mistake to lay out a plan "based upon the capture or holding of specific geographical points" because doing so is "likely to impose a rigidity of action upon the commander," and he had no desire to straitjacket a creative subordinate. Instead, Ike believed a superior should assign a "general mission" to a "qualified commander" so that he would be "completely unfettered in achieving the general purpose of his superior."

Military commanders always seek what they call force multipliers—anything that leverages available resources, that amplifies their effect. Assigning general missions to qualified people is a force multiplier because doing so creates an environment flexible enough for the exercise of creative imagination. Given this freedom, a qualified subordinate will produce above and beyond expectation. Overly specific missions—symptoms of micromanagement—are force reducers, because they confine the imagination. Instead of two heads working a problem, you have at best just one and a fraction, the subordinate merely duplicating much of what the superior has already done.

It takes courage to give freedom to others. After all, those others may fail. Yet an organization condemned to shuffle in lockstep has already failed, whereas an organization driven by the freedom of a general mission may well find the room to succeed and to succeed far beyond expectation.

◆ ◆ ◆

Lesson 42

Every Positive Action Requires Expenditure

[E]very positive action requires expenditure. The problem is to determine how, in space and time, to expend assets so as to achieve the maximum in results.

—*Crusade in Europe*

Early in the North African campaign, Ike heard a story about how a young staff officer refused a brigadier general permission to transport part of his command via half-tracks (lightly armored vehicles with conventional tires on front wheels and tank treads instead of rear wheels) more than seven hundred miles from Oran to a place called Souk-el-Arba. The staff officer objected because the trip would consume half the useful life of the half-tracks. Ike observed that the young officer was not to blame for "this extraordinary attitude." He had been trained "through years of peace, in the eternal need for economy, for avoiding waste." What he had yet to accept was "the essential harshness of war," which is "synonymous with waste." Nor "did he understand that every positive action requires expenditure."

The first step for you as a decision maker is to accept reality as it currently exists, even if it differs from what you are accustomed to. Once you have accepted and understood that reality, you must further accept that every positive action requires expenditure. Depending on the nature of current reality, the expenditure may be greater or smaller than you are accustomed to. "The problem," Ike reasoned, "is to determine how, in space and time, to expend assets so as to achieve the maximum in results." Once this has been decided on, "then assets must be spent with a lavish hand," especially, in the case of war, "when the cost can be measured in the saving of lives."

True economy is never static. It is pegged to the variables of a changing reality. True economy is never one sided—a matter of saving or spending. It is, rather, a process of giving value to obtain value. In the reality of peacetime, driving a half-track seven hundred miles may be a foolish waste. In war, if using up a half-track will save lives, it is a bargain. To be an effective leader, you must adjust to reality as it exists and then persuade others to make the same adjustment, even if this adjustment requires a painful divorce from a comfortable past.

◆ ◆ ◆

Lesson 43

Weigh Every Risk Against Every Reward

Direct risks of destruction . . . are much lower . . . but . . . we do not have a gambling chance to achieve a really worthwhile strategic purpose.

—Secret cable to George C. Marshall, August 25, 1942

After Ike and his staff had labored to produce a plan for Operation Torch and had submitted it to the Combined Chiefs of Staff (the Anglo-American high command), planners in the War Plans Department submitted an alternative plan to Marshall, who asked Eisenhower for his opinion. Ike's evaluation of the alternative proposal was contained in a single razor-sharp sentence, which reveals much about how he made decisions: "Direct risks of destruction of the attacking force are much lower under the proposed [alternative] plan than in the one as now outlined and submitted to the Combined Chiefs of Staff, but broad strategic risks are equally great and under the new proposal we do not have a gambling chance to achieve a really worthwhile strategic purpose."

In evaluating a course of action, weigh *every* risk against *every* reward. It may be fatal to base your decision on partial information, on a partial evaluation of the available information, or on a single risk or a single reward. Look at everything and formulate the evaluation in as complete and concise an expression as possible. Ike's sentence has the elegance and clarity of a mathematical equation— and as much truth: as to immediate risk, the alternative proposal is better than the current plan; as to "broad strategic risks," the two plans are equal; but as to the opportunity for realizing a significant reward—"a really worthwhile strategic purpose"—only the original plan, initially risky though it is, offers a "gambling chance." The equation is cold and hard, to be sure, but the answer is unmistakable: a risky plan that has a "gambling chance" of producing a worthwhile strategic purpose is far more valuable than a relatively safe plan that has no chance of producing anything of strategic value.

◆ ◆ ◆

Lesson 44

Stick to the Plan

Unforeseen and glittering promise on the one hand and unexpected difficulty or risk upon the other present constant temptation to desert the chosen line of action in favor of another.

—*Crusade in Europe*

"A foolish consistency," Ralph Waldo Emerson wrote, "is the hobgoblin of little minds." A careful writer, Emerson thought about each word he used, including, in this case, the adjective modifying the subject noun. Whereas adherence to a *foolish* consistency never constitutes effective leadership, consistency is at its very heart.

"History," Eisenhower wrote, "has proved that nothing is more difficult in war than to adhere to a single strategic plan." He noted that "glittering promise . . . and . . . unexpected difficulty" offer "constant temptation to desert the chosen line of action." To yield to such temptation, more often than not, is wasteful of resources, opportunity, and time, as well as very harmful to morale.

As a leader, you cannot afford to maintain commitment to a course of action that is clearly failing. That would be, at the very least, a foolish consistency. But the essence of leadership is inherently conservative. Unless there is truly overwhelming evidence of failure of the current course or truly overwhelming evidence of success offered by a new opportunity, the leader's task is to hold everyone to the chosen course, which, in the absence of overwhelming evidence against it, is the most likely road to success.

◆ ◆ ◆

Lesson 45

Never Confuse Tactics with Strategy

The doctrine of opportunism, so often applicable in tactics, is a dangerous one to pursue in strategy.

—Crusade in Europe

Leadership is about making judgments, and one of the key judgments to make concerns when to think strategically and when to think tactically. Confusing the two modes of thought may be fatal.

The object of strategic thinking is to create long-term plans from which the organization will not deviate except in the most extreme of circumstances. The object of tactical thinking is to implement those plans in real time and in the real world. The first process is all about stability; the second, flexibility.

Ike continually found that his principal task was to keep his top commanders from abandoning the agreed-upon strategy when this or that opportunity or crisis happened to present itself. At the same time, he encouraged all his subordinates to recognize and exploit tactical opportunities as they emerged. By thinking in strictly segregated terms of strategy and tactics, a leader can combine steadfastness of purpose with flexibility of response. The difficulty is to know when to act on an apparent opportunity and when to pass it by. When a transient circumstance tempts the leader and the enterprise to jettison the plan, it is almost certainly a seduction to be resisted, no matter how difficult it may be to do so. When, however, a transitory event offers a way to improve or enhance the realization of the underlying plan, the leader should recognize it as a tactical opportunity to be acted on.

◆ ◆ ◆

Lesson 46

Be Calm, Clear, and Determined

Deviation from fundamental concepts is permissible only when significant changes in the situation compel it. The high commander must therefore be calm, clear, and determined.

—*Crusade in Europe*

Good plans are "founded in fact and intelligent conclusions." Once a plan is made, it "must be fixed and clear." The purpose of a plan is to advance whatever has been determined to be the fundamental concepts. The intention of a plan is to be adhered to. Barring significant changes in the situation, an effective leader holds his or her organization to proceed in accordance with the plan, countering the natural tendency of large groups in high-stakes actions to deviate by responding impulsively to momentary events and issues.

Ike believed that the most effective way to keep everyone on course was not by "adherence to fixed notions of arbitrary command practices," but by an "ability to lead and persuade." For Eisenhower, persuasion, not the mere assertion of authority, no matter how loftily ordained, was the key to leadership. He believed that the foundation of persuasion was confidence, an attitude that could be created, first and foremost, by the calm, clear, and determined demeanor of the leader as conveyed through everything he said and did.

◆ ◆ ◆

Lesson 47

Remember to Breathe

I am just about as busy as a man can be and am always in the middle of a thousand problems.

—Letter to his brother Arthur B. Eisenhower, August 27, 1942

"With surprisingly little delay a copy of the letter you wrote to [brother] Edgar on August 11th reached me here in London. It was a real treat to have so much news of the family, and I thank you sincerely for taking the trouble to write. . . . You are quite right in assuming that I am just about as busy as a man can be and am always in the middle of a thousand problems. However, the writing of short letters does not really take my time—it is my only relaxation and, frequently, the few minutes I take off to write informally to a friend or one of the family will serve to clear up things that I have been thinking about for a couple of hours. In the same way, the receipt of letters is a bright spot in many a high-pressure day."

When you reach the point that you believe your days are too full to accommodate a word from family and friends, you've reached the point when your life is too full to accommodate—your life. And that is a dangerous point.

Perhaps no one in history has ever had more to do, day to day, than Dwight Eisenhower in World War II, but he never allowed his life to become too full for family, friends, and other emissaries of the reality beyond his headquarters. He knew that he could not afford to lose touch with that reality and looked to periodic contact with it for relief, refreshment, and even the opportunity to gain a fresh perspective on the work at hand.

No matter how busy you are, remembering to breathe, at least once in a while, can have only a healthy effect on you and your enterprise.

◆ ◆ ◆

Lesson 48

The Answer Is Always People

It is not the problem itself that always presents the greatest difficulty—it is the trouble one has in finding people of sufficient caliber to tackle the job intelligently.

—Letter to George Van Horn Moseley,
August 27, 1942

No problem is solved without the right people to solve it, and Ike found himself getting "exceedingly weary of the little people that spend their time worrying about promotions, personal prestige, prerogatives and so on, rather than forgetting everything in the desire to get on with the work." He saw his leadership task as "finding people of sufficient caliber to tackle the job intelligently," which meant finding people willing "to get on with the work" rather than dissipate energy in looking after themselves and themselves alone.

But what to do when all you seem to find are "the little people"?

You lead them, mentor them, persuade them to become bigger until they are of sufficient caliber to get on with the work and get on with it intelligently. Fail in this, and no problem will be solved.

◆ ◆ ◆

Lesson 49

Don't Throw a Good Man Away

[Send] him out with his troops.

—*Crusade in Europe*

Eisenhower asked for George S. Patton Jr. to lead the critical amphibious landings at Casablanca during Operation Torch. Accordingly, General Marshall ordered Patton to London, where Ike
briefed him. "Hardly had [Patton] returned to Washington before I
received a message stating that he had become embroiled in such a
distressing argument with the Navy Department that serious
thought was being given to his relief from command."

Ike knew Patton well, that he "delighted to startle his hearers
with fantastic statements" and that he alienated many, but he also
knew that Patton was "essentially a shrewd battle leader who invariably gained the devotion of his subordinates." Ike put getting
along with others very high on his list of requisites for a commander, but he saw in Patton qualities that trumped even this. At the
same time, he recognized that Patton was indeed a "problem child"
(as he later called him). Asked to choose between two unaccept-
able alternatives, Ike refused both. Instead, he offered a third course
that recognized the problem, solved the problem, *and* retained a
good man: he suggested "that if [Patton's] personality was causing
any difficulty in conferences the issue could be met by sending him
out with his troops and allowing some staff member to represent
him in the completion of planning details."

Provide a distraction. Sidestep. Invent a new job. Do whatever
must be done to avoid throwing a good man away.

◆ ◆ ◆

Lesson 50

End the Day

I feel like the lady in the circus that has to ride three horses with no very good idea of exactly where any one of the three is going to go.

—Letter to George S. Patton Jr.,
August 31, 1942

During the planning of Operation Torch, Ike was pulled in various directions by a variety of British and American commanders, not to mention Prime Minister Winston Churchill. By the end of August, as he confessed in a letter to his friend and trusted field commander General Patton, the stress was telling on him. "I am in somewhat of an irritable mood," he wrote, "because last night, when I hit the bed, I started thinking about some of these things all over again and at two-thirty I was still thinking."

We all spend a sleepless night now and then, worrying about the problems of the day, but Ike had a hard time forgiving himself for having done so: "I suspect that I am just a bit on the weak-minded side when I allow myself to do that, but any way it doesn't happen often." Clearly, Ike believed in the importance of compartmentalizing, mentally and emotionally separating the business of the day from the rest of his life, so that when the day ended, it was truly at an end and did not carry over into the night. Problems are solved by clear thinking and sharp analysis, not by nocturnal rumination. Allow yourself to be robbed of sleep, and you allow yourself—as well as your enterprise—to be robbed of your full effectiveness the next day. Before you begin the night, make certain to end the day.

◆ ◆ ◆

Lesson 51

Demand Satisfactory Performance

The time has passed for dilly-dallying.

> —Secret memorandum to Harry C.
> Butcher, September 15, 1942

In a memorandum to his naval aide, Commander Butcher, Ike noted a meeting he had with his immediate subordinates prior to the launch of Operation Torch concerning the urgent necessity of instituting "instructional programs that would insure a knowledge of elementary discipline and military courtesy on the part of all officers." Without these elements, Ike believed, no advanced, demanding, or complex military operation could be successfully carried out. This being the case, he felt thoroughly justified in defining as "satisfactory performance" the ability to instill discipline and the observance of military courtesy throughout his command. With that definition established, Ike set the requirement in the most uncompromising of terms, pointing out "that the time had arrived when commanders of such units as are not coming up to standard, must be relieved"—that is, fired.

As a leader, you must set certain unambiguous, mandatory, and nonnegotiable standards. Set them a notch higher than you realistically believe you need, then define meeting them as your sole measure for "satisfactory performance." Finally, demand that they *be met*. You will find, perhaps surprisingly, that no one will grumble, provided that the standards you set are declared and defined in objective terms and with crystal clarity.

◆ ◆ ◆

Lesson 52

Make Performance the Measure

*I informed them that success or failure in this task will be . . .
the measure of the individual's value.*

—Memorandum to Harry C. Butcher,
September 15, 1942

In his memorandum to his naval aide Butcher, Ike reported that he had taken special pains "to impress upon all the principal officers of the theater the importance of devoting everything to preparations for [Operation] Torch." He did this by telling them that "success or failure in this task will be, so far as I am concerned, the measure of the individual's value."

It was a stark and unsparing formula, which left no doubt about the leader's expectations. Ike promised: "if each of these officers were successful in carrying out the mission given, there would be no limit to the representations I would make the War Department on their behalf." And he also warned: "on the other hand, failure would mean only that the officer's usefulness was ended." Moreover, "I urged them particularly to impress this idea on all subordinates."

Ike was a great manager and motivator. He did not deal in threats, but in facts. He explained to the officers that Operation Torch "was not an ordinary task in which reasonable effort and reasonable measures had any application." It was a task that required maximum effort, an effort that would call upon the whole being of each leader involved. Such an effort would be the measure of their value as leaders. This said, Ike advised his top subordinates to present the very same formula to *their* subordinates. In this way, he intended to plant the seeds of a truly maximum effort throughout the entire organization.

Challenge those you lead. Persuade them to deliver their personal best by reminding them that their work is a measure of themselves. Promise a realistic and worthwhile reward, but also apprise them of the equally real consequences of failure. Present nothing as a threat, a plea, or an opinion. Offer only the hardest of hard facts, in which performance is the final measure, and success or failure the only arbiters of enduring worth.

◆ ◆ ◆

Lesson 53

Keep Score

In war about the only criterion that can be applied to a commander is his accumulated record of victory and defeat.

— *Crusade in Europe*

Evaluate performance as objectively as possible. In war, evaluation of performance is a matter of weighing victories against defeats. As complex an undertaking as a great war is, sooner or later, everything that is done and that is not done comes down to a single product: triumph or surrender.

Business is just as complex and, in the end, just as simple as war. All business enterprises, no matter how vast, speak the same simple language. The language of business is money. Sooner or later, everything a business is and everything a business does is expressed in money earned, money saved, money spent, and money lost. As a military commander is judged by the simple yardstick of victory versus defeat, so the leader of a business enterprise is judged by his or her impact on the bottom line. Everything else is mere opinion and quite beside the point.

◆ ◆ ◆

Lesson 54

"The Commander and Unit Are Almost One and the Same Thing"

I have developed almost an obsession as to the certainty with which you can judge a division, or any other large unit, merely by knowing its commander intimately.

— Letter to Vernon E. Prichard,
August 27, 1942

Ike reminded his West Point classmate Brigadier General Vernon E. Prichard how "we have had pounded into us all through our school courses that the exact level of a commander's personality and ability is always reflected in his unit," but, he confessed, "I did not realize, until opportunity came for comparisons on a rather large scale, how infallibly the commander and unit are almost one and the same thing."

Never forget that any organization is the magnified reflection of its leader.

2

FROM AFRICAN VICTORY
TO SICILIAN CONQUEST

Promoted to lieutenant general in July 1942, Eisenhower was named to command Operation Torch, the Allied invasion of French North Africa. Launched on November 8, 1942, this first major Allied offensive of the war had a rocky start, as the poorly prepared American army suffered humiliating defeats in its two initial encounters with Erwin Rommel's infamous Afrika Korps. This was bad enough, but Eisenhower also drew a storm of protest for his collaboration with the Vichy French admiral Jean-François Darlan. Nevertheless, it was the ultimate result that counted most, and, ultimately, victory in North Africa was won by the Allies, under Eisenhower.

Up to this point, Eisenhower had revealed himself a master at working with the diverse and demanding personalities of the U.S. Army officer corps. Now, in the invasion of North Africa and the conduct of fighting there, he had also to lead and coordinate the efforts of America's ally, the British. Among the American officer corps, Anglophobia amounted to a malignant disease. What one of Ike's most senior commanders, Mark W. Clark, recorded in his diary was all too typical: "I was about to agree with Napoleon's conclusions that it is better to fight Allies than to be one of them" (quoted in Carlo D'Este, *Eisenhower: A Soldier's Life*. New York: Henry Holt, 2002, p. 314). In the British camp, even Winston Churchill, American on his mother's side and a great friend of the United States, remarked that "the only thing worse than having allies was not having them." Eisenhower put it in words at once more vivid and more homely. His job, he said, was like "trying to arrange the blankets smoothly over several prima donnas in the same bed."

Promoted to four-star general in February 1943, Eisenhower next directed Operation Husky, the Anglo-American invasion of Sicily, which commenced on July 9. General George S. Patton Jr.'s Seventh Army took Palermo on July 22, the Italian Fascist Council removed Benito Mussolini from office on July 25, and, on August 17, Patton took Messina, which completed the Allied conquest of Sicily. Eisenhower now prepared to launch Operation Avalanche, the Allied landings at Salerno on the Italian mainland.

Ike had already proved himself as an organizer and a manager. Now he would have to coordinate armies in actual combat. The lessons here are about leading while learning. They concern on-the-job training at the very highest level and for the highest possible stakes.

◆ ◆ ◆

Lesson 55

Leap

We are standing, of course, on the brink and must take the jump—whether the bottom contains a nice feather bed or a pile of brickbats!

—Secret communication to George C.
Marshall, November 7, 1942

About to launch Operation Torch, Ike did what every leader must do at the very point of taking action: resolve to accept the consequences, whatever they may be. The time for worry was over. The time for action was now. As he explained to General Marshall, Ike took satisfaction in the self-assurance that "we have worked our best to assure a successful landing, no matter what we encounter."

For Marshall's benefit, Ike reviewed the preparatory steps behind the leap he was now leading. "As I look back over the high pressure weeks since July 24th, I cannot think of any major item on which I would now, if I had the power, change the decision that was made at the time." The ability to make such a statement—and mean it—is a reliable gauge of one's real confidence in a course of action about to be taken. Ike continued, "Every member of the staff, British and American, has slaved like a dog"—another good sign. Indeed, Ike believed "that we have established a pattern for Combined Staff [cooperation between British and American officers] that might well serve as a rough model . . . in the future."

Ike listed four factors that contributed to his optimism about the impending operation. "The greatest single feature," he wrote, "was the fact that there was one responsible head." Ike believed above all that only by concentrating authority in a single commander—namely himself—could this complex alliance composed of often disputatious and highly individualistic subordinate commanders be made to work. The alliance involved plenty of meetings and a plethora of committees and study groups. Ike listened to them all, but the final decisions were always his and his alone. Only by accepting this finality, Ike firmly believed, could plans be translated into effective action. He pointed out to Marshall that the "British government made absolutely certain that commanders and staff officers, detailed to the expedition, had no mental reservations about their degree of responsibility to the Supreme Commander." Moreover, he was grateful that the Combined Chiefs of Staff—the committee made up of top U.S. and British officers—"on both sides of the water, preserved the attitude that they had placed responsibility in one individual and refused to interfere in matters properly pertaining to him."

These, then, were the first three of the four factors that gave Ike the confidence to take the leap. In truth, all three were really a single factor: full and final authority vested in one supreme commander. The fourth factor was Ike's belief that "the officers detailed to the Staff and to command positions, were the ablest that could be found."

Ike was so thoroughly convinced that the single-command method—the placing of final authority in one responsible individual on whose absolute authority everyone absolutely agrees—was essential to the success of the alliance that he sought to preempt the consequences of possible failure. "If, of course, some unexpected development should make this operation appear as a failure, much of the work that has been done will be discredited by unthinking people, and the methods that have been followed will be cited as erroneous. I do not believe that a final success or failure . . . should blind us to the fact that before this war is won the type of thing that we have been doing for the past many weeks will have to become common practice between the British and American services."

◆ ◆ ◆

Lesson 56

Promote

You are hereby authorized to promote instantly officers of your command . . . when they have demonstrated outstanding ability to command in actual combat.

—Radio message to Patton,
Fredendall, Ryder, and Doolittle,
November 9, 1942

Ike believed in recognizing leadership performance instantly, partly to reward it, but mostly to get the best men into command positions as soon as possible. To make this happen, he gave to Generals Patton, Fredendall, Ryder, and Doolittle, his principal field officers, the authority to make the necessary promotions, which included field promotions of enlisted men to second lieutenants as well promotions of officers up to and including the grade of colonel.

Ike saw a pressing need for combat leaders, so he restricted carte blanche promotion authority to cover only those in combat. "This authority does not, repeat, does not include promotion of staff officers," whose job put them behind a desk rather than a gun.

Identify the leaders you need in the context in which you need them, cut red tape as required, and get them into place without delay.

◆ ◆ ◆

Lesson 57

Demand and Support

The only tough nut is left in your hands. Crack it open quickly and ask for what you want.

—Secret radio message to George S.
Patton Jr., November 10, 1942

During the initial phase of Operation Torch, General Patton was assigned to take Casablanca. Ike sent his old friend a pointed radio message on November 10, addressed familiarly to "Dear Georgie," but unmistakably meant to be a sharp spur to Patton's flank: "Algiers has been ours for two days. Oran defenses crumbling rapidly. . . . The only tough nut is left in your hands." What to do with it? "Crack it open quickly." That was Ike's order and demand. But it was not the end of the sentence. The rest went like this: "and ask for what you want."

Eisenhower rarely gave an order in isolation. He routinely hitched each demand to a promise of 100 percent support. *Do it. I'll back you.* It was the perfect formula for leadership that yielded results.

◆ ◆ ◆

Lesson 58

Express Your Gratitude

The real purpose of this message is to express to you again my deep appreciation for the perfect support you have continuously given us.

—Cable to Winston Churchill,
November 11, 1942

After the Torch landings had proved successful and the campaign was progressing well, Ike cabled Prime Minister Winston Churchill his "deep appreciation for the perfect support you have continuously given us." Ike chose his words carefully: *perfect support* given *continuously*. He took pains to show that his appreciation was truly deep, in that he fully understood the nature of the support that was being given to him. Moreover, Ike became even more specific: "I particularly want to register once again my complete satisfaction with the selection of individuals you and the British Chiefs of Staff have made to serve as my principal command and subordinates."

Expressing gratitude is not merely a matter of etiquette; it is a means of perpetuation. Positive feedback engenders continued performance at a high level. No one works at his or her best in a vacuum. Respond to top-level performance with understanding and appreciation—deep appreciation—and you will reinforce that performance. Take it for granted, and you risk bringing it to an end.

◆ ◆ ◆

Lesson 59

Cure Victory Fever Fast

I am disturbed by the apparently bland assumption that this job is finished.

> —Secret cable to Walter Bedell "Beetle"
> Smith, November 12, 1942

Early in Operation Torch, Ike found himself peppered with proposals for departing from the accepted operational plan and diverting forces to a variety of new objectives. He was aware that these suggestions were the result of an impression on the part of leaders who were remote from the battle front that "this job is finished" and that forces were therefore available for other tasks. "It would take only five minutes actually on the ground to convince anyone that nothing could be further from the truth."

Before the war was over, the tendency to convert good news into a false assurance of victory achieved would become all too familiar to Eisenhower. He would call it victory fever, and he came to know it as an enemy as dangerous as any Nazi with a gun. The cure for victory fever was neither a scolding nor an overreaction of panic. As he wrote to "Beetle" Smith, "I am not crying wolf nor am I growing fearful of shadows." The cure was the reestablishment of a sound perspective on the situation, which was this: "We are just started on a great venture and I must insist that there be nothing now but the firmest and most intense support, in order that a good beginning may not be destroyed by any unwarranted assumptions." A good beginning is a wonderful thing, but confusing it with final victory is fatal. Ike's duty at this moment was to ensure that such confusion was quickly cleared up and victory fever cured once and for all.

A leader pushes, pulls, and steers. Often, however, his or her most important job is to let everyone know just where the enterprise stands here and now, lest people think they're somewhere else.

◆ ◆ ◆

Lesson 60

Eye on the Prize

Give them some money if it will help.

> —Secret communication to Mark W.
> Clark, November 12, 1942

Operation Torch landed the Allies on the North African colonial territory of France. At the time, this region was defended by forces of the French Vichy government, which was ostensibly allied with the Axis—Germany and Italy. Ike knew that the actual support for the Axis among the Vichy officers was very soft, and he wanted to do everything possible to win Vichy compliance with Operation Torch rather than provoke opposition to it. As he put it, he did not want to waste on the Vichy bullets that were better used on the Germans and Italians.

Acting on his own initiative and authority, Ike negotiated with the most powerful Vichy authority in the region, Admiral Jean-François Darlan, securing his cooperation in return for the Allies' acknowledgment of his authority in North Africa. Charles de Gaulle, the most important leader of the Free French forces, and several other Allied leaders objected to Ike's dealings with Darlan, whom they considered a collaborationist traitor. It is no exaggeration to point out that Eisenhower risked losing his job. Ultimately, however, he secured the approval of both President Roosevelt and Prime Minister Churchill for his dealings with Darlan.

Ike did not expect the Vichy forces to fight the Germans and Italians, but he wanted to ensure that they would not fight the Allies, that they would cooperate with the occupation, and that they would act to keep order among the natives of the region. "It is important," he wrote to Mark Clark, the general who served as his emissary to the Vichy French in the region, "that we do not create any dissension among the tribes or encourage them to break away from existing methods of control." The last thing the Allies needed was to have to fight the French, the native North Africans, *and* the Germans and Italians. "To organize this country in support of the war effort, we must use French officials and we do not want any internal unrest or trouble."

The problem was that the French colonial officials were hardly selfless or unified in their objectives. This was a source of anger and frustration, but Ike did not allow his feelings either to lead to stalemate or to find expression in ways that would alienate the officials. Doubtless holding his nose, he ordered Clark to "Give them some money if it will help." Ike was not willing to compromise on the objective of victory. He was, however, quite willing to make compromises to achieve that objective. It was distasteful to deal with the Vichy French, not only because of the prevailing sentiment that they had betrayed the honor of France but because it was nearly impossible to determine from day to day where each Vichy official stood. The situation was in flux, and the ranks of the colonial officers were rife with opportunists. Nevertheless, Eisenhower decided that the quickest, surest, and most economical route to total victory lay through a series of compromises, including even bribery. Flattering words and the disbursement of cash were both cheaper and more effective than bullets in dealing with the Vichy of North Africa. Ike's objective was victory, and he meant to achieve it by whatever means he judged necessary, even if these were not always the accepted means of a soldier.

Leadership requires a combination of flexibility and rigidity. Even more important, it requires knowing where and when to bend and where and when to be absolutely unbending.

◆　◆　◆

Lesson 61

Register Your Vote of Confidence

I have not the slightest doubt that any such demands will be met just as efficiently and cheerfully as they have in the past.

—Letter to Carl Spaatz,
November 12, 1942

The principal purpose of this letter was to alert General Spaatz that "we shall have to make new and unexpected demands upon you [as theater commander of the of the Army Air Forces] because, as usual, circumstances never develop quite as planners anticipated." Ike began the letter by promising "to make a special point of recording with the War Department my boundless appreciation for the way you and your splendid organization have responded to every demand ever made upon you," and, after warning that new demands would surely be made, Ike concluded by remarking that he did not have the "slightest doubt that any such demands will be met just as efficiently and cheerfully as they have in the past."

On the face of it, Eisenhower would seem to be offering a pretty one-sided proposition: *Thanks for what you've done. You're going to*

*have to do even more. I have every confidence that you will do it as well
as you have in the past.* But Ike knew his man as a high achiever, and
he knew that the greatest incentive you can offer a high achiever is
the opportunity to achieve at an even loftier height. The secret is
to ask for more and more, bolstering your request with the confident
expectation of receiving total satisfaction. Set the bar high, vote
your confidence, then set the bar higher.

◆ ◆ ◆

Lesson 62

Become Partners

I will take prompt steps to correct the difficulty.

—Letter to Auguste Noguès,
November 15, 1942

With great skill, Ike managed to secure the cooperation of Vichy
French forces during the invasion of North Africa. Early in the
operation, it was anybody's guess how Vichy commanders would
react to the Allied landings: Would they cooperate with the Axis
and lead resistance against the "invaders"? Would they remain passively neutral? Or would they actively assist the Allies?

Ike seized the initiative in negotiating with the chief French
military authority in the region, Admiral Jean-François Darlan, and
his right hand in the army, General Auguste Noguès. After securing an agreement with Darlan and Noguès, he took steps to cement
amicable relations. His approach was to create common cause with
the French commanders—to make them his partners. To Noguès,
he wrote asking that the general "bring to my early attention any
instances in which you consider that any part of the forces under
my command are failing to contribute their full share in producing
the amity and cooperation you and I are seeking." The language
here is telling: he invites Noguès to alert him to failures among

Allied officers and enlisted men. In this, Ike takes full personal responsibility for correcting any problems; however, he also emphasizes that the objective is a shared one: "the amity and cooperation *you and I* are seeking." He continues: "I know you are animated by the same impulses [that animate me]."

Recruit allies by inviting both cooperation and criticism and by presenting yourself as the person on whom your prospective partner can absolutely rely for aid and loyalty. Define common goals and values, expressing your confidence that, by acting together, you and your partner can realize them.

◆ ◆ ◆

Lesson 63

Do Your Job, Not Someone Else's

I am far too busy to give my time to anything that does not have to do with my present job.

—Secret cable to Walter Bedell "Beetle"
Smith, November 17, 1942

Ike mentioned to his chief of staff, General Smith, that he agreed with Prime Minister Churchill's recommendation that he "have nothing whatsoever to do with international political relationships" because "I am far too busy to give my time to anything that does not have to do with my present job."

Ike had a big and complex job, but it was, he knew, a job that did have defined limits, and although the nature of the job continually tempted him to overstep those limits, he was determined to resist temptation. Effective leadership requires both knowing your job and knowing what is *not* your job. Armed with this clear knowledge, always do your job and not someone else's.

◆ ◆ ◆

Lesson 64

Watch Your Language

I have deliberately used understatement.

—Secret cable to George C. Marshall,
November 17, 1942

"In order to promote cooperative action between this expedition [the Allied force invading North Africa] and available French units, particularly while we need their help in Tunisia," Ike wrote to his boss, General Marshall, "I have tried to avoid the creation of animosities that would naturally spring up between the two sides if we should publicly announce or regard ourselves as the conquerors of a defending French Army. Consequently I have deliberately used understatement in describing publicly some of the earlier operations, although in certain instances the fighting [between the Allied invaders and the French defenders] was quite sharp as is shown from our present estimate of U.S. Army losses alone of 531 killed, 1,054 wounded, and 237 missing."

Some histories of World War II depict the initial stages of the Allied landings on North Africa as a cakewalk, implying that resistance from Vichy French forces was negligible. This impression, even among some historians, was created in part by Eisenhower's reports, which, as he explained, deliberately underplayed the extent and seriousness of the initial battles. Eisenhower was less interested in portraying a glorious martial conquest than he was in using language that would allow the French to save face and enable French commanders to see their way clear to laying down their arms and cooperating with the Allies. To use a modern term, Ike "spun" the invasion story in order to ease the conversion of the Vichy French in North Africa from enemy to something just short of ally. If words could substitute for bullets—and save lives in the process—Ike would use words, even if the words he used did not quite correspond with reality.

All things being equal, Abraham Lincoln's advice that honesty is the best policy is surely true. Yet all things are not always equal, and although outright lies and distortions can rarely be justified, a leader must sometimes massage present circumstances with language intended to shape a more favorable future. Morally and even legally, this may require treading a fine line, yet it is never a good idea to use language that, no matter how truthful, forecloses the future. Sometimes it is necessary to bend and brighten the truth in order to preserve the possibility that reality may, in good time, be made to coincide with what is at present a description more hopeful than accurate.

◆ ◆ ◆

Lesson 65

Consider the Source

Before the war was over I became accustomed to this tendency of individuals far in the rear to overevaluate early success and to discount future difficulty.

—*Crusade in Europe*

The person closest to the action, who receives data unfiltered, is the person whose opinion counts most. Ike understood that the farther you were to the rear, the more you thought you knew; you believed you had the "big picture." In fact, he discovered, the farther you were to the rear, the less reliable was your information. Moreover, Ike concluded from experience that those in the rear tended to "overevaluate early success and to discount future difficulty." The problem for Ike was that those farthest to the rear were the bosses, the political leaders to whom even he had to answer.

As a hands-on leader, you are in the best position to evaluate progress or lack thereof. A big part of your job is continually to persuade those above—and behind—that this is the case. However, if there is one thing that may be more difficult than persuading others of this fact, it is convincing yourself. After all, those at the top and rear got there by being smart—maybe (you think) smarter than you. But always remember that the quality of information—and, therefore, the value of judgments based on it—has nothing to do with who is smarter. It has everything to do with proximity to the operation at hand.

◆ ◆ ◆

Lesson 66

Persuade Them to Let You Do Your Job

God knows I'm not . . . trying to be a kingmaker.

—Secret cable to Walter Bedell "Beetle"
Smith, November 18, 1942

Ike was widely criticized for striking a deal with the Vichy French admiral Jean-François Darlan, whom Free French leaders deemed a traitor, but who, Ike knew, was the only official in French-controlled North Africa capable of exercising authority over Vichy forces in the region, French colonial administrators, and the native population. When Eisenhower endorsed Darlan's authority over the Vichy-controlled colonies in exchange for the admiral's pledge of cooperation with the Allies, some accused Ike of exceeding his brief and acting the kingmaker. At this, Ike bristled, explaining to his chief of staff "Beetle" Smith that he was by no means a kingmaker, but was "simply trying to get a complete and firm military grip on North Africa, which I was sent down here to do." He did not want to fight Germans, Italians, *and* Vichy, too. His objective, he explained, was to "get Tunisia quickly," so that the Axis would not have "time to do as it pleases in that region," including inciting Spain to abandon its neutrality and openly join its cause. "The potential consequences of delay are enormous," he warned Smith, "because this battle is not repeat not yet won."

Ike assured Smith that he did "not expect any encouragement and hurrahs from the rear, but I regret that I must use so much of my own time to keep explaining these matters."

A frustration universal among those entrusted with great responsibility is the discovery of the limitations of that trust. Much of the time, a leader's hardest job is persuading those above him to let him do his job. Such persuasion may require a great deal of tedious explanation and seemingly endless repetition of the text of your job description. Yet you have to do it and do it vigilantly to prevent the inevitable shrinkage of your sphere of authority, influence, and action.

◆ ◆ ◆

Lesson 67

Win the Battle Any Way You Can

I will tie units into knots if I can win a battle that way.

—Radio message to George S. Patton Jr.,
November 26, 1942

In his effort to capture Tunisia from the Germans and Italians as quickly as possible, Ike cobbled together some army units in unorthodox fashion, creating a number of "mixed" units, which combined infantry and armor. This ran contrary to accepted procedure, and Ike admitted to General Patton that he "abhor[red] mixed units as much as anyone," but, he continued, "I will tie units into knots if I can win a battle that way."

Decide on the must-do objectives, then do what you must to attain them. If this means adopting ad hoc or unorthodox methods—and you are persuaded that these will give you the edge in attaining the objective—don't hesitate to start coloring outside the lines.

◆ ◆ ◆

Lesson 68

Be in Touch—Constantly

I have liaison officers constantly in the forward area.

—Secret cable to Walter Bedell "Beetle"
Smith, November 27, 1942

As supreme commander during the North African campaign, Ike took his place not at the front, the "forward area," nor at the extreme rear, in Washington or London, but somewhere in between, between the field officers at the front and the politicians and planners in the Allied capitals. And Ike knew his place. But he also knew that it was vital for him to remain *constantly* in touch with the front, and he did this through liaison officers, whose job it was to serve both as his conduits to the field commanders and as his eyes and ears—independent of those commanders—in the field.

As a leader, you need to avoid micromanagement on the one hand and remote management on the other. You occupy a middle position, between your subordinates and your bosses, or between those who execute your policies and directives and those to whom you are immediately responsible, such as investors and customers. You cannot afford to stay too far back or too far forward, but you must remain constantly in touch with both the rear and the forward area. Like Ike, you need an adequate and accurate means of liaison—the next best thing to the impossible ideal, which is to be everywhere at once.

◆ ◆ ◆

Lesson 69

"Shove Along the Fellow Who Can Really Do the Job"

I am constantly being importuned to promote this fellow or that fellow because he had curly hair or had a nice mother.

—Letter to Mabel "Mike" Moore,
December 4, 1942

Ike sympathized with the situation of Gordon Moore, his brother-in-law, who felt he deserved more rapid promotion in the army; however, he did point out to Mabel "Mike" Moore, Gordon's wife, that one of his own great burdens was being saddled with "the type of fellow who is always looking for advancement." Ike told Mike that whereas he was "pretty hard-hearted about" promoting people just for the asking, he was "certainly quick to shove along the fellow who can really do the job."

If you have it in your power to make merit promotions, be certain that the promotions you make really are merit promotions—and then don't be stingy with them. The better the people who are closest to you in responsibility, the more effectively you will lead the enterprise. Promotion of cronies or promotion for the sake of being perceived as a nice guy is destructive to the enterprise and, of course, to your ability to lead. Promoting people on any basis other than demonstrated ability is at best an act of unwarranted faith and, at worst, one of vain stupidity. Go ahead, be hard-hearted, as long as you are also evenhanded. There is no contradiction in acting both carefully and generously.

◆ ◆ ◆

Lesson 70

Value Experience over Prestige

No individual regardless of personal qualifications could serve at this time . . . except a man that has lived through the hectic experiences of the past few weeks.

—Secret cable to George V. Strong,
December 4, 1942

Major General George V. Strong, G-2 (head of intelligence) at the War Department, suggested to Ike that New York's brilliant, colorful, and much-loved Mayor Fiorello LaGuardia could be drafted to relieve the supreme commander of much of the burden of dealing with a host of civilian agencies and individuals swarming over North Africa. Ike replied to the suggestion in no uncertain terms: "Do not repeat not consider it advisable at this time further to complicate my staff problems and procedure by drafting of Mayor LaGuardia. No individual regardless of personal qualifications could serve at this time as head of my civil section except a man that has lived through the hectic experiences of the past few weeks."

As Eisenhower saw it, the man with the experience was Robert D. Murphy, a State Department diplomat who was FDR's personal representative to the Vichy officials in North Africa. Unbidden, Murphy had become Ike's political adviser, and, because he had the ear of the president, he had to be listened to. Certainly Ike was not always thrilled to have Murphy questioning his decisions and even undercutting his authority in dealing with the always ambiguous Vichy; yet Ike was convinced that it was better to have Murphy, drawbacks and all, heading up his civil affairs section than it was to introduce someone entirely new. Despite his shortcomings, Murphy had experience. He knew all the players, and he was familiar with the complex issues. Ike favored this experience over prestige, and he successfully resisted Murphy's displacement by LaGuardia.

Never rush to shed an experienced manager, even when somebody more glamorous or even more promising appears on the horizon. Continuity and experience weigh very heavily in the balance against any other quality that may be offered. To be sure, it is a mistake to hold on to someone who is not up to the job, but it is a far bigger error to trade, on a casual basis, experience for promise.

◆   ◆   ◆

Lesson 71

Don't Get Sucked into the Whirlpool of Power

The pressure of work on a job like this seems to result in making personal activity resemble a whirlpool, with the individual constantly getting closer to the center and, therefore, with his contacts limited progressively to fewer and fewer people.

—Letter to Paul A. Hodgson,
December 4, 1942

Ike saw that a danger of "supreme" authority was the almost inevitable contraction of your universe to an inner circle of advisers and subordinates. Because you were in contact with them virtually all the time, you had less and less contact with those outside the circle. Caught in this whirlpool, you became progressively removed from reality.

"I find myself resenting this," Ike wrote his old friend and West Point roommate, "and frequently try to break out of its clutches, at least mentally, by wondering what someone else would say or think about particular questions."

This was, in fact, a brilliant solution. If the high pressure of his job made it inevitable that he would deal almost exclusively with the men of the whirlpool, Ike was determined to maintain his contact with reality at the very least through an exercise of the imagination.

Call it a whirlpool, a think tank, an inner circle, or an ivory tower, you have to get beyond it and outside it, using whatever means of escape you can grab hold of. Nothing is more fatal to leadership than mistaking a coterie for reality. Contact with "the outside" is key.

◆   ◆   ◆

Lesson 72

Don't Let Them Take the People You Need

I can not repeat not concur at this time in solution requiring frequent presence of [Mark] Clark in London.

—Secret cable to George C. Marshall,
December 5, 1942

When General Walter Bedell "Beetle" Smith was transferred from London to Algiers, General Marshall was concerned that Prime Minister Winston Churchill would not have an officer of appropriate rank and prestige to keep him informed of the fluid situation in North Africa. Marshall suggested that Clark turn over command of the Fifth Army to Lloyd Fredendall and then go to London, at least for a time. Although Ike made clear that he realized the "importance of keeping Prime Minister informed," he deemed Clark indispensable to combat operations in North Africa and therefore objected to the recommendation for reassignment. Ike carefully detailed the reasons for his objection, which centered on Clark's role in organizing the Fifth Army and in overseeing its training. Moreover, Ike noted that he "may need Clark for special emergency missions at any time."

Mark W. Clark, Ike believed, was a combat resource far too valuable to misuse as a liaison officer, even to so exalted a figure as Winston Churchill. He conveyed this to Marshall in no uncertain terms. Unwilling, however, to leave his boss with nothing but a negative, he suggested an alternative: "A better solution from my standpoint would be to have Smith spend one week, out of each three in London or if necessary every alternate week, which can be arranged without serious dislocation of work here."

Don't submit passively or automatically to any "suggestion" or "recommendation" from on high. Consider it, question it, and, if necessary, object to it. Make your objection clear, and always frame it in terms of the good of the organization. It is rarely either persuasive or productive to offer nothing but an objection. Supply an alternative or two and provide a supporting rationale for what you suggest. Rejecting a "suggestion" from your boss requires fortitude, self-confidence, and resolve on your part. Remember, however, that both you and your boss have a common interest in advancing the entire organization. In this you are not antagonists, but teammates. Moreover, if you present yourself as a problem solver—by offering an alternative along with your objection—you need not fear being perceived as a dissident. On the contrary, you will be regarded as an asset indispensable to the total victory you and your boss seek.

◆ ◆ ◆

Lesson 73

Everyone Works

Throughout the rear areas, soldiers should be just as busy as they are in the forward ones.

—Memorandum to Walter Bedell "Beetle" Smith, December 5, 1942

Ike wanted no resources wasted. Soldiers in the rear areas were not there to idle but to be worked: "If they are not training, they must be working—there are a thousand things to do and commanders must get after them." He wanted them engaged not in busywork but in perfecting bases of operations, transforming them from "improvised facilities" to permanent ones, the better to enable continued action at the front. Even though Eisenhower did not propose makework activities, the mere fact of work was almost as important as what the work accomplished. Ike needed to keep his entire organization active, so as to maintain a sense of urgent and collective enterprise. The leader who allows any of his assets to lie idle at the very least diminishes the cohesiveness and group identity of the organization. At worst, he dooms it to disintegration.

◆ ◆ ◆

Lesson 74

The Fine Balance

The flashy, publicity-seeking type of adventurer can grab the headlines and be a hero in the eyes of the public, but he simply can't deliver the goods in high command. On the other hand, the slow, methodical, ritualistic person is absolutely valueless in a key position.

—Notes for Harry C. Butcher,
December 10, 1942

One of the hardest lessons Ike learned from the North African campaign was that the ideal leader had to strike a "fine balance" between the flashy adventurer-hero and the slow, methodical, ritualistic manager. Ike concluded that "rich organizational experience and an orderly, logical mind are absolute essentials to success," whereas mere flamboyance is fatal. Yet order and logic alone were not sufficient to lead a successful military enterprise. A commander had to balance flash with reason, heroism with order. Even more, he had to be able to "absorb the disappointments, the discouragements and the doubts of his subordinates and to force them on to accomplishments, which they regard as impossible."

Just how difficult was it to maintain the required balance? At this stage in the war, Ike judged that "Among the American Commanders, Patton I think comes closest to meeting every requirement made on a commander," yet before too long, Ike would have reason to criticize Patton's impulsiveness and lack of self-control. Even worse, he rated just below Patton Lloyd Fredendall, commanding general of II Corps. But Fredendall would soon preside over an ignominious defeat at the Battle of Kasserine Pass, and Ike would remove him, replacing him with Patton. The fact is that very few leaders—perhaps none—maintain the required balance all the time. Realistically, the best that can be hoped for is adequate balance most of the time.

◆ ◆ ◆

Lesson 75

The Hardest Thing

[W]aiting for other people to produce is one of the hardest things a commander has to do.

> —Notes for Harry C. Butcher,
> December 10, 1942

To his trusted naval aide, Commander Harry C. Butcher, Ike confessed that his difficult experience commanding Operation Torch and the campaign in North Africa had taught him the necessity of waiting for others "to produce," and it had also taught him that this is one of the hardest things a leader must do.

Delegation of responsibility is necessary in an organization of any size and complexity, but it is, by definition, a surrender of control and authority. As a leader, you can only instruct and supervise so much. At some point, you have to cut others loose and trust them to do the job assigned. The interval between assignment and fulfillment can be torture for you, as you will now find yourself responsible for operations and events that are out of your hands—and, if you are doing your job, *must* be out of your hands.

◆ ◆ ◆

Lesson 76

Upward the Buck Is Passed

[S]ubordinates don't even realize that they are simply pouring their burdens upon the next superior.

> —Notes for Harry C. Butcher,
> December 10, 1942

Ike was jumped over 366 more senior generals when he was made supreme commander of the Allied effort in North Africa, but he viewed the power he was thus given as more of a burden than a prerogative. A leader had "day and night to absorb the disappointments, the discouragements and the doubts of his subordinates." Moreover, the orders he gave them did not so much add to the responsibilities of subordinates as it "relieved [them] of a great load of moral responsibility." Subordinates, Ike pointed out, "don't even realize that they are simply pouring their burdens upon the next superior." As Queen Elizabeth I observed concerning leadership in her 1601 "Golden Speech" to Parliament, "To be a king and wear a crown is a thing more glorious to them that see it than it is pleasant to them that bear it."

◆ ◆ ◆

Lesson 77

Be Ruthless with Deadwood

The easiest thing for us would be merely to load these people on returning ships.

> Secret letter to George C. Marshall,
> December 11, 1942

War Department rules dictated that officers found deficient in their ability to perform their duties be subjected to a long, formal process before being relieved of command, demoted, or reassigned. Ike wrote to General Marshall, noting that "everybody that is worth his salt [was] working at top speed. . . . The result is that there is simply no time or opportunity to convene the [required] boards and go through the lengthy process [prescribed by regulations]." This being the case, Ike proposed only two alternatives. The first was "for us to dispatch to the United States, by any returning transportation, all officers found unsuitable, sending to the War Department such evidence as can be rapidly obtained of the particular type of failure of which the man is guilty." The second "would be to give to the Theater Commander . . . an arbitrary authority" to reduce officers in rank and reassign them to different duty. Of the two alternatives, the first was somewhat distasteful to Ike because it involved passing the buck to the War Department; however, it did represent the "easiest thing for us." Ike's overriding concern was to weed out non-performing, underperforming, and badly performing officers, getting rid of them by the most expedient means possible. He could not afford deadwood in his organization.

A good leader is loath to throw anyone away, yet no organization can afford to keep carrying deadwood. It is crucial, therefore, to find an effective compromise among expedient dismissal, rehabilitation, and fair treatment of the individual. In finding this compromise, however, you must chiefly consider the good of the organization, without which everyone fails.

◆ ◆ ◆

Lesson 78

People Come Before Things

[G]ood training depends on ingenuity and enthusiasm and intelligent direction and example rather than upon material resources.

—Message to Anglo-American senior commanders, December 11, 1942

Ike wanted to ensure that everyone in his command was put to work productively. When they were not working, men in the rear areas were to be training. To the complaint that training facilities did not exist, Ike responded, first, that "Training facilities may not exist but they can be created," and, second, that "good training depends on ingenuity and enthusiasm and intelligent direction and example rather than upon material resources."

Never allow facilities and equipment to be put ahead of your human resources, and never allow the absence of "material resources" to be used as an excuse for the failure to exercise human resources. As long as "ingenuity and enthusiasm and intelligent direction and example" are available, there is no excuse for the failure of productivity.

◆ ◆ ◆

Lesson 79

You Are Your Own Moral Compass

The only thing that a soldier can use for a guide is to try to do what appears right and just in the moment of the crisis.

—Letter to his son, John S. D. Eisenhower,
December 20, 1942

Many criticized Ike for working with Admiral Jean-François Darlan, the Vichy leader of French North Africa. "Apparently, the people who have been creating the storm do not like Darlan," Ike wrote to his son. "The answer to that one is 'Who does?'" Ike made the decision to deal with rather than fight Darlan because, "at the moment of crisis," he believed it was the "right and just" decision. "That is one reason we train people all their lives to be soldiers, so that in a moment of emergency they can get down to the essentials of the situation and not be too much disturbed about popularity or newspaper acclaim."

The right decision may or may not be the most popular decision. A decision made in a moment of crisis might, in the fullness of time, prove to be the wrong decision. The point is that it *is* a decision, which has to be made. In a crisis, the failure to decide in a timely fashion almost always has graver consequences than making a less-than-perfect or even a wrong decision. And, in a crisis, there is rarely time to conduct an opinion poll.

◆ ◆ ◆

Lesson 80

Emphasize Execution

It is in the application . . . that we fail.

—Secret memorandum to Russell P.
"Scrappy" Hartle, January 15, 1943

In operations to retake Tunisia from the Axis, Ike was disappointed by the performance of the troops, whom he found deficient in training. "The defects in training in elementary subjects are the most outstanding lessons learned in this campaign. The mistakes made in maneuvers nearly two years ago are now being repeated on the battlefield." As an effective leader-manager, Eisenhower was not content to deliver criticism unaccompanied by analysis. He told Hartle that he could find "no great fault . . . with our training doctrine or methods," but "It is in the application of them that we fail." The need, he felt, was to "impress upon our junior officers . . . the deadly seriousness of the job, the absolute necessity for thoroughness in every detail."

Too often, leaders at the top concern themselves exclusively with plans and policy, with "doctrine or methods," to the exclusion of monitoring the execution of orders, principles, plans, and policies. Plans and policy mean nothing until they are implemented and implemented adequately. Ike correctly believed that execution was the job of junior officers, and when he perceived a failure of adequate execution, it was to these officers that he turned his attention. *They* needed to be counseled to train their troops harder and to lead them in continual practice so that the old mistakes would not be repeated.

The leadership remedy for inadequate execution is not a revision of plans and policies, nor is it micromanagement. It is focusing on the level of management most directly responsible for ensuring the adequacy of execution. Motivate this middle level to ensure the continuity of the vital link between headquarters (plans and policies) and the front lines (execution).

◆ ◆ ◆

Lesson 81

Leadership as Thoroughness

Thoroughness—thoroughness achieved by leadership and constant attention to detail—will pay maximum dividends.

—Secret memorandum to Russell P. "Scrappy" Hartle, January 15, 1943

This sentence concludes Eisenhower's letter to General Hartle concerning deficiencies in the training and discipline of American troops—problems that became all too apparent to Ike during the campaign to capture Tunisia.

On the surface, there is hardly anything radical here. Who could argue with "thoroughness," "constant attention to detail," and "leadership"? Yet *leadership* is rarely found as the third leg of a triad that includes *thoroughness* and *attention to detail*. Ike believed the three were inextricably linked. The task for leadership, in this three-way arrangement, is to inculcate and execute thoroughness and attention to detail without micromanaging. In short, the leader must ensure that his immediate subordinates do their jobs, so that nothing slips through. The broad, bold strokes popularly associated with leadership are not sufficient. Without losing sight of the big picture, the leader must ensure thorough execution of all the details. It is not easy, and certainly it is not a solo act. Leaders do not lead companies or projects. They lead people. In large organizations, they lead the people who lead the people. Allow a single link to break, and execution itself breaks down.

◆ ◆ ◆

Lesson 82

What's in a Name?

I am going to name him as "Deputy Commander for Ground Forces."

—Message to George C. Marshall,
January 17, 1943

General George C. Marshall, the army chief of staff, suggested to Eisenhower that he use General George S. Patton Jr. "as a sort of deputy." Ike wrote to Marshall to let him know that he was considering the matter and had "tentatively come to the conclusion that I am going to name him as 'Deputy Commander for Ground Forces.'

This will give him the necessary authority and will allow me to use his great mental and physical energy in helping me through a critical period. On the other hand, it will avoid the difficulties that might be involved should I call him 'Deputy Commander-in-Chief,' which would imply an influence in Naval and Air matters, and might be resented."

Many managers treat job titles cavalierly. After all, it's substance, not some label, that counts. Right?

That is not the way Ike saw it. He took the time and thought to translate "some sort of deputy" into a very specific title—not for reasons of empty ceremony, but to create a useful job description, a label meant to inform the bearer (as well as those who deal with him) of the precise scope and limits of his job.

Do everything you can to define and demarcate authority, paying special attention to where one person's job leaves off and that of another begins. We depend on labels every day to keep us from taking the wrong medicine, eating the wrong food, or using the wrong motor oil. Good labels also keep us from using the wrong people for the job.

◆   ◆   ◆

Lesson 83

Make This One Very Simple, Very Difficult Demand

All I demand is that every man do his best.

> —Memorandum to Walter Bedell "Beetle"
> Smith, January 26, 1943

"All I demand is that every man do his best; if he does that, he need have no fear of his standing with his superiors and of the certainty that he will be constantly brought up to serve in positions of increasing responsibility and authority."

Sometimes leadership consists of making very simple demands that may be very difficult to carry out. Asking a subordinate for his or her "very best" may be the hardest demand you can possibly make. What Ike sought was a commitment from each person to make a maximum effort directed toward a single goal: "We must all realize that we are fighting a tough war and everything we do, day and night, must be directed toward the winning of that war. Training, morale, self-respect, smartness, saluting, respect for Allies— each of these subjects has, in its own way, some bearing upon the efficiency of an army. That is what I am interested in."

◆ ◆ ◆

Lesson 84

Preach Simplicity, Practice Simplicity

As much as we preach simplicity in the Army, I sometimes feel it is the one thing most frequently violated in our own thinking.

—Letter to Thomas T. Handy,
January 28, 1943

"Every once in a while Staff Officers get all confused in a bunch of charts and drawing lines on blank paper," Ike wrote to his friend General Handy. "I take a fiendish delight in ripping them to pieces and breaking up their little playhouses."

Dwight Eisenhower dealt in plans all day, every day. He had great respect for planners. But even when he was locked for hours and days on end in a dreary headquarters, remote from the battlefield, he never mistook planning for an end in itself. A plan is not real. It is a means to what is real, a means to an end.

A plan should be a window or a door. One way or the other, it must open out onto reality. It must not be merely a pretty picture, opaque to what lies outside it. A plan should be sufficiently complex to address reality, but absolutely no more complex than is necessary to do so. The best plans are the simplest *possible*, which means the simplest that get the job done. Fall in love with plans, and you will never make them this simple. Ike resisted such romances, and when he saw them growing in others, he nipped them in the bud—or, as he put it, took a fiendish delight in breaking up their little playhouses.

◆ ◆ ◆

Lesson 85

Package Your Criticism

There is no one else of my acquaintance, particularly any of my old seniors, to whom I would write so freely and frankly on such a subject.

—Letter to George S. Patton Jr.,
February 4, 1943

Eisenhower valued Patton as what he called one of his "fighting generals," but (as he wrote in 1944), he also regarded him as a "problem child." Patton was impulsive in speech and had an often self-destructive need to shock and offend others. As his boss, Eisenhower was determined to do what he could to curb this trait, but although Patton was clearly under his command during the North African campaign and beyond, both Patton and Eisenhower were well aware that Patton had been Ike's senior. Ike took pains to preserve this fact of his personal history with Patton, who had been a friend and mentor, yet he could not afford to yield any of his present authority. Customarily, Ike delivered criticism as straightforwardly as he delivered praise. With Patton, however, because issues of friendship and seniority threatened to foul the chain of command, Ike was careful to package his criticism in a form that delivered it whole, yet without giving offense.

He began by pointing out how, as time passed, the Allies would increasingly realize the need for a "*fighting* General . . . people such as yourself." Then he continued: "We must not forget, however, that superiors will frequently shy off from a man on account of impressions and I am anxious in your case that this does not occur."

Ike was careful to use the first person plural, *we*, rather than first person singular, *I*, and the second person singular, *you*. He wanted to put himself in Patton's corner rather than set up a situation of opposing sides. Having established an alliance, he continued with an observation: "You are quick-witted and have a ready and facile tongue." This is a compliment—sort of. "As a result, you frequently give the impression that you act merely on impulse and not upon study and reflection." This is a criticism, but Ike immediately qualifies it: "People that know you as I do are quite well aware of the fact that much of your talk is a smoke-screen, but some of those in authority, who have a chance to meet you only occasionally, do not have this knowledge." Now that the criticism and its context have been set up, Ike offers what he is careful to call "advice . . . (if you want it)," namely "to 'count ten before you speak.'" And here is his *real* point: "This applies not only to criticism of the Allies, a subject on which I am adamant, but to many others."

Ike could not allow anyone—even a fighting general, an old friend, a respected former senior—to sabotage working relations with the British. He became blunt: "A man once gave to me an old proverb. It was this: 'Keep silent and appear stupid; open your mouth and remove all doubt.'" But, once again, he carefully qualified his remark: "I do not mean that this applies to you, as you damn well know, but I do mean that a certain sphinx-like quality upon occasion will do one hell of a lot toward enhancing one's reputation." To further remove the criticism from the arena of personality, Ike took a step back: "All of this free advice I am dishing out is not, as you will probably guess, just the product of my own reflection. Rather, it has been gleaned from my interpretation of things said by some of our distinguished visitors and then placed in my own homely words."

Many managers glibly claim that friendship ends where business starts. They should know better. It is rarely easy and often impossible to separate professional conduct from personal feelings. We do not— and certainly should not—shed our humanity and personal history when we enter the office in the morning. But every leader has to come to viable terms with friendship and other issues of personality and personal history in the workplace. The triumph of professionalism must not come at the expense of insulting or embarrassing anyone, yet personal issues cannot be allowed to trump the requirements and welfare of the enterprise. Navigating these murky waters sometimes requires considerably more words than the few sharp orders you would like to give.

◆ ◆ ◆

Lesson 86

Cure Staff "Obesity and Elephantiasis"

I am determined to kick out of here all matters that involve petty patronage.

> —Letter to George C. Marshall,
> February 8, 1943

"I am constantly impressed by the . . . tendency of all staffs to crowd around the center of local power," Ike wrote to Marshall. Instead of devoting themselves to "their own operational duties," he complained, staff officers constantly try to get in on "administration." The result? A staff afflicted with "diseases that include obesity and elephantiasis." The cure? "Apparently only a sharp knife, freely wielded, provides any cure."

Ike admitted "the impossibility of working without adequate staffs," but he noted their tendency to expand and bog down as too many rising officers seek the fruits of "petty patronage" at the center of power: the various headquarters under Ike's command. His ideal for any headquarters was a lean staff, which did nothing more or less than facilitate the connection between the highest level of command and the commanders in the field. Anything else not only wasted manpower but actually clogged the arteries of the enterprise, bloating it and slowing it down. Eisenhower's solution was periodically to pare down his headquarters.

Few leaders would disagree with Eisenhower on the problems created by a top-heavy organization. Yet even fewer leaders are willing to voluntarily reduce the number of staff who report directly to them. The function of a staff is to achieve transparency, to move orders from the top to the people on the front lines, and to move feedback from the front up to the top. Overfill this staff layer, and it inevitably becomes increasingly opaque, creating blindness when acute vision is most necessary.

◆ ◆ ◆

Lesson 87

Kill Committees

I will be constantly on my guard to prevent any important military venture depending for its control and direction on the "committee" system of command.

—Letter to George C. Marshall,
February 8, 1943

Ike wrote to his boss Marshall to express concern over the "inevitable trend of the British mind toward 'committee' rather than 'single' command." Ike always insisted on being accepted by his American as well as his British colleagues as the single source of command for Allied operations. This did not mean that he failed to ask for advice or to heed his subordinate and field commanders, but he wanted to be in the position of making the final decisions and issuing the final orders. Committees, he believed, consumed too much time and, even worse, diffused responsibility, which made it difficult to create rapport, loyalty, and timely compliance among a disparate group of field officers.

What do you do with a committee? You kill it. Or at least you ensure that it never acts in anything other than a study, reporting, and advisory role. No leadership decision should issue from or depend on a committee.

◆ ◆ ◆

Lesson 88

"Throw Him Out"

For God's sake don't keep anybody around that you say to yourself "He may get by"—he won't. Throw him out.

—Letter to Leonard T. Gerow,
February 24, 1943

It is easy to fire someone who consistently fails. It is more difficult to shed the subordinate to whom you give the benefit of the doubt: "He may get by." It is these twilight members of the enterprise that Ike thought most dangerous, because although they had almost no chance for successful rehabilitation, they also had a tendency to slip through the cracks and thereby evade the ax. For Ike, nothing was more destructive to victory than an empty uniform, an officer who is present but cannot be relied on to produce excellence as a matter of routine.

◆ ◆ ◆

Lesson 89

Value the Lessons, Learn the Lessons

There are a thousand lessons now reposing in the minds and memories of tank drivers, sergeants, captains, colonels and generals, that would be of the utmost value to people carrying the responsibility for preparing future battle formations.

—Letter to Vernon E. Prichard,
March 1, 1943

The Battle of Kasserine Pass was the kind most commanders would like to forget. The first major fight between the German and the American armies, it resulted in a humiliating defeat for the U.S. II

Corps. If Ike was embarrassed, he didn't let on. Instead, he observed that "we have now on the front some organizations . . . that have just been through a type of battle for which we have not been fully prepared." Far from simply putting this disaster behind him and his army, Ike wanted to learn from it, to collect the "thousand lessons" to be had from everyone who fought.

All experience is valuable, and no experience is more valuable than a mistake. Ike was determined to capture, collect, and analyze the fruit of error and success alike. It was bad to suffer losses, of course, but the worst loss was losing an opportunity to learn. Lose that, and you lose the future.

◆ ◆ ◆

Lesson 90

Confidence

I would not leave you in command . . . one second if you did not have my confidence.

—Letter to Lloyd Fredendall,
March 2, 1943

After Lloyd Fredendall's II Corps took a disastrous beating at the Battle of Kasserine Pass, Fredendall lost confidence in his subordinates and they in him. After the battle, Ike addressed this issue in a letter to him. It is clear that he was talking to himself as much as to his subordinate:

[I]t is necessary to show confidence in a subordinate; to let him do
his job. This means that ordinarily a subordinate is given a mission
commensurate with the size, strength and efficiency of his unit,
and then he is allowed to execute it. It is frequently most difficult
for the superior to keep his fingers out of the subordinate's pie. I am
sure you can believe that I have had great difficulty in resisting this

impulse myself; but the subordinate must feel that the senior trusts him, has confidence in him, if that subordinate is to do his best work. I would not leave you in command . . . one second if you did not have my confidence.

Even as he wrote these words, Ike became aware that he had, in fact, lost confidence in Fredendall. The issue had less to do directly with his having been defeated in an important battle than with what that defeat said about Fredendall's fatal flaw. To his friend General Joseph McNarney, Ike wrote on the same day as the letter to Fredendall: "Fredendall has many fine qualities; his greatest weakness is handling personnel. As quickly as you get a sensitive person under him, you have something to watch and watch carefully." To General Marshall, just one day later, Ike wrote that Fredendall "is tops—except for one thing. He has difficulty in picking good men and, even worse, in getting the best out of subordinates; in other words, in handling personnel."

Even with this flaw—and it takes very little thought to conclude it to be a fatal flaw—Ike did not want merely to discard Fredendall. "He is too good to lose," he wrote Marshall, "but his assignment is critical at this moment" because II Corps must succeed as "an *independent* American organization" capable of conducting "a speedy attack." What to do? "I have discovered that a man must take the tools he has and do the best he can with them. . . . I must either find a good substitute for Fredendall or must place in his command a number of assistants who are so stable and sound that they will not be disturbed by his idiosyncrasies."

In the end, Eisenhower sent Fredendall back to the United States to handle a noncombat training assignment. In his place as commander of II Corps, Ike chose George S. Patton Jr., who quickly transformed this defeated, dispirited bunch into a disciplined and victorious fighting force.

◆ ◆ ◆

Lesson 91

Get out of Your Command Post

One of the things that gives me the most concern is the habit of some of our generals in staying too close to their command posts.

—Letter to Lloyd Fredendall,
February 4, 1942

Ike was not a perfect manager. One of the darkest of his blind spots was Lloyd Fredendall, the commanding general under whom II Corps had suffered a humiliating defeat at the Battle of Kasserine Pass. Ultimately, Eisenhower did decide to replace Fredendall with Patton, whom he brought in specifically to "rehabilitate" the unit and, in a very real sense, restore to the U.S. Army its pride as a fighting force. Yet it took Eisenhower a very long time to realize that Fredendall was simply not equal to a major combat command, even after Fredendall took engineers away from important work on front-line fortifications to build an elaborate subterranean headquarters for his own protection. Ironically, when Ike wrote to Fredendall, cautioning him to "watch . . . very, very carefully among all your subordinates" the tendency to avoid the front lines, he seemed quite unaware that the biggest offender in this regard was Fredendall himself. Despite this failure of insight on Eisenhower's part, his advice to Fredendall was solid: "Ability to move rapidly is largely dependent upon an intimate knowledge of the ground and conditions along the front. As you well know, this can be gained only through personal reconnaissance and impressions. Generals are expendable just as is any other item in an army; and, moreover, the importance of having the general constantly present in his command post is frequently overemphasized. The same thing applies to commanders of all grades, and I sincerely hope that you will make this a matter of primary interest in the handling of your forces."

Communications on the fly have advanced to such a state in the twenty-first century that any leader can afford to be away from the office and out in the field for a long time without danger of losing touch with "headquarters." Fredendall was a bad general, but he had a good reason for avoiding the front lines: a person could get killed out there. What's your excuse?

◆ ◆ ◆

Lesson 92

Personnel Management

You must not retain for one instant any man in a responsible position where you have become doubtful of his ability to do his job.

> —Memorandum to George S. Patton Jr.,
> March 6, 1943

I have no intention of throwing valuable men to the wolves merely because of one mistake.

> —Letter to George C. Marshall,
> December 17, 1943

Between these two statements—the first issued as a directive to Patton, the second in a report to Marshall concerning the highly embarrassing mishandling of publicity following Patton's infamous slapping of two shell-shocked soldiers in Sicily (see Lesson 129 in Chapter Three)—is contained all you need to know about the theory and practice of effective personnel management.

Like any top manager, Eisenhower measured performance ultimately by results. It was the results Patton produced—victory at minimal cost—that persuaded Eisenhower to retain this subordinate despite sometimes outrageous behavior and consequent damaging publicity. Patton's "mistakes"—his lapses in public conduct, his provocative public pronouncements—would have provided any manager ample reason to fire him. Yet the results Patton consistently produced reinforced Eisenhower's confidence in him. Ike therefore defended Patton, even protected him, not because he was an old friend (which he was), but because he proved himself valuable time and time again. Had that value, objectively measured by results, ever diminished, it was just as certain that Eisenhower would have fired Patton in a heartbeat. In the most positive and affirmative way possible, he made this chilling but absolutely essential point clear to his subordinate and friend:

> You need have no doubts whatsoever about enjoying my fullest confidence. I mention this again because it affects your handling of personnel under you. You must not retain for one instant any man in a responsible position where you have become doubtful of his ability to do his job. We cannot afford to throw away soldiers and equipment and, what is even more important, effectiveness in defeating our enemies, because we are reluctant to damage the feelings of old friends. This matter frequently calls for more courage than any other thing you will have to do, but I expect you to be perfectly cold-blooded about it; and you may be sure that as long as you remain in command of that Corps, your decisions with respect to personnel will be fully backed up.

By instructing Patton in the "cold-blooded" calculus of high-stakes personnel management, Eisenhower also served notice on him that *his* tenure depended exclusively on the results he produced. There was no threat intended, just the hard facts of a necessarily hard bargain.

◆ ◆ ◆

Lesson 93

Hold No Grudge

An offense once committed and punished is, so far as I am concerned, forgotten.

—Letter to Lincoln Barnett,
March 12, 1943

Life magazine reporter Lincoln Barnett violated a war zone censor-ship order in filing one of his reports. For this, Eisenhower ordered him out of North Africa. Realizing that his offense had been a seri-ous one, Barnett wrote to Ike to thank him for not making the pun-ishment even more severe. Eisenhower wrote back, explaining that he refused to hold a grudge, that "Neither the offender nor those who are compelled to take action in the case should allow it to assume such an importance, thereafter, that it precludes the possi-bility of washing clean the slate." Ike advised Barnett not to "let [the incident] ruin your future usefulness; on the contrary, you should now go ahead as if the thing had never happened and re-establish yourself."

Misdeeds should not be allowed to slide, but neither should they be allowed to usurp the present or foreclose the future.

◆ ◆ ◆

Lesson 94

No Cronies Need Apply

A man delivers or, if I can find out about it, he gets out.

—Letter to John H. Dykes,
March 15, 1943

Eisenhower abhorred cronyism. When Dykes, a former West Point roommate, wrote to Ike with the observation that he doubtless had to "make room for lots of officers commissioned for some reason other than their value to the service," Ike replied that he should "disabuse [his] mind of any [such] thought. I don't do any such thing."

Eisenhower judged officers on their capacity to do the job— their performance—period. As he wrote in a memorandum to his field officers on March 15, "The only valid reason for advancing an individual is to improve the quality of our military leadership and so produce greater battle and general efficiency in the American

Forces." He wanted to "use promotions to extend the influence of *officers who have produced effective results and who have not yet reached the limit of their productive capacity.*"

◆ ◆ ◆

Lesson 95

Outlaw Prejudice

[E]xecute . . . orders . . . without even pausing to consider whether the order emanated from a British or American source.

—Letter to George S. Patton Jr.,
April 5, 1943

Ike was well aware that anti-British prejudice existed in the American ranks just as there was anti-American prejudice in the British army. His response? Outlaw it with a "policy of refusing to permit any criticism couched along nationalistic lines. Ike called for "true cooperation and unification of effort" born of "frank, free, and friendly understanding amongst all," American and British. "This, once accomplished, will insure that every subordinate throughout the hierarchy of command will execute the orders he receives without even pausing to consider whether the order emanated from a British or American source."

Whatever else it may be in legal and moral terms, prejudice is an obstacle to profit and productivity. No organization can thrive in coexistence with this waste of effort, energy, and attention. There is no reason for a manager to make any effort to understand prejudice—that merely compounds the waste—but there is every reason to take whatever steps are necessary to purge it and, once purged, bar its reentry.

◆ ◆ ◆

Lesson 96

The Hard Way

Trained but not properly trained. . . . That bunch learned a lesson, the hard way.

> —Letter to George C. Marshall,
> April 5, 1943

Ike quoted a letter he had received from an officer, who commented on experienced versus inexperienced troops. A new artillery unit "moved in next to us about a week ago, dug in beautifully, dispersed nicely, then turned around and drove a truck into an area that [we] wouldn't think of going into. Result, one 2½ [ton truck] wrecked by a mine. A bunch of their men ran over there, someone stepped on an anti-personnel mine and killed three of them."

That was a lesson learned "the hard way." The officer continued, "They'll learn a lot more before they're through, probably the same way. Too bad that we can't train them right before they come up." The officer called for "more realism" in training: "to hell with the blank ammo. Maybe you'll kill off a hundred or so in training a division by using the real stuff, but you'll save many more than that when they get in the real thing."

Harsh training under realistic conditions is hard, but the consequences of failing to train this way are much harder. Demand a great deal from those you intend to prepare for leadership, and demand it now, before it is too late.

◆ ◆ ◆

Lesson 97

Be a Crusader

I do have the feeling of a crusader in this war.

> —Letter to Everett Edward Hazlett Jr.,
> April 7, 1943

Command at Eisenhower's level was hardly immune to the infamous "fog of war," the inevitable confusion that comes when masses of men are committed to combat. Yet he was never uncertain of the overall goal of his mission, which he considered, unambiguously, a crusade: "It seems to me," he wrote his childhood friend Hazlett, "that in no other war in history has the issue been so distinctly drawn between the forces of arbitrary oppression on the one side and, on the other, those conceptions of individual liberty, freedom and dignity, under which we have been raised in our great Democracy."

Confusion, uncertainty, and doubt are part and parcel of leading any substantial enterprise. Successful leaders are not immune to these unpleasant sensations, but, nevertheless, they define some set of values central to the battle yet also above and beyond it, values that do not change and that are always certain. From this foundation, they prevail.

◆ ◆ ◆

Lesson 98

Secure the Necessary Results

You must be tough with your immediate subordinates and they must be equally tough with their respective subordinates.

—Letter to Omar N. Bradley,
April 16, 1943

Dwight Eisenhower was not pleased with the pace of progress in the Allied conquest of Tunisia, and he advised Omar N. Bradley, now in command of II Corps, to "be tough." Ike was appalled that a general had reported to him that very morning "that a battalion of infantry, working under him, requested permission to withdraw and reorganize because it had a total of *ten killed* during an attack." Casualties, Ike knew, were to be expected. They were the price of victory. And the time had come to be willing to trade casualties for victory. "We have reached the point where troops *must* secure objectives assigned by Commanders and, where necessary, we must direct leaders to get out and *lead and to secure the necessary results*."

Resolve requires not only a resolve to win but a resolve to pay the price of winning. Resolve also requires that the leader demand, without equivocation, that the price be paid by everyone at every level of the organization. Ike made the demand, and he left no room for failure. "I know we can do this," he concluded to Bradley.

◆ ◆ ◆

Lesson 99

Know Who Knows Best

[T]he people that reported on him were much closer to his actual performance than I was.

—Cable to George C. Marshall,
April 24, 1943

Ike relieved the commander of the First Armored Brigade, Brigadier General McQuillin, and sent him back to the States to train troops. He explained to General Marshall that "I think he will never be an inspirational leader nor anything more than an average soldier," but he went on to observe that "the people that reported on him were much closer to his actual performance than I was and they believe that his return [to the United States] should be considered as nothing more than a part of the rotation policy [rather than as the removal of an inadequate officer]."

Without discounting his own opinion, Ike scrupulously included the opinion of those who had actually observed the officer in question, because he believed that a firsthand assessment had great value, even if it differed from his own assessment, which was made from a more remote perspective. Give value to the opinions of those in the best position to know, even if they are subordinate to you and you do not agree with them.

◆ ◆ ◆

Lesson 100

Shorten "Ritualistic" Orders

We are sure you will find the divisional and corps staff officers of particular value because these people have learned to shorten ritualistic orders, so as to speed up movement and action.

—Cable to George C. Marshall,
May 15, 1943

Eisenhower insisted on regularly rotating combat officers back to the United States, mainly to help train new officers for combat. In sending some staff (administrative) officers back to the States for work at the War Department, Ike assured General Marshall that Marshall would find them useful because, due to the demands of actual combat, "these people have learned to shorten ritualistic orders" and thereby "speed up movement and action."

Experience teaches us what we need—and, as Eisenhower well knew, it also teaches us what we do not need. Sometimes that second lesson is more valuable than the first. Look for ways to separate ritual from necessity. Then separate them.

◆ ◆ ◆

Lesson 101

On Duty and Discipline

[T]he only unforgivable sin in war is not doing your duty when you know what it is.

—Letter to his son, John S. D. Eisenhower,
May 22, 1943

Ike mentioned or discussed discipline in a great many of his wartime letters and papers, but he defined it most succinctly in a letter to

General Vernon E. Prichard on June 2, 1943, and in a letter to his own son, John, on May 22. To Prichard, he observed that "Discipline is nothing in the world but the absolute certainty that every order issued by the leader will be obeyed." To John, he drew a very instructive connection between duty and discipline.

> Dear Johnnie,
>
> I am sorry you lost your [West Point] roommate, but you are wrong in thinking that he should not be discharged for failure to get his calculus lessons. By your own account, he was bright enough to do the job if he would apply himself; the only unforgivable sin in war is not doing your duty when you know what it is. To attempt to say that the duty is unimportant and inconsequential and, therefore, one may neglect it, is to be guilty—at least in principle—of the biggest crime a soldier can commit. The salute, for example, may not be important but any soldier knowing that it is his duty to salute and failing to do so, should be severely punished. Some day you will be commanding a platoon or a battery. The one thing you are going to depend upon is a certain knowledge that every soldier in your unit will do what you tell him, whether you are watching him or not. If you cannot be certain, then you do not have a unit and you have failed to develop a battleworthy organization.

At this point in his letter, Ike drops the word *duty* and substitutes *discipline*, suggesting that, for him, the two were simply equivalent: "We sometimes use the term 'soul of the army.' That soul is nothing but discipline, and discipline is simply and certainly that every man will obey orders promptly, cheerfully and effectively. . . . If your roommate was too indifferent to study and get his lessons, he has no business in the army, certainly not as an officer."

(Ike softened his view considerably in a letter he sent to his son on February 19, 1944. He said that he was glad to learn that his friend was back at the academy, "and from what you tell me of his antics I have a suspicion that he will be exactly the type we ought to have in the Army—a fellow with some imagination and initiative.")

◆ ◆ ◆

Lesson 102

School Stops Here

One criticism I have of all the schools where they tried to pound into my head some military erudition, is that I was never given a hint of what a headache could come out of a quarter of a million prisoners of war, when transportation facilities are clogged and evacuation from the theater can be at the rate of only about thirty thousand a month.

—Letter to George C. Marshall,
May 15, 1943

School stops where experience begins. With the successful conclusion of the North African campaign, Ike was faced with something no American military school had ever contemplated: 250,000 POWs to process, contain, and transport. His response? Grumble just a little, take care of the problem, and make notes to help the next class.

◆ ◆ ◆

Lesson 103

Make It Personal

In making any recommendation for promotion of an officer, the responsible authority will . . . include a statement that he will be glad to have—under his command—the officer recommended for promotion, in the grade for which recommended.

—Memorandum to Everett S. Hughes,
May 29, 1943

Take every opportunity to compel personal responsibility. Ike ordered General Hughes, his deputy theater commander, to communicate "to all American officers immediately subordinate" to him the memorandum just quoted. Ike's message? *You—personally—are expected to live with the results of what you ask for, order, or otherwise make happen.*

◆ ◆ ◆

Lesson 104

Opinions

In the last analysis, no battles are won with headlines, although I appreciate that wars are conducted by public opinion.

—Letter to Charles D. Herron,
June 11, 1943

Ike rejected the well-intentioned suggestion of General Charles D. Herron that he hire a personal public relations officer. "I abhor the idea insofar as it implies that I should consciously seek publicity. . . . By giving credit to others and by being reasonably self-effacing, an Allied Commander eliminates competition for publicity and consequent jealousies thus engendered."

Ike's business was winning battles, and he believed that "no battles are won with headlines." He did admit, however, that "wars are conducted by public opinion," but that was not his business. As a soldier, he fought battles. Conducting wars was up to politicians. This distinction brought to his mind "one other thought: If I were to follow the precept indicated by employment of a personal press agent I am fearful it would . . . lead to decisions being taken in the light of their effect upon me personally." Ike thought that "this would be ruinous to good military operations."

Eisenhower was, in fact, sensitive to the press and public opinion, but he never wanted to be in the position of deliberately playing for either. Public opinion follows the actions you lead, and that is something you must cope with and manage. But it is "ruinous" ever to allow public opinion to lead you in any of your action decisions.

◆ ◆ ◆

Lesson 105

No Born Leaders

The one quality that can be developed by studious reflection and practice is leadership.

—Letter to his son, John S. D. Eisenhower,
June 19, 1943

In contrast to George S. Patton Jr., who felt himself born to lead men into desperate battle and who believed that all great leaders are leaders by virtue of their destiny, Dwight Eisenhower thought that leadership could be acquired, learned through "studious reflection and practice." When his son, a West Point cadet, expressed disappointment at having been promoted to ordinary cadet sergeant rather than given the distinction of promotion to color sergeant, Ike replied that it did "not indicate that you are lacking in the qualities of leadership" and explained that these qualities could be acquired. He went on to demystify leadership, telling his son that it was nothing more than the ability to "get people to working together, not only because you tell them to do so and enforce your orders but because they instinctively want to do it for you. . . . You do not need to be a glad-hander nor a salesman, but your men must trust you and instinctively wish to win your approbation and to avoid things that call upon you for correction."

◆ ◆ ◆

Lesson 106

Improvise and Compromise

The broader problems of war have a habit of presenting themselves without a pedigree of precedent.

—Letter to his brother Milton S.
Eisenhower, June 29, 1943

"I must say that, at times I've been puzzled by an apparent lack of understanding, at home, of the direct and intricate relationship that existed last winter between the military and political problems of North Africa," Ike wrote to his brother. What "puzzled" him was the public's inability to appreciate the need for improvisation as well as compromise and their assumption that complex problems could always be resolved by the application of a simple right-or-wrong morality. The North African campaign, he explained, was an unprecedented situation that had to be resolved through difficult and even distasteful compromises between military and political priorities:

> In this instance, a large Allied force invaded an officially neutral territory, but one in which there were known to exist definite Axis influences and glaring examples of deplorable racial and political discrimination that not only cried aloud for quick correction, but were of the type that our people were determined the war should eliminate. Every dictate of conscience and of upbringing in a free country urged us all to attempt immediately drastic and arbitrary reformation. But it was also necessary to conduct an exceedingly risky campaign, far to the eastward of our original landings, and considering the size of our available mobile force, as of that time, we had to have the active cooperation of French forces. Otherwise, we would have had to sit still and permit the Axis to take over and defend all Tunisia and eastern Algeria. Had we done that, and surrendered the airfields of that region to the Axis, we would still be fighting the Tunisian campaign next Christmas. The coordination that had to be established was between, on the one hand, a degree of military success that would let us get on with the war, and, on the other, as rapid a governmental reform as we would show the world the good faith of the Allies in crusading for liberal forms of government, but would not disrupt all local tranquility and group relationships, which would, in turn, have paralyzed military movement and thus inordinately delayed the reformation process. I repeat, we then needed the positive cooperation of

French forces, not merely passive non-resistance. The size of the eventual military victory certainly justified the policy of evolution rather than revolution in the political field.

Like any other tool, compromise can be misused, even destructively so. Yet it is an essential tool, often indispensable in achieving anything of value. Ike was not afraid to use it.

◆ ◆ ◆

Lesson 107

A Good Man

He is an outstandingly good man.

> —Letter to George C. Marshall,
> July 21, 1943

When Brigadier General Albert C. Wedemeyer was being rotated back to the States from the Sicilian campaign, Ike wanted General Marshall to know that "during the early stages of the Sicilian fighting," Wedemeyer, a "desk officer" from the Army War Plans Division, had asked "for demotion to the grade of colonel in order that he could command a regiment [in front-line combat]. While he was not demoted, his offer of service was snapped up on the spot and he actually commanded a regiment of the 45th Division during certain stages of the fighting. He is an outstandingly good man, of course, and I tell you about this particular incident simply because I doubt that he will tell it himself."

As Ike well knew, sometimes your duty is behind a desk, not a gun, but he admired a desk officer who was not content with remaining remote from the action and hungered for the experience of combat. Ike knew that Wedemeyer was not after glory, but craved the connection with reality that all too often is broken somewhere between the front lines and headquarters. It is a craving shared by all truly effective leaders.

◆ ◆ ◆

Lesson 108

Prepare Mentally and Physically

[M]easures . . . must be intensified and carried on continuously
to the end that the morale, determination and fighting qualities
of all units are of the highest, and each soldier has acquired a
definite and practical knowledge of the true reasons for which
he is fighting this war.

> —Memorandum to all commanders,
> July 23, 1943

General Eisenhower distributed to all commanders a portion of a
secret letter he had received from George C. Marshall, concerning
the problem of preparing men mentally and well as physically for the
rigors of war. Marshall was disturbed by a survey that suggested a
majority of recruits did not fully understand what was at stake in
World War II and, therefore, were not fully committed to fighting it:

It is of great importance . . . that every member of the Army be
prepared mentally as well as physically to pursue his training under
extremely rigorous, warlike conditions. It is important that each
man enters into combat with the determination to close with the
enemy and destroy him, accepting the inevitable casualties with
grim determination to bring the war to a conclusion as quickly as
possible. In a recent survey of several divisions only 38% of the
enlisted personnel thought that the task remaining to us before
Germany and Japan are defeated is an extremely tough job involving heavy losses of men and materials. Less than half the enlisted
personnel questioned believed that they were more useful to the
nation as soldiers than they would have been as war workers. In the
last stages of training, only 30% of those questioned felt they were
ready and anxious to get into the fighting. A considerable number
were hopeful that they would not have to go overseas. A majority of
the men felt that they did not hear enough talks on "what this war is

all about," and the officers agreed that there was not enough instruction along this line. It is evident that the distribution of additional
information materials in a routine manner will not provide a satisfactory solution. The interest which junior officers will give to such matters varies in direct proportion to the emphasis placed by the higher
commanders. Nothing can compensate for the zealous initiative on
the part of the higher commanders. Your will and your personal convictions will determine the state of mind of your command. Undue
optimism is to be avoided, but a firm attitude of assurance in our ultimate success and the ability to meet any task imposed is essential to
leadership for the character of fighting in which our troops will soon
be engaged. The morale of the Army and the tremendous task with
inevitable hardship and losses about to be undertaken make this matter of critical importance demanding energetic leadership.

Eisenhower instructed his commanders to heed Marshall's directive by ensuring that everyone under their command became a
committed "crusader" in a war of good against evil. Ike knew that
the army was no democracy, but he believed that soldiers fighting
on behalf of a democracy not only deserved to know why they were
fighting but actually *needed* to know in order to fight effectively.
Many officers believed that a soldier's place was not to understand,
but merely to obey. Ike believed that true obedience—cheerful, efficient, and vigorous—was predicated on understanding. That principle was at the core of his leadership philosophy.

◆ ◆ ◆

Lesson 109

Know Your Craft

[T]he Field Artillery man is forced to learn the teamwork
between the Infantry and the Field Artillery, and in so doing
becomes well rounded for Divisional service.

—Letter to his son, John S. D. Eisenhower,
August 7, 1943

Like all cadets about to graduate from West Point, John Eisenhower was faced with the decision as to which branch of the Army he should join. "From your letters," his father wrote,

> it appears that you are swinging back toward the Infantry. It is a fine branch, as would naturally be my opinion. I do believe that the Field Artillery offers certain advantages over the Infantry, one of which is this—the Field Artillery man is forced to learn the teamwork between the Infantry and the Field Artillery, and in so doing he becomes well rounded for Divisional service. In other words, it is essential that he know a great deal about the characteristics of Infantry—its limitations, its needs and its capabilities. On the other hand, the Infantry Officer is very frequently tempted to look upon the Field Artillery as something a bit technical and to pay no attention to the details of Field Artillery handling. He just insists that he must have so much fire at such and such a place and leaves it up to the Field Artillery to get it there.

Ike was grooming his son for leadership, his eye on the divisional level, which encompassed the specialized units of infantry, field artillery, and so on. He believed a leader at this level had to be something of a generalist, with a thorough knowledge of all the branches under his command. He had little patience for leaders who looked upon their units as so many black boxes—devices that take in orders and spit out results—without feeling the need to know what actually goes on inside of them.

◆ ◆ ◆

Lesson 110

Evaluating Leaders

Foreseeing a future need of yours for senior U.S. commanders who have been tested in battle, I have been watching very closely and earnestly the performance of American commanders here.

—Letter to George C. Marshall,
August 24, 1943

At the conclusion of the campaigns in North Africa and Sicily, Ike sent General Marshall his assessment of his top three field commanders.

First and foremost was Patton, who "has conducted a campaign where the brilliant successes scored must be attributed directly to his energy, determination and unflagging aggressiveness. The operations of the Seventh Army in Sicily are going to be classed as a model of swift conquest by future classes in the War College in Leavenworth. The prodigious marches, the incessant attacks, the refusal to be halted by appalling difficulties in communications and terrain, are really something to enthuse about. This has stemmed mainly from Patton." What Ike admired most about Patton was his drive: "He never once chose a line on which he said 'we will here rest and recuperate and bring up more strength.'"

Balanced against these remarkable achievements were "unfortunate personal traits," including a "habit of impulsive bawling out of subordinates, extending even to personal abuse of individuals." Ike was thinking about the notorious "slapping incidents," in which Patton physically struck not one, but two enlisted men who were suffering from battle fatigue. (See Lesson 129 in Chapter Three.) "Aside from this one thing, he has qualities we cannot afford to lose unless he ruins himself. So, he can be classed as an army commander that you can use with certainty that the troops will not be stopped by ordinary obstacles."

Next in order, Ike listed Omar N. Bradley. Bradley was the soul of dependability: "running absolutely true to form all the time. He has brains, a fine capacity for leadership and a thorough understanding of the requirements of modern battle." Although Bradley did not evoke for Eisenhower the remarkable list of achievements he had attached to Patton's name, Ike noted, "He has never caused me one moment of worry."

The third commander Ike singled out was Mark W. Clark, "the best organizer, planner and trainer of troops that I have met. . . . He inspires an intense loyalty in all his staff and in his subordinates."

This letter provides remarkable insight into Dwight Eisenhower's concept of command leadership. Clearly he admired all three men—Patton, Bradley, and Clark—yet one cannot help reaching the conclusion, after reading this letter, that Ike's ideal leader would have combined the qualities of *all three* men: the drive and energy of Patton, the reliability of Bradley, and the people skills of Clark. Perhaps these describe Dwight David Eisenhower himself.

3

SUPREME COMMANDER

After directing the assault on Sicily and early operations on the Italian mainland, Eisenhower returned to London to plan the invasion of France. The greatest amphibious attack in history, D-Day, June 6, 1944, involved the landing of 156,000 troops (850,000 more would follow over the next days and weeks) and the coordinated action of more than 5,000 ships and 13,000 aircraft. Eisenhower instigated and oversaw the creation of the plans and approved their every detail. One of his most daunting tasks was persuading Churchill, haunted by the near annihilation of the British army at Dunkirk early in the war, to sign on to the invasion. (Eisenhower succeeded, Churchill finally declaring to FDR, "I am in this thing with you to the end, and if it fails we will go down together.")

In addition to massive and massively bewildering logistical problems, including a chronic, pressing shortage of landing craft, Eisenhower had the usual cast of prima donnas to contend with as well as the ongoing demands of the stalemated campaign on the Italian mainland, the bitter fruit of Churchill's "soft underbelly" strategy. Moreover, George S. Patton Jr., whom Eisenhower recognized as his most brilliant field commander, essential to the success of the Normandy campaign, repeatedly managed to outrage the press and the public with his compulsively outspoken behavior.

After months of intensive planning and build-up, all the while juggling jarring personalities and maintaining absolute secrecy while directing a brilliant campaign of disinformation to mislead the Germans, Eisenhower was ready to launch the invasion, pending the cooperation of the weather. Under the best of conditions, crossing the English Channel was treacherous. In stormy conditions, it was suicidal. A gale on June 4 forced Eisenhower—the only man who could give the launch order—to postpone the invasion. He knew that each hour of delay risked losing the all-important element of surprise, and to delay beyond June 6 would also mean moonless nights and, for the next three weeks, high morning tides. Paratroopers needed the moonlight for night jumps, and high tides would render German mines and underwater obstacles invisible, making close-in amphibious landings all but impossible. When his RAF weather officer, Captain J. M. Stagg, predicted better albeit iffy weather for June 6, Eisenhower turned calmly to his aides: "I am quite positive we must give the order. I don't like it but there it is." Ike recorded a proclamation to be broadcast to the world on the day of the invasion. "Soldiers, Sailors and Airmen of the Allied Expeditionary Forces," it began. "You are about to embark on the great crusade. . . . The hopes and prayers of liberty-loving people everywhere march with you." And he quickly scrawled another message, which he folded then tucked into his wallet, so that it would be ready for broadcast, if necessary. "Our landings in the Cherbourg-Havre area have failed to gain a satisfactory foothold," it began, "and I have withdrawn the troops. . . . If any blame or fault attaches to the attempt it is mine alone."

Following the successful completion of the D-Day landings and the very hard-fought breakout from the beachheads and through the "hedgerow country" that followed, Eisenhower's job became increasingly fraught with the conflicting demands of world politics and military strategy. His task became one of delicate compromise in which the stakes were the life or death of all his soldiers and the future balance of political power in the world. Militarily, Eisenhower's overriding objective was the destruction of the Nazi armies. Devoting time and resources to the occupation of cities often conflicted with this key objective, yet Eisenhower had to manage the liberation of Paris even though this diminished his ability to press the battle against the enemy army. He had continually to parry attempts by General Montgomery, backed by Churchill, to concentrate forces narrowly against the German front. Eisenhower instead called for a broad-front strategy, which would make for a slower advance, but which would destroy more of the enemy's forces. While alternately fighting and mollifying Montgomery and Churchill, Eisenhower found himself having to mediate between his two principal ground commanders, Omar N. Bradley, the blunt American, and Bernard Law Montgomery, the imperious Brit, who were themselves locked in bitter conflict.

The lessons in this chapter chiefly address the myriad difficulties of managing high-stakes, high-risk operations, with emphasis on inspiring excellence; maintaining focus and intensity; coping with conflicting, egocentric, high-level subordinate commanders; and taking ownership of triumph as well as tragedy.

◆ ◆ ◆

Lesson 111

Moving the Unmovable

I expect you to do your part.

—Cable to Pietro Badoglio,
September 8, 1943

On September 3, 1943, a representative of Marshal Pietro Badoglio, who had become head of state after the Italian Fascist Council had ousted Benito Mussolini, signed an armistice between Italy and the Allies. At 1:00 A.M. on September 8, he sent a message to Eisenhower in effect retracting the armistice "due to changes in the situation brought about by the disposition and strength of the German forces in the Rome area." Badoglio feared that an immediate armistice would "provoke the occupation of the capital and the violent assumption of the government by the Germans." Ike replied immediately and in no uncertain terms:

I intend to broadcast the existence of the armistice at the hour originally planned. If you or any part of your armed forces fail to co-operate as previously agreed I will publish to the world full record of this affair. Today is X-day and I expect you to do your part.

I do not accept your message of this morning postponing the armistice. Your accredited representative has signed an agreement with me and the sole hope of Italy is bound up in your adherence to that agreement. . . .

Plans have been made on the assumption that you were acting in good faith and we have been prepared to carry out future operations on that basis. Failure now on your part to carry out the full obligations of the signed agreement will have most serious consequences for your country. No future action of yours could then restore any confidence whatever in your good faith and consequently the dissolution of your government and nation would ensue.

To the Combined Chiefs of Staff and the British Chiefs of Staff, Ike sent a message on the same day, that he had "determined . . . not to accept the Italian change of attitude." On the very next day, September 9, he was able to assure the chiefs: "Due to my refusal to accept evasive and dilatory action on the part of the Italian government, Badoglio went through with his part of the armistice program last evening," and, on this day, Allied troops landed on the Italian mainland at Salerno. Operation Avalanche, the invasion of the Italian mainland, was under way.

Ike cabled Badoglio on September 10:

The whole future and honour of Italy depends upon the part which her armed forces are now prepared to play. The Germans have definitely and deliberately taken the field against you. . . . Now is the time to strike. If Italy rises now as one man we shall seize every German by the throat. I urge you to issue immediately a clarion call to all patriotic Italians. They have done much locally already but action appears to be uncoordinated and uncertain. They require inspired leadership and, in order to fight, an appeal setting out the situation to your people as it now exists is essential. Your excellency is the one man that can do this.

It was a stirring appeal, but it elicited no response from Badoglio, and while Italian resistance fighters played an important role against the Germans, the regular Italian armed forces could not be employed effectively in the Allies' Italian campaign. By simply refusing to accept any excuses or backsliding, Ike had succeeded in compelling Badoglio to honor the armistice—a major achievement—but even he could not forge a reliable military ally out of the remnants of the demoralized and disorganized Italian armed forces.

There is a limit to what can be done in moving the unmovable, but you must make the attempt. Never yield what is right and what has been agreed to in good faith. Stand your ground. Get the other party to blink.

◆ ◆ ◆

Lesson 112

Accept All the Responsibility, but Not Necessarily All the Blame

This decision was solely my own, and if things go wrong there is no one to blame except myself.

—Memorandum to Harry C. Butcher,
September 14, 1943

Ike gave the go-ahead for Operation Avalanche, the invasion of the Italian mainland via landings at Salerno, despite the Combined Chiefs of Staff having turned down his request for additional landing craft and B-24 bombers. "In the face of these refusals, doubts were frequently expressed in this headquarters as to the wisdom of going on with AVALANCHE. I felt that the possible results were so great that even with the meager allotments in landing craft, particularly LST's and in Air Force, we should go ahead." Ike continued, "This decision was solely my own, and if things go wrong there is no one to blame except myself." But he added, "It is only fair to say, however, that all three Commanders-in-Chief backed up the idea and it is also only fair to say that they have striven in every possible way to make good these deficiencies through redoubled efforts in using what we have." This being the case, Ike concluded: "I have no word of complaint concerning any officer or man in the execution of our plans."

You cannot always get the resources you want. When that is the case, you must weigh risk against reward in deciding whether to proceed with an action for which you are not optimally prepared. Ike made the decision and took responsibility for it, noting, however, that others supported his judgment and delivered their utmost effort to execute the course of action decided upon. As for complaining, Ike refused to do it. Calculated risk is business as usual in war and in many other enterprises.

Make your calculations, then make your decision and take ownership of it—but get all the support you can. Once the operation is under way, stop whining and make it work.

◆ ◆ ◆

Lesson 113

Solve the Human Equation

This problem involves the human equation and must be met day by day.

—Memorandum to Lord Louis
Mountbatten, September 14, 1943

Immediately after his appointment as supreme Allied commander for Southeast Asia, Lord Louis Mountbatten wrote to Eisenhower, seeking his advice on "the duties and tribulations with which a Supreme Allied Commander is faced." Ike replied with an extensive memorandum that stressed what he identified as the true source of leadership authority—or "unity of command," as it was called: the concept of a single supreme commander responsible for all Allied activities in a theater of the war. Although, Ike wrote, the "basis for allied unity of command is found in directives issued by the Combined Chiefs of Staff,"

> [T]he true basis lies in the earnest cooperation of the senior officers assigned to an allied theater. Since cooperation, in turn, implies such things as selflessness, devotion to common cause, generosity in attitude, and mutual confidence, it is easy to see that actual unity in an allied command depends directly upon the individuals in the field. . . . It will therefore never be possible to say the problem of establishing unity in any allied command is ever completely solved. This problem involves the human equation and must be met day by day. Patience, tolerance, frankness, absolute honesty in all dealings, particularly with all persons of the opposite nationality, and firmness, are absolutely essential.

A leader must solve, on a daily basis, the human equation. He must "strive for . . . the utmost in mutual respect and confidence among the group of seniors making up the allied command."

> All of us are human and we like to be favorably noticed by those above us and even by the public. An Allied Commander-in-Chief, among all others practicing the art of war, must more sternly than any other individual repress such notions. He must be self-effacing, quick to give credit, ready to meet the other fellow more than half way, must seek and absorb advice and must learn to decentralize. On the other hand when the time comes that he himself feels he must make a decision, he must make it in clean-cut fashion and on his own responsibility and take full blame for anything that goes wrong;

in fact he must be quick to take the blame for anything that goes wrong whether or not it results from his mistake or from an error on the part of a subordinate.

Eisenhower explained that the position of supreme Allied commander was unique, "not really a commander . . . if you are thinking of the picture you have of commanding a battle fleet or a destroyer flotilla"; however, neither "is he a figurehead or a nonentity. He is in a very definite sense the Chairman of a Board, a Chairman that has very definite executive responsibilities—some of which I have rather hastily hinted at above. He must execute those duties firmly, wisely and without any question as to his own authority and his own responsibility."

Eisenhower took particular pains to explain to Mountbatten that he could not cling to "the British system of command," which "has proved that it can work where *only British Empire forces* are involved" and "cannot work where sizeable U.S. and British forces are placed together in one theater to achieve a common objective." The problem?

Just consider what would happen if you had 6 Commanders-in-Chief, all reporting to the Combined Chiefs of Staff. Or suppose you had only 3—say two British and one American. Who would carry on all the tasks that are separate from the actual military operation in progress, and whose voice would be authoritative in dealing with the Combined Chiefs of Staff? The point I make is that while the set-up may be somewhat artificial, and not always so clean-cut as you might desire, your personality and good sense *must* make it work. Otherwise *Allied* action in any theater will be impossible.

In short: there is no such thing as leadership by committee.

◆　◆　◆

Lesson 114

Test Them

*[B]attle leadership is the test for which we have trained profes-
sional officers.*

> —Cable to George C. Marshall,
> September 19, 1943

Major General Earnest Dawley is being immediately relieved as
commanding general of the VI Corps . . . . Dawley is a splendid
character, earnest, faithful and well informed. There is nothing
against him except that he cannot repeat not exercise high battle
command effectively when the going is rough. He grows extremely
nervous and indecisive. . . . I feel that battle leadership is the test
for which we have trained professional officers. They were given
wartime rank to meet wartime jobs and if they cannot measure up
to the standards required then we must reduce them to peace rank.

Ike realized that to "Dawley this will be a heartbreaking thing
because he has done his best. . . . Unless you have some specific
position in which you want to use Dawley in his current rank I suggest that you give me authority to reduce him to his regular [peace-
time army] rank . . . and return him to the United States."

Dawley was a friend, and relieving him was not easy for Eisenhower, but he had failed what Ike deemed an objective test—battle
leadership—and that left no alternative. He wrote to Dawley on
September 22:

I want you to know, definitely, that your relief from the VI Corps
does not reflect in the slightest degree upon your character, your
loyalty, or your sincere devotion to duty. It was brought about by
the simple fact that under conditions of extraordinary battle stress
you do not, in the opinion of your superiors, function as efficiently
and as calmly as is called for in the position of Corps Command. In

all fairness to you I must say that your particular test imposed conditions of a most rigorous character.

I realize that your reduction to your permanent rank and return to the United States will be a great blow to you, and, because of my long friendship with you and my admiration for your character and devotion to duty, it is extraordinarily painful for me to have to approve this action in your case. I hope, however, that you will take this decision as the good soldier you are and try to remember that anyone who does his full duty in this war will always have the approval of his own conscience, no matter what decisions may be made as to his disposition.

◆ ◆ ◆

Lesson 115

To Reshuffle or Not to Reshuffle?

The relief of a combat leader is something that is not to be lightly done in war.

—*Crusade in Europe*

Lieutenant General Mark W. Clark, commanding the U.S. Fifth Army in Italy, recommended that one of his corps commanders be relieved as ineffective. Ike never rushed a subordinate to the chopping block. His greatest concern was that removing a commander indicated "to troops dissatisfaction with their performance; otherwise the commander would be commended, not relieved." The possibility of demoralizing an entire corps had to be "weighed against the hoped-for advantage of assigning to the post another, and possibly untried, commander." Yet Ike believed that "really inept leadership must be quickly detected and instantly removed."

Typically, when a manager contemplates firing a subordinate, his first concern is for the man or woman who is about to be removed. Ike appreciated the issue of what he called "academic justice for the leader," but the only truly relevant stakes were the "concern for the many and the objective of victory." The feelings, even the future, of the leader who now finds himself in the cross-hairs matters little compared to the "lives of thousands."

A corporate reshuffle must not be entered into lightly, not because it may work an injustice on an individual leader, but because it may undermine an entire enterprise. By the same token, when a manager proves inept, no personal consideration should impede his or her immediate departure.

◆ ◆ ◆

Lesson 116

"Dear Johnnie"

It is now only a matter of a few months until you graduate.

—Letter to his son, John S. D. Eisenhower,
September 20, 1943

To his son at West Point, Ike wrote a long letter filled with homey advice on leadership. He began with the practical, advising his boy to invest in what is most useful, not what looks nice. His advice on making an investment in an eiderdown sleeping bag provides a lesson in the importance of value over price:

> Since the early part of your service will be under war conditions, you should think carefully about the nature of the uniforms and equipment you buy. The first rule is don't buy too much, particularly of things that look like they would just be "nice to have around." You should always have one little pack *that you can carry yourself* that will provide existence [subsistence] and a reasonable degree of comfort no matter if you get separated from the rest of your baggage. Good shirts, good trousers and good shoes are far more important than blouses, stiff caps and ceremonial sabers. You should get the very finest sleeping bag you can buy. These are made of eiderdown and are quite expensive. Their virtue is that they are

light in weight and will pack up into a very small roll. I think a fine eiderdown sleeping bag will cost you about $40.00, but don't be tempted into buying a $15.00 kapok sleeping bag if you can possibly get hold of an eiderdown one.

Ike continued with an important rule of thumb for uniforms: "Your actual field uniform will ordinarily be of the [standard-]issue variety. In action officers should look just as much like their men as they possibly can." There are two reasons for this: first, the field uniform is a means by which an officer identifies with his men; second, an undistinguished field uniform gives the enemy less of a target. Identify yourself ostentatiously as an officer, and you're liable to get shot.

From field uniforms, Ike moved on to dress items:

But such other things as you buy, namely, shirts, trousers and one good blouse, should be of the very best material and workmanship that you know of. In the long run these are much more economical than the cheaper hand-me-down variety. The thing to do is to learn to live simply and to get along with bare necessities, but to do it in such a way that you are always neat and thus an example to your men as well as a rather pleasing young lieutenant for your captain to look at.

Identify with your subordinates, but distinguish yourself in the eyes of your superiors.

While he was on the subject of establishing good relations with a superior officer, Ike pointed out one disadvantage of being a West Point graduate, and he suggested a way to transform it into an advantage:

It is entirely possible—even highly probable—that you, as a well trained and instructed lieutenant, will report to a captain for duty who has had very few months actual service in the Army. He will know far less of discipline and possibly even of the operation of weapons, of sanitation and of many other essential subjects than you do. Nevertheless, do not be too free with advice. Within your own sphere—that is, in your own platoon if you are given one— apply every bit of knowledge that you have but do not make the mistake of telling the captain how he should run his job. When he asks for information or advice, give it in a respectful, pleasant manner and don't be afraid of showing your enthusiasm for any task he gives you. Seniors like to have subordinates that react enthusiastically upon being detailed to an additional and often onerous duty. A young lieutenant of this kind may become very easily the "willing horse" in the company or the battalion and very quickly get all the most difficult jobs to do and be working far more hours than anyone else. That is the greatest compliment you could get, and you will find that when this happens your captain and battalion commander will be trying their best to get you promoted.

The surest way to satisfy a boss is to present yourself as the solution to any one of his many problems.

Ike believed an officer should possess an intimate knowledge of the weapons of war:

Don't be afraid to do the dirty work yourself of improving your own expertness with every weapon with which you have anything to do. If you are in an infantry platoon, make certain that you know everything there is to know about the rifle and never neglect a chance to practice your marksmanship. The same applies to the tommy gun, the carbine, the pistol, the bayonet, the grenade and the 60 mm. mortar, as well as the "bazooka." Should you be in a heavy weapons company it is equally important that you become, if possible, more expert in the use of every single weapon than any one of your men is in any one of them.

Fitness must not be neglected: "Your physical toughness and endurance you must watch every day. You must not break yourself down; particularly must every soldier be very, very careful of his feet, no matter what his branch."

Ike advised his son not to be limited by the limitations of those above him: "If you should find that your captain's knowledge of minor tactics is a bit meager, I think you will also find that you can train your own platoon accurately and properly without ever violating the general instructions of the captain."

He counseled awareness and preparedness above all else:

> In action on maneuvers never forget the importance of reconnaissance; reconnaissance to the front, to the flanks and sometimes even to the rear, in order that you may know exactly and at all times where you can send a message in a hurry. Make your platoon runners become as tough and as hardy and as good trail finders as the American Indian was. Be constantly ready to fight, either to the front, to either flank or, if necessary, to repel a sudden assault from the rear. Always study the ground. Learn to follow the lines of the ground through which your main body is protected and which your scouts by reconnaissance and watchfulness can cover. Learn also that the low flying airplane doesn't like the fire of ground troops. Teach your men that dispersion and volume of fire is almost a certain protection against the dive bombers.

Like his former senior and present subordinate, George S. Patton Jr., Ike disdained foxholes and trenches: "In an advance be rather wary about digging in too quickly. Once men get the feeling of safety that a slit trench provides it is hard to get them started again in the advance." However, "when you must remain in one place for a considerable time either in defense or merely awaiting the bivouac . . . the slit trench . . . is a great comfort if a few stray bombs start to come down." Digging trenches provides an opportunity to build teamwork: "don't ever let your men think they are too tired or too lazy to provide shelters for everybody."

Finally, Ike counseled, be a leader to *your* men:

Always try to make your whole platoon look upon you as the "old man." If the platoon or any member of it has done anything badly, try to keep any senior from jumping directly onto your men. Let them jump on you and don't present any alibi because if the man failed it was probably due to your lack of prior instruction and fore-sight. If you get a hopeless individual, one who is nervous under fire and shows signs of a neurotic state of mind, you must get rid of him by reporting him to the captain, but the average American will respond to intelligent and sympathetic instruction and will absolutely admire a leader that takes all the blame on his own shoulders and gives the credit to the sergeants and the corporals.

◆ ◆ ◆

Lesson 117

Give a Thoughtful Gift

If you should like it . . . I will be glad to send it to you.

—Letter to Ernest J. King,
September 20, 1943

Ike took time to write to Admiral King to tell him that he had, during the Sicilian landings, "asked the Photographic Section of the Air Force to make me as extensive a [photo] mosaic as it could of the beaches, after daylight on the morning of [the Salerno landings]. My thought was that through some such thing there might be developed a number of lessons some Staff Section could dig out and apply in the future." Once Ike had received the mosaic, however, it occurred to him "that if there is any value in it at all, the Navy Department would be in the best position to extract such value and pass it on to others." Accordingly, Ike offered the mosaic to King, who eagerly accepted it.

◆ ◆ ◆

Lesson 118

"The Spirit Which Makes Him Stick to His Job"

While I can appreciate the great desire of your husband and yourself to have him with you during his father's illness, I also find very commendable in your son the spirit which makes him stick to his job, no matter how great his own personal desire might be to be at home at this time.

—Letter to Mrs. John Logan,
September 22, 1943

Parents often wrote to Eisenhower, and, as often as he could, the supreme Allied commander replied personally—especially when the subject was of special interest to him. When Mrs. John Logan of Knoxville, Tennessee, wrote to Eisenhower (on August 5, 1943) to request emergency leave for her son, who was serving in the Sixteenth Engineers Battalion, because her husband had suffered a heart attack and was dying, Ike "had him called in [to tell him] that an exception might be made in his case and he would be allowed to go home." Ike now reported to Mrs. Logan that her son's "decision was that under present circumstances it would be inadvisable for him to leave his job here and return."

Ike explained: "While I can appreciate the great desire of your husband and yourself to have him with you during his father's illness, I also find very commendable in your son the spirit which makes him stick to his job, no matter how great his own personal desire might be to be at home at this time." Ike softened the blow with an expression of his very personal empathy, mentioning that he had "had an exactly similar situation in my own case, and could not go to see my father." He did not tell Mrs. Logan that the event was the death of David Jacob Eisenhower, on March 10, 1942. At the time, Ike wrote in his notebook: "I have felt terribly. I should like so much to be with my Mother these few days. But we're at war! And war is not soft—it has no time to indulge even the deepest and most sacred emotions."

❖ ❖ ❖

Lesson 119

A Policy of Risk

I do not see how any individual could possibly be devoting more thought and energy to speeding up operations or to attacking boldly and with admitted risk than I do.

—Cable to George C. Marshall,
September 24, 1943

To complaints from some British colleagues that the pace of operations in Italy was too slow, Ike replied by pointing out his adherence to a policy of "attacking boldly" and taking "admitted risk." Just the day before sending this cable to Marshall, he had sent a cable to Prime Minister Winston Churchill thanking him for his "personal telegram . . . . I am particularly delighted that you so clearly recognize [the dangers of] but nevertheless unqualifiedly approve of the policy of taking risks. I intend to adhere to this policy." Any effective leader must. Risk is the fuel of achievement.

❖ ❖ ❖

Lesson 120

Wishful Thinking

It is a rather odd thing . . . that no matter how much one foresees and prepares for an adverse situation, wishful thinking always intervenes following on early success and there results . . . a too hopeful spirit of optimism, which is badly shattered when the enemy reacts exactly as you figured he would.

—Letter to Thomas T. Handy,
September 26, 1943

Operation Avalanche, the Allied landings at Salerno, had begun very well, in defiance of calculations that predicted formidable German resistance. When that resistance finally materialized during the initial inland advance from the beaches, the shock of some officers approached panic. Ike understood that this was nothing more than the shattering of wishful thinking, an affliction that comes even when difficulty has been foreseen and prepared for. As he wrote to British general John G. Dill on September 30: "Of course one always hopes for more than he has any reasonable right to expect and such hopes always get a great stimulation when initial success accompanies any venture."

Ike Eisenhower was celebrated for a smile that radiated optimism, and he not only valued optimism but demanded it in all of his officers. Yet he also knew that optimism was a very potent medicine and that like any powerful drug, it could become dangerous. His solution was never to banish hope, but always to manage it. This was the case at Salerno, and it would be the case at the end of 1944, during the penultimate crisis of the European war, the Battle of the Bulge, when Ike had to fight the Germans as well as what he called victory fever, a dangerous disease within his own ranks.

◆ ◆ ◆

Lesson 121

Be Human

We are all intensely human, and war is a drama, not a game of chess, so a wide grin, particularly in [a] trying situation, is often worth a battalion.

> —Letter to Geoffrey Keyes,
> September 27, 1943

Ike appointed Geoffrey Keyes to succeed Omar N. Bradley (who had succeeded George Patton) as commander of II Corps. He wrote to Keyes that he had "no doubt at all as to your tactical ability, your fighting qualities, and your complete and intense loyalty."

But I do have a word of suggestion along a line that would possibly never occur to you, nor possibly to your immediate senior. It is this:

don't be afraid to show pleasant reactions in your contacts with your subordinates. Be quick to give credit and, wherever possible, shove a bit of the limelight on to a Division Commander where you could easily have absorbed it all yourself. Every commander is made, in the long run, by his subordinates. We are all intensely human, and war is a drama, not a game of chess, so a wide grin, particularly in [a] trying situation, is often worth a battalion. Mere efficiency on your part will sometimes not be enough! An informal, but always sincere expression of commendation—even if given in an offhand manner—is sometimes called for even when the particular subordinate may have been guilty of some mistakes. You do not need to be told that I am not advocating that you court popularity. Such a habit is fatal. I am merely talking about honest, open-handed, pleasant readiness to give the subordinate more than his full share of the credit for any and every success and to sustain him in reverses.

Please do not think that because I have given this paragraph of advice that I have any doubts of your ability to command that Corps. If I had any such doubts I would have put in someone else, but I do believe—based, as I said, purely upon personal impression and stray remarks picked up here and there—that you could advantageously think over and possibly practice some of the suggestions I have made. In other words, I am talking about something that I believe should transform an admittedly good commander into a brilliant one.

◆ ◆ ◆

Lesson 122

Move Your Headquarters

It is always a good thing to move a headquarters when its personnel begin to get so well "dug in" [that they] become too much concerned with the conveniences of living [and] grow away from troops and from the real problems of war.

—Crusade in Europe

As the Allied campaign progressed in mainland Italy, Ike decided to move his entire headquarters to a location near Naples. One reason was simply to be closer to the scene of operations, another was "to permit concentration of command and logistical systems solidly in proximity to the battle line," and a third reason was to shake up management, the headquarters staff. When leaders and managers become too comfortable, too well "dug in," they focus on issues of comfort and convenience, losing touch with the "real" issues, the business of the world outside of headquarters.

Business, like war, is dynamic. When management digs in, it loses touch with a world in continual motion. Get too comfortable, and you become disengaged, more concerned with shadows on the wall than with the people outside the wall. Make yourself—and others—uncomfortable from time to time. It's an important part of leadership.

◆ ◆ ◆

Lesson 123

Up to Your Ears? Lay Down the Law

I have to lay down the law as to exactly how much I will do.

—Letter to Paul A. Hodgson,
September 30, 1943

"Today I am up to my ears in a bunch of inconsequential plans all centering on taking care, during the next few days, of three very prominent visitors and their assorted staffs."

No manager can fail to sympathize with such a burden.

"I like to see people and have a chat with them but when individuals of this kind arrive there is all the bother of planning conferences, dinners, sleeping accommodations, transportation and a bunch of other details. Naturally, I have a staff to take care of these things but staff officers frequently get so enthusiastic in such things that they commit me to a far greater participation than I like, so I have to lay down the law as to exactly how much I will do."

A big part of leadership is management of time. Devote too much time to "inconsequential plans," and the results can be fatal to you and your enterprise. Devote too little of it to the same plans, and (as Ike admitted) you may "sometimes [be] thought churlish," impolite, and unpleasant. Knowing when to lay down the law as to exactly how much you will do in what amounts to essentially social situations requires fine judgment. Actually laying down that law requires the resolve to risk being judged "churlish."

◆ ◆ ◆

Lesson 124

Hold on to Whatever Works

The idea is . . . so unthinkable that I feel certain nothing of this sort is intended.

—Cable to George C. Marshall,
October 1, 1943

The . . . reason for writing this note is a rumor that there is intended some over-all reorganization of air forces that would transfer control of at least part of our air forces, to London. The idea is, to us here, so unthinkable that I feel certain nothing of this sort is intended. However, any such eventuality would be so far-reaching in effect that I want to give you my views about it. . . .

In the first place, direct operational control of the forces in this theater could not be efficiently done from London. Local factors, including the daily condition of airfields, locations of bombs and fuel, and weather, both over the fields and over the target areas, must all be considered from day to day, sometimes from hour to hour. So, merely on the grounds of practicability the proposal would appear to be unsound.

But there is a far more serious aspect to it than this. We have gone a very long ways in this theater to prove that Allied unity of command can be made to work.

For Eisenhower, "Allied unity of command"—the vesting of final military authority in a single supreme Allied commander—was the linchpin of the war in Europe. It was a principle and policy he jealously guarded, vigorously defended, and would not compromise.

> This is something that originally required demonstration. The mere designation of a commander for such a set-up does not prove the case at all. The progress we have made in this direction has been the result of hard work, constant watchfulness and a continuous process of education. I am sure, though, that for a long time every senior commander here has accepted this principle as a matter of personal conviction, and everything we do is governed by this conviction. Effective and continuous coordination between the air, ground and naval forces is the direct result. To introduce any forces into this theater that are not under the command of the Allied Commander-in-Chief would be destructive of this principle. In my opinion the effect would be most far-reaching. Moreover, the resultant confusion would be serious.

Leadership requires an open mind and a high degree of flexibility. It also requires knowing when the mind must close and the spine become absolutely rigid.

◆ ◆ ◆

Lesson 125

Stick to Your Knitting

I live by one doctrine: All of us have now one job to do, which is winning the war.

—Letter to his brother Arthur B.
Eisenhower, October 20, 1943

Arthur Eisenhower wrote to his brother to tell him that statements were appearing in various papers to the effect that Dwight D. Eisenhower would make a good president. Ike shot back, disavowing any ambition other than to win the war: "For a soldier to turn from his war duty for any reason is to be guilty of treachery to his country and disloyalty to his superiors. The President is my Commander-in Chief. Nothing could sway me from my purpose of carrying out faithfully his orders in whatever post he may assign me."

When personal ambition collides with commitment to the enterprise you lead, only one ethical choice is possible. Stick to your knitting. Honor your commitment. Do the job you've been hired to do.

◆ ◆ ◆

Lesson 126

Inspire Morale

All the truly great armies in history had a cause that inspired the individual to remarkable heights of courage and endurance.

—Letter to William L. Lee,
October 29, 1943

In response to a letter from his friend, who complained about problems he was having training his troops, Ike wrote that "every day, in a position such as mine, brings new lessons. . . . I have talked to you in the past about discipline and perfection of training. . . . Alongside them, and equally important, is morale."

Ike defined morale not as "mere pride of unit or 'esprit de corps,'" but as the product of "confidence in leaders, in training, in discipline, in unit and individual comrades" and "a deep-seated conviction in every individual's mind that he is fighting for a cause worthy of any sacrifice he may make." Recognizing that "all the truly great armies in history had a cause that inspired the individual to remarkable heights of courage and endurance," Ike insisted that the individual soldier's understanding of the cause had to be intensely particular and personal, not a vague compound of such abstractions as "liberty" or "patriotism":

Professional soldiers do not like to get too sentimental about such things as the flag and love of country. But it is essential that every soldier realizes clearly that the privileged life he has led in our democracy is under direct threat. His right to speak his own mind, to engage in any profession of his own choosing, to belong to any religious denomination, to live in any locality where he can support himself and his family, and to be sure of fair treatment when he might be accused of any crime—all these would disappear if the forces opposed to us should, through carelessness or over-confidence on our part, succeed in winning this war. I believe that once a soldier has thoroughly assimilated these basic truths, he has something that will stay with him throughout the war no matter how tired he gets of mud, lice, monotony and filth.

If you would inspire the members of your organization, you must make the values and objectives of the enterprise crucially important in the lives of each member. Between the individual and the group, identification must be extensive and intimate. Discuss values and objectives often—and in detail that is meaningful to the individuals who make up your enterprise.

◆ ◆ ◆

Lesson 127

"Personal from General Eisenhower . . ."

During the year just past, you have written a memorable chapter in . . . history.

—Message to American forces,
November 8, 1943

Following his own advice on the necessity of thoroughly informing and inspiring the men and women under his command, Ike issued the following congratulatory review of the year's achievements in the form of a small pamphlet distributed to every officer and enlisted soldier in his command. The message combines approval, evaluation, assessment, and thanks, with a look toward the future:

Personal from General Eisenhower to all men and women of the American Military and Civil Forces in the North African Theater: We have reached the first anniversary of initial British-American landings in this theater.

You came here to take part in a crusade to eliminate ruthless aggression from the earth and to guarantee to yourselves and to your children security against the threat of domination by arrogant despotism.

During the year just past, you have written a memorable chapter in the history of American arms, a chapter in which are recorded deeds of valor, of sacrifice, of endurance and of unswerving loyalty. You have worked effectively and in friendly cooperation with the Armies, Navies and Air Forces of our Allies and have established in a foreign land a reputation for decency and dignity in conduct. Hour by hour your efforts are contributing toward the ultimate defeat of mighty military machines that hoped to conquer the world. You are just as surely the protectors and supporters of American democracy as your forefathers were its founders.

From my heart I thank each of you for the services you have so well performed, in the air, on the sea, in the front lines and in our ports and bases.

All of us salute with reverence the memory of the comrades we have lost, as we earnestly pray that Almighty God will bring comfort to their loved ones.

But we must now look forward, because for us there can be no thought of turning back until our task has been fully accomplished.

We are on the mainland of Europe, carrying the battle, daily, closer to the vitals of the enemy. More Americans and more of our Allies will continue to follow steadily into the fight. All of us will work together as one. With the gallant and powerful Russian Army pounding the European enemy on the East and with growing forces seeking out and penetrating weak spots in his defenses from all other directions, his utter defeat—even if not yet definitely in sight—is certain. Victory will likewise be ours in the far off Pacific, where Allied Forces are already on the offensive and where unconquerable China, awaiting the time when the full power of the Allies may come to her assistance, continues to defy one of the most powerful and vicious of our enemies.

The heart of America supports our every endeavour. Reports of sporadic troubles on the home front are occasioned by the ill-considered actions of a relatively few individuals. Let us always remember that our great nation of 130,000,000 people is ceaselessly working and sacrificing to provide us weapons, equipment and supplies, and to send us an increasing flow of reinforcements. Our Allies march forward with us. The God of Justice fights on our side.

Let us, then, strengthen ourselves for the tasks yet lying ahead. With high courage let us redouble our efforts and multiply the fury of our blows so that we may the more quickly re-cross the seas to our own homeland with the glorious word that the last enemy stronghold has fallen and with the proud knowledge of having done, in our time, our duty to our beloved country.

◆ ◆ ◆

Lesson 128

Teach a Practical Lesson

If I were teaching military hygiene, I would simply take [the example of] an infantry company from the time it was mobilized on through its training period into a campaign, and describe all the things the officers and men had to do to preserve their health.

—Letter to his son, John S. D. Eisenhower, December 3, 1943

Ike good-naturedly kidded his West Point cadet son about a low grade in a subject called "military hygiene." After admitting that his own standing in the subject was probably lower than his son's, he went on to offer as a criticism of "much of our training program . . . the uninteresting way in which subjects are presented. I personally see little use in the ordinary officer being able to identify the various types of mosquitoes. He hasn't time to do it even if he could. The important thing is to consider all mosquitoes as enemies and take the necessary steps to get rid of them and guard against them."

Ike thought military education should be practical and directly relevant to the needs of the student. "Any student learns anything easiest when he is most interested." Education is a leadership responsibility, and an effective leader will want to create a program of effective education. The goal is not so much to keep it simple as it is to keep it useful, which means relevant, which means interesting.

◆ ◆ ◆

Lesson 129

The Greatest Blunder

The greatest blunder in war is indecisiveness, slowness and hesitation. The leader that will take upon his own shoulders the awful burdens of battle responsibility and still act quickly and decisively saves lives—all others, even if personally kind and sympathetic—are guilty of useless expenditure of life.

> —Letter (marked "Personal and
> confidential") to June Jenkins Booth,
> December 14, 1943

"For certain types of action," Eisenhower wrote in *Crusade in Europe*, George S. Patton Jr. "was the outstanding soldier our country has produced." For the role of army commander, "he personally was ideally suited." But he was also one of the most difficult of the legion of very difficult people Eisenhower had to lead and had to manage. As with a hero of Greek tragedy, the very elements of Patton's genius in war were nearly his undoing in public. Ike understood this. He continued in *Crusade in Europe*: "His emotional tenseness and his impulsiveness were the very qualities that made him, in open situations, such a remarkable leader of an army. In pursuit and exploitation there is need for a commander who sees nothing but the necessity of getting ahead; the more he drives his men the more he will save their lives."

Tenseness and *impulsiveness*. From July 10 through August 17, 1943, Patton drove the U.S. Seventh Army relentlessly through the difficult but triumphant invasion of Sicily, not only defeating the Italians and Germans but also besting his British rival, Bernard Law Montgomery, whom he beat to the key Sicilian port of Messina. Then, near the very pinnacle of his triumph, on August 3, Patton called at the front-line Fifteenth Evacuation Hospital to visit with wounded troops. Amid the shattered young men was one Private Charles H. Kuhl, without apparent injury.

What was the problem? Patton asked him.

"I guess I can't take it," Kuhl replied.

That answer was the match to a fuse.

Patton exploded in curses, called Kuhl a coward, and ordered him out of the hospital tent. Stunned, the private did not move. The general, who was holding his leather gloves in his hand, lashed out. Some witnesses later reported that he struck Kuhl across the face with his gloves. Others, with greater accuracy, noted that the slap was across Kuhl's helmet and delivered with sufficient force to knock it off his head. All agreed that Patton then lifted Kuhl by the shirt collar and sent him out of the tent with a kick in the rear.

Outrageous as this incident was, it received no immediate public notice. But then, on August 10, during a visit to another evac hospital, Patton encountered another victim of battle fatigue.

"It's my nerves," Private Paul G. Bennett complained to the general.

"What did you say?"

"It's my nerves. I can't stand the shelling any more."

"Your *nerves*. Hell, you are just a goddamned coward."

Laying his hand on his trademark ivory-handled Colt revolver, Patton muttered, "I ought to shoot you myself right now." He unholstered the weapon, waved it in front of the terrified soldier's face, then delivered a sharp slap.

This second incident was impossible to keep quiet, and it ignited a firestorm of public and professional criticism even from the highest levels. Eisenhower's boss, army chief of staff General George C. Marshall, left the decision to Ike, but the pressure mounted on all sides to relieve Patton of command.

Eisenhower resisted the pressure. He directed (but did not order) Patton to make the rounds of every Seventh Army unit and apologize for the incident. Eisenhower knew it was a humiliating punishment intensely painful to Patton, but it was better than firing a commander he believed would continue to prove among the Allies' most effective instruments of war.

Once Ike had decided to retain Patton, no other military commander dared to second-guess him, but doubts, criticism, condemnation, and concern continued to pour in from politicians, the press, and private individuals. One communication Eisenhower received was a letter from a lady named June Jenkins Booth, who wrote that she had one son in the service and another slated to go the following year. She hoped that Patton would not remain in command, where he might "repeat his fits of temper on another unfortunate victim." She appealed to the supreme commander, writing that she would "die of worry" if her sons had to serve under "such a cruel, profane, impatient officer."

Eisenhower not only took the time to read Mrs. Booth's letter but answered it "within the hour of its arrival at my Headquarters." He wrote:

> As a matter of fact, no mother of an American soldier has yet written me a letter who did not receive a prompt reply, because no one can be more appreciative than I of the tremendous sacrifices made by the mothers of America for the cause for which we fight. My own son will take his place in the battleline next June, which is an added reason for my feeling very close to those other parents whose sons are already in or are soon to enter the armed services.

The all-important details of his business, Eisenhower understood, were the individual lives on which that business depended. Each life was someone's son.

"War is a sad, a desperate and a tragic business," Eisenhower explained to Mrs. Booth. "The chief concern of any man in my position is to meet the heavy responsibilities placed upon him by his government in such a way as to avoid the unnecessary loss of a single American soldier."

Business, including the tragic business of war, is always an unyielding economic proposition: the purchase of necessary ends at the cost of precious treasure. Good business makes this transaction with the least possible expenditure, and if you are an effective executive, you strive to manage costs while also gaining the necessary ends. This is the art of realizing maximum value. Yet however you manage them, you know and accept that there *will* be costs.

In war, the general explained to the mother, value consists in achieving victory while avoiding the *unnecessary* loss of a single American soldier:

> Even with the greatest of skill and the finest of leadership, the cost is heavy enough for us to bear—both as a nation and individually. If to these losses are added those that come about through blundering, then indeed does the tragedy become almost unbearable.
>
> The greatest blunder in war is indecisiveness, slowness and hesitation. The leader that will take upon his own shoulders the awful burdens of battle responsibility and still act quickly and decisively saves lives—all others, even if personally kind and sympathetic—are guilty of useless expenditure of life.

"The ideal leader," Eisenhower admitted to Mrs. Booth, "is one who invariably acts kindly and with consideration and is still decisive and bold." The implication was unmistakable: Patton had shown himself to be far from the ideal. "You are quite right in deploring acts such as his and in being incensed that they could occur in an American army." He continued, "But in Sicily General Patton saved thousands of American lives. By his boldness, his speed, his drive, he won his part of the campaign by marching, more than he did by fighting. He drove himself and his men almost beyond human endurance, but because of this he minimized tragedy in American homes."

In short, Patton had proved he could achieve value. Therefore, he was himself valuable, despite his formidable liabilities.

"I decided [that Patton] should not be lost to us in the job of winning this war . . . even though the easy thing for me would have been to send General Patton home. I hope that, as the mother of two American soldiers, you will understand."

Results trump personal peccadilloes. Stand by your man, even if you sometimes have to hold your nose.

◆ ◆ ◆

Lesson 130

Grease Each Point of Friction

This is directly contrary to my policies and must cease at once.

—Cable to Carl Spaatz,
December 23, 1943

After hearing that General Carl Spaatz of the Army Air Forces had reserved recreational facilities on Capri "exclusively for air force officers," Ike fired off a cable ordering an immediate end to this and directing that the facilities be opened to "all British and American personnel in this area, particularly from combat units."

Identify even apparently small points of friction, then act to lubricate them. Seemingly slight affronts have a nasty tendency to blossom into major insult and injury.

◆ ◆ ◆

Lesson 131

Separate Administration from Application

My experience here amply justifies the statement that no man should be held responsible for the actual handling of an army in the battlefront and at the same time meet the problems that are constantly arising as the senior American representative in this theater.

—Cable to George C. Marshall,
December 25, 1943

Ike insisted on separating the functions of administration and application. He believed that each of the two functions demanded 100 percent commitment, which was beyond the capacity of any single commander. The administrator had to operate with regard to those in the field as well as those in the rear—the politicians and statesmen. The field commander's responsibility was to his troops below him and to the theater commander above him. These spheres of loyalty were frequently in conflict.

Shirtsleeves managers often complain about front-office administrators, insisting that they themselves could do the job better. From the narrow perspective of a particular department, this may well be true, at least in the short run. But as Ike discovered through experience, it is far more effective to have at least two layers of leadership—one hands-on, the other guiding the hands-on leader and coordinating his efforts with those of other hands-on men. This arrangement implies—indeed, calls for—a hierarchy of the kind Ike insisted on.

◆ ◆ ◆

Lesson 132

Protect the Individual, Protect the Organization

[B]e very careful.

—Memorandum to Everett S. Hughes,
December 27, 1943

Ike sent a brief memo to Everett S. Hughes, his deputy theater commander, which began, "Yesterday I had a letter from the parent of one of our soldiers, who alleged that her son, a recruit of only 13 weeks' training, was in this theater and presumably about to go into combat."

It was remarkable enough that Eisenhower had taken the time to read a letter from the parent of a recruit, but far more significant was the use he made of what he read. Instead of dismissing the letter, however sympathetically, as an expression of concern from just one more worried parent out of millions, he used it to formulate a key piece of personnel policy: "I think our replacement system should be very careful in determining the age and length of the training period of all recruits so that whenever any of these particular type of cases are uncovered, the man should be sent to a [non-combat] service unit and get out of the rigors of combat until he is more fully developed."

Ike's decision protected the individual as well as the organization. Inexperienced soldiers not only get themselves killed but endanger others. Inadequately trained personnel do not simply dilute the effectiveness of an organization; they actively reduce it, because their uncertainty and their mistakes require labor to fix— if they *can* be fixed. The sink-or-swim approach resembles Russian roulette more than it does bold management.

◆ ◆ ◆

Lesson 133

Use What Inspires You

A prayer that I once heard a company commander repeating to his men, on a wet, cold night, just before starting a march to the front line, struck me more forcibly than almost any other I have heard.

—Letter to Gerald Mygatt,
December 28, 1943

When Major Gerald Mygatt wrote to Eisenhower with a request that he compose a prayer for the *Soldiers' and Sailors' Prayer Book* (New York, 1944), the general replied with this:

> Almighty God, we are about to be committed to a task from which some of us will not return. We go willingly to this hazardous adventure because we believe that those concepts of human dignity, rights and justice that Your Son expounded to the world, and which are respected in the government of our beloved country, are in peril of extinction from the earth. We are ready to sacrifice ourselves for our country and our God. We do not ask, individually, for our safe return. But we earnestly pray that You will help each of us to do his full duty. Permit none of us to fail a comrade in the fight. Above all, sustain us in our conviction in the justice and righteousness of our cause so that we may rise above all terror of the enemy and come to You, if called, in the humble pride of the good soldier and in the certainty of Your infinite mercy. Amen.

Public prayer is not appropriate in most secular enterprises; nevertheless, leaders should recognize and address the spiritual dimension of any serious endeavor. In leadership, use what inspires you and share what inspires you. The only influence to avoid is the surely destructive force of cynicism.

◆ ◆ ◆

Lesson 134

Facilitate, Don't Aggravate

In giving these views, I merely wish to remove any political difficulties that may occur to you in order that you can launch the best military operation.

—Cable to Harold Alexander,
December 29, 1943

By the end of 1943, the Allied invasion of Italy was stalled at the so-called Winter Line, German defenses just south of Rome. Prime Minister Winston Churchill sponsored a plan called Operation Shingle, which was seconded by Franklin D. Roosevelt and Joseph Stalin. The operation, which stepped off on January 22, 1944, was an Allied amphibious landing in the area of Anzio and Nettuno, Italy, and was intended to outflank the Winter Line. The operation culminated in the costly Battle of Anzio.

During the final preparations for Operation Shingle, Ike cabled the overall commander of the Mediterranean theater, the British general Harold Alexander, in response to Alexander's intention to "employ one British and one U.S. . . . division" in the initial assault. Ike reminded Alexander of the "disadvantages of employing a mixed corps"—a corps under one commander but compounded of an American and a British division— disadvantages that "are particularly applicable" in a "self-contained" operation. Ike "wondered whether or not" Alexander had been influenced in his decision to use a mixed corps by strictly political factors. If so, he advised that such factors should not "be allowed to outweigh the military advantages of launching your assault by any troops you believe best fitted and most available. I hope your decision will be guided solely by your convictions as to feasibility of the operation and the best way, from the tactical viewpoint, to do it." Eisenhower stressed that "in giving these views," he wanted only "to remove any political difficulties that may occur to you in order that you can launch the best military operation."

On the one hand, second-guessing key subordinates, who should enjoy a high degree of autonomy and autonomous responsibility, is poor leadership. It not only telegraphs a lack of faith in the subordinate but also betrays the insecurity of the leader. If a subordinate repeatedly gives you good reason for second-guessing, it is time to look for a new subordinate. On the other hand, you are not obliged to leave everything to any subordinate. An effective leader does not hesitate to communicate advice, provided he or she can do so in a positive way that facilitates rather than aggravates and that offers help rather than induces doubt. In his masterful cable to Alexander, Ike accomplished two objectives: (1) he reminded Alexander of the dangers of a mixed corps, and (2) he explicitly released Alexander from the political necessity of using a mixed corps.

Ike gave advice, then he provided the means by which Alexander could act on that advice without feeling that his authority or judgment was being questioned, much less overridden.

◆ ◆ ◆

Lesson 135

Micromanagement or Brilliant Management?

I do not look with favor on risking your neck.

—Secret cable to Bernard Law
Montgomery, December 29, 1943

For most of today's top executives, a single word figures as an unforgivable obscenity: *micromanagement*. No one wants to sully the skirts of his or her coat with the mud of mere details. Prevailing management practices would rather risk losing contact with the foot soldiers than permit an executive to descend into the daily mire for fear that it might become a quagmire.

Ike Eisenhower's understanding of the difference between management and micromanagement was profound. Personally he had always craved a "field command," direct combat leadership of troops in battle, but what he was given instead was the more remote task of commanding the commanders. He accepted it. He understood that he was the CEO, not the plant manager, but when he recognized a critical detail, he made the time to manage it.

Learning that Bernard Law Montgomery, the British general he had tapped to serve as the overall commander of ground forces in the upcoming D-Day invasion of Europe, "intended to make the ocean hop from Africa to England via [his] Dakota plane," Eisenhower dispatched Secret Cable no. 20670, marked "Personal from Commander in Chief to General Montgomery." The plane the British called the Dakota was what the Americans designated simply as the C-47, the military version of the Douglas DC-3, the enormously popular twin-engine civilian passenger transport that had been flying reliably since the mid-1930s. There was no question that it was a rock-solid aircraft. Eisenhower himself would credit it, along with the bulldozer, jeep, and 2½-ton truck, as having been indispensable to victory in Europe. Nevertheless, the supreme commander cabled Montgomery: "While I realize that such [over-water] trips are made by these planes constantly, I do not look with favor on risking your neck on a two engine transport, particularly since your plane has not been regularly on this particular flight."

Engrossed in planning on the largest scale, Eisenhower nevertheless zeroed in on a key operational detail. Flying over water in a twin-engine aircraft put passengers at risk—and Montgomery was one passenger the Allied cause could not afford to put at risk.

Identifying and focusing on such a detail is in itself a remarkable piece of management. But then Eisenhower took it to the next level. It is one thing to point out a problem; successful management also requires providing a solution. Eisenhower continued his cable: "From Marrakech to England there is a regular service of the big C 54 planes (four engine). I can arrange the very highest priority for you and whatever small staff may be accompanying you personally and I strongly urge that you allow me to do this."

Nor did the supreme commander stop here. Having pointed out a problem as well as having provided a solution, Ike sought to ensure follow-through with appropriate action. "Will you please answer at once?" he added.

Montgomery replied on December 29 and did, in fact, agree to depart from Marrakech on a four-engine C-54. It's not all about the details. It's all about the *right* details.

◆ ◆ ◆

Lesson 136

The Credible Cheerleader

[M]erely compare your present position and prospects in this great conflict with your position and outlook in the late Fall of 1942.

> —Farewell message to "All Men and Women Serving in or with Allied Forces in the Mediterranean Theater," January 1, 1944

At the end of 1943, Eisenhower was ordered to step down as over-all commander of Allied forces in the Mediterranean theater so that he could assume the office of supreme commander of Allied forces in Europe, the position from which he would direct Opera-tion Overlord, the cross-Channel invasion of the continent. On January 1, 1944, he issued a farewell message to the troops of the Mediterranean.

As any effective leader would, he praised those he had led, cred-iting them with the success of the enterprise. But Eisenhower was more than just an effective leader. He possessed a positive genius for motivation. Cheerleading is key to motivation, and Eisenhower knew that optimism, like pessimism, is infectious. He also under-stood that self-confidence, like self-doubt, flows downward through an organization from the very highest levels of command. So it was important for a commander to exude the positive feelings born of faith in victory. Yet Ike was also well aware that this was not enough. You can't just *order* soldiers to feel confident. The downward perco-lation of confidence cannot be commanded. It must be created.

To create the collective emotion of victory, Eisenhower did more than lead an empty cheer. "Although tempted to review again the many advantages that have accrued to the Allied cause through your bravery and fortitude, I believe all these will come home to you if you will merely compare your present position and prospects in this great conflict with your position and outlook in the late Fall of 1942."

Great leaders share the secret of great salesmen. The pitch they craft *shows* more than it *tells*. Instead of offering hollow adjectives, Ike asked his troops to think for themselves by comparing the present *reality* to the reality of just a short time ago. Offering a before-and-after picture, Eisenhower pointed out that back in fall 1942,

> [T]he British Eighth Army was making its final preparations to attack the enemy, who was standing only a short distance west of Cairo. Vast Allied armadas were approaching Northwest Africa in complete ignorance as to whether good fortune or complete disaster awaited them. Battered Malta was being defended only by the bravery of her almost entirely isolated garrison. No Allied ship could transit the length of the Mediterranean. Our fortunes appeared at a low ebb.

But today:

> All this is changed—changed by your skill, your determination and your devotion to duty. Enemy action against our convoys in the Mediterranean is limited to harassing and submarine efforts. You have established yourselves on the mainland of Europe. You are still advancing.

The operative pronoun is *you*, and the subject is *what* you *have done*. This is meaningful, credible cheerleading, not an assemblage of encouraging words but a crisp presentation of irrefutable firsthand evidence.

From pictures of the past and present, Ike advanced into the future: "You, along with the other Allied Forces fighting on many fronts, have already achieved the certainty that, provided every soldier, sailor and airman, and every citizen in our homelands continues incessantly to do his full duty, victory will be ours." Here the commander showed himself to be a master of the communicative power of tense. The sentence builds the "certainty" of the future ("victory *will be* ours") on the accomplished facts of the past perfect ("*have* already *achieved*"), and both are leavened by a proviso in the conditional present ("*provided* every soldier, sailor and airman, and every citizen in our homelands *continues* incessantly *to do* his full duty"). In place of hopes and hollow words, Eisenhower furnished the syntactical certainty of a verbal equation that added up past and present to derive the sum: an essentially inevitable future.

Leading a complex endeavor requires managing the present while also bridging the past and the future. You have to pilot the organization through time as well as space, providing the group with an awareness not only of where it is but of where it came from and where, based on the facts of past and present, it is destined to arrive.

◆ ◆ ◆

Lesson 137

Know the Stakes

I know that this attack must *succeed.*

—Letter to George C. Marshall,
January 17, 1944

Operation Overlord was the code name for the Allied invasion of France via the beaches at Normandy. History would remember it as D-Day—the beginning of the Allied victory in Europe.

Overlord had been a long time coming, especially because the British, having earlier failed twice in assaults on the Continent, were cautious about making a third attempt. Ike possessed what any adequate leader of a great enterprise must possess: a thorough awareness of what was at stake in the operation. "I clearly appreciate," he wrote to Marshall, "that the coming venture is the decisive act of the War from the viewpoint of the British-American effort. I know that this attack *must* succeed." In a cable to the Combined Chiefs of Staff a few days later, on January 23, he declared that Operation Overlord "marks the crisis of the European war. Every obstacle must be overcome, every inconvenience suffered and every risk run to ensure our blow is decisive. We cannot afford to fail."

These were bold words—but they were only words, after all. The real measure of Eisenhower's leadership was his ongoing struggle to maintain Allied focus on Overlord. He wanted to supplement the Normandy landings with additional landings on the French Riviera in an operation initially code-named Anvil and later dubbed Dragoon. Anvil-Dragoon would require diverting some forces from the struggling Italian campaign; the British, however, did not want to make that sacrifice. Ike argued vigorously for Anvil-Dragoon as a means of "increasing our insurance in obtaining the first foot-hold on the beaches" of Normandy, and he declared his determination "to uncover every single expedient for increasing the initial weight of the OVERLORD attack before I am willing to recommend any great weakening of the ANVIL project."

In the end, Ike had to put off the Riviera landings until August 1944, some two months after the landings at Normandy. Eisenhower had done his best to preserve what he considered the ideal strategy—a simultaneous assault on Normandy and the Riviera—but, failing this, he did everything he could to ensure that the single-pronged attack on Normandy would be exploited to the maximum. The invasion, of course, succeeded without the simultaneous Riviera invasion; nevertheless, military historians have since debated the wisdom of postponing Anvil-Dragoon.

Work *toward* the ideal, but work *with* the real. The greater the stakes, the more important this is.

◆ ◆ ◆

Lesson 138

Act "According to Ritual"

I think the whole thing should be handled according to ritual so that there can be no flare-back.

—Letter to his brother Milton S. Eisenhower, January 20, 1944

Like George S. Patton Jr.'s bull terrier, named William the Conqueror but commonly answering to Willie, Ike's Scotty, Telek, was no dog of war. If Patton had wanted a fearless and feisty pup, what he got in Willie was a faithful but decidedly sheepish companion. As for Eisenhower, he was happy to have an engaging pet who had nothing at all of the warrior in him. To a reporter who asked him why Telek formed part of his "staff" at Telegraph Cottage, the villa outside London that served as Eisenhower's headquarters, the general replied, "You can't talk war to a dog, and I'd like to have someone or something to talk to, occasionally, that doesn't know what the word means! A dog is my only hope."

When Telek had a litter of puppies early in 1944, Ike decided to send one to Buddy and Ruth, the children of his brother Milton. As usual, this sounded simpler than it proved to be, as livestock imported from abroad was subject to a thick catalogue of laws and regulations, including a period of quarantine. "I feel sure the authorities would allow you to do his quarantine period back at Kansas State College," Ike wrote Milton, but was scrupulous to avoid even the appearance of any attempt to skirt the rules or obtain privileged treatment: "and I think the whole thing should be handled according to ritual so that there can be no flare-back."

The infamous, celebrated—and finally hilarious—"scandal" over FDR's Scotty, Fala, would not occur until that summer, when Roosevelt was accused by Republican politicians and the Republican-dominated media of dispatching, at great expense and peril, a U.S. Navy warship to retrieve Fala after he had been inadvertently left behind during a presidential visit to troops in Alaska's Aleutian Islands. Although the rumor echoed to the very halls of Congress, the president had, in fact, never lost his dog, let alone sent a navy ship after him.

No, Eisenhower needed no presidential example to alert him to the hazards of "flare-back." He instinctively understood that although rank hath its privileges, there is often a high price to pay in casually exercising them. The higher your rank, the more important it is to demonstrate your absolute willingness to be governed even by the homeliest of the organization's "rituals."

The famously ostentatious George S. Patton Jr., whose gorgeous uniforms and ivory-handled revolver deliberately and unmistakably distinguished him from the olive-drab troops he led, nevertheless laid it down as a principle of command that "In cold weather, General Officers must be careful not to appear to dress more warmly than the men." Ike's attitude toward the gift puppy was very much of a piece with this principle.

By all means, distinguish yourself from those you lead—there must be no mistaking your identity, your office, and your authority—yet bind yourself to the same rights, rules, and hardships that govern the most junior of your subordinates. You are all citizens of the same community and strivers in the same endeavor.

◆ ◆ ◆

Lesson 139

Never Marry an Idea

After detailed examination of the tactical plan I clearly understand Montgomery's original objection.

> —Secret Cable to George C. Marshall,
> January 22, 1944

The pressure on Eisenhower to formulate and finalize plans for the cross-Channel invasion of Europe was tremendous. Under such conditions, the temptation to wed himself to the first apparently workable solution was nearly impossible to resist. The British general Bernard Law Montgomery was notoriously cranky, argumentative, and contrary. It would have been easy for Eisenhower to dismiss his objections to plans he himself endorsed, but, as supreme Allied commander, Eisenhower was never seduced by what was easy. The prickly Montgomery's objections prompted him not to turn against his British subordinate but to make a renewed and "detailed examination of the tactical plan." This led him not blithely to confirm his earlier faith in the plan but instead to see its shortcomings from Montgomery's point of view and, what is more, to acknowledge and act on them. Eisenhower now understood that "Beaches are too few and too restricted to depend upon them as avenues through which all our original build-up would have to flow. We must broaden out to gain quick initial success, secure more beaches for build-up and particularly to get a force at once into the Cherbourg peninsula behind the natural defensive barrier separating that feature from the mainland. In this way there would be a reasonable hope of gaining the port in short order." Eisenhower concluded, "We must have this."

Despite the pressures imposed by time, bosses, and customers, never rush to the altar with any one idea. Hug a particular plan too tightly, and you can see nothing else. Ike made it his business to keep looking, even after decisions had ostensibly been made, and he held no plan so dear that he allowed it to escape change when he saw that change was what "we must have."

◆ ◆ ◆

Lesson 140

Look Beyond Ego to Focus on Issues

I have no recourse except to do my very best.

—Letter to John W. Burn, January 23, 1944

On January 23, 1944, General Eisenhower received a handwritten letter, dated January 17, from a John W. Burn of Horley, Surrey.

Dear Sir,
    While I offer you personally a welcome to England, I do not do so as C[ommander] in C[harge] of the Allied Forces because I consider that either [British] General [Bernard Law] Montgomery

or [General Sir Harold] Alexander should have held that position. Remember we have been in this war for over four years. Twelve months we stood alone. Our troops have done some very hard fighting, especially in Africa where we chased Rommel for over a thousand miles out of Africa. If for some reason a British general was not desired we should have preferred a Russian General to lead the Allied Forces in the same way as they have led their wonderful Army in Russia. We are all very pleased that Mr. Churchill has seen that wonderful Frenchman, General Charles DeGaulle [sic], who is now in his right place as head of all loyal Frenchmen. Perhaps some day your country will recognize his stirring qualities.

Ike could have been forgiven for either throwing the letter in the trash or replying with more than a touch of impatience. But he did neither. Instead, he personally dictated a disarmingly thoughtful response:

Dear Mr. Burn:

I well understand the feelings that prompted you to write your letter of the 17th of January. Moreover, I am the first to agree with you that anyone of the Generals you suggested, and possibly even anyone of a number, would have been a better selection than that actually made for the accomplishment of my task. However, I hope you will agree that as long as this duty has been placed upon me by Great Britain and the United States, I have no recourse except to do my very best to perform it adequately.

The reply not only was a model of humility but also made use of its humility to look beyond ego and focus attention on the issue at hand: leading an Anglo-American army to victory.

In the next paragraph, Eisenhower turned that very issue back upon his critical correspondent:

I hope also, that the mere fact that you do not agree with the two Governments in their selection of the Commander will not

prevent you from doing everything that it is possible for you to do
to help win this war speedily and conclusively, so that we may
have an end of destruction and carnage.

Instead of picking up the gauntlet flung down before him and
accepting the role Burn attempted to thrust on him, that of adver-
sary, Eisenhower made common cause with the writer, effectively
pointing out that he, John W. Burn, shares the same duty as the
commander in chief.

All complex enterprises operated for high stakes present a mul-
titude of problems as well as opportunities. Conflicting egos descend
on these like a fog, rendering the problems far more hazardous and
the opportunities far less visible. You can't afford to ignore personalities; after all, business is first and last about people. Yet to do meaningful, effective, profitable business, you have to sweep aside the fog
of ego in order to see, bright and sharp, the problems and the opportunities that are the bottom line of any worthwhile endeavor.

◆ ◆ ◆

Lesson 141

Say What You Must to Get What You Need

*To get what we want I am perfectly willing to avoid terms and
language that may startle anyone.*

—Letter to Henry "Hap" Arnold,
January 23, 1944

To the chief U.S. Air Force officer in Europe, Hap Arnold, Ike
wrote that "there can be no evasion of the certainty that when the
time comes the OVERLORD Commander must have the full power to determine missions and priorities for the attacks by all forces,"
including the air forces. This meant that air commanders would
have to concede their ultimate authority to the overall commander
of Operation Overlord. Ike knew that no commander is eager to

give up authority, and he knew that this was especially true in the case of air commanders asked to yield to ground commanders. For this reason, Ike was willing to spin the requirement so as "to avoid terms and language that may startle anyone," but he wanted nonetheless to make the requirement—an absolute requirement—absolutely clear to Arnold.

Decide what you must have, then invent the language to get it. Remember that your object is not to assert your authority with words that challenge the authority of others, but to express yourself in a way that simply gets what you want without raising undue alarm.

◆ ◆ ◆

Lesson 142

Turn Apology into Opportunity

I truly thank you for the trouble you took in reporting to me the incident.

—Letter to Maxwell Taylor,
January 24, 1944

On January 23, 1944, Eisenhower received a letter from one Maxwell Taylor of Hertfordshire. Aware that "the matter of Anglo-American understanding" was close to the general's heart, Taylor wrote to report an incident he had witnessed that very morning. A cigar-smoking American officer boarded the lower level of an English double-decker bus, where he was approached by a "rather fussy and perhaps ridiculous Englishman," who informed him that smoking was not allowed inside and that he should go upstairs to the open-air top deck. The officer growled, "Don't be so typically English; you ought to be in an institution," and an argument ensued, which prompted Taylor to observe, "I do feel that your compatriots, especially senior officers, are doing their country an ill-service by such tactlessness."

General Eisenhower replied:

> I truly thank you for the trouble you took in reporting to me the
> incident related in your letter of January 23. My only regret is that
> I do not have the name of the offending American officer; if I did,
> I assure you that he at least would never again be guilty, in this
> Theater, of such a breach of good manners and of such direct
> assault upon the good relations that must obtain between our two
> countries.
>
> You are completely right in assuming that the matter of
> maintaining a firm Anglo-American partnership for the purpose
> of winning this war lies close to my heart. There is no single thing
> that I believe more important to both of our countries, and I
> request merely that if ever again you are witness to such an inci-
> dent, you will make such effort as you can to identify the offending
> individual.
>
> Thank you again.

In the 2,696 printed pages of Dwight Eisenhower's wartime correspondence, hundreds of pages are devoted to letters in answer to
soldiers' family members and various other private citizens. Almost
always, Eisenhower displayed an uncanny faculty for replying to
very particular and apparently personal concerns in ways that reveal
far-reaching, even universal implications. Here, for example, the
supreme commander took time to address what most would deem a
very small incident in a very big war. The supreme commander
apologized on behalf of his brother officer, but, more important, he
amplified the apology into an opportunity to reaffirm and reinforce
the Anglo-American alliance he knew was key to winning the war
against a common enemy.

When you—or somebody for whom you accept responsibility—
makes a mistake, you have to say you are sorry. That's very important.
But it is even more important to turn the apology into something
both positive and active. In this case, Ike expressed his regret that he
was unable to discipline an officer whose identity was unknown, but

he effectively recruited the letter writer into the "Anglo-American partnership" by asking him to make an effort to identify any individual who might in the future offend against the "good relations that must obtain between our two countries." He made common cause with a person who otherwise would have had good reason to feel nothing except offense and injury. He transformed an unfortunate incident, an occasion for apology, into an opportunity to reassert the loftiest principles on which a great enterprise, the alliance of two mighty powers for the common good, was founded.

◆ ◆ ◆

Lesson 143

Salve

The incident . . . leads me to seek in advance your cooperation in being instantly ready to apply salve instead of an irritant onto fancied hurts that may arise out of individual personality or conviction or of mere lack of understanding on the part of some person.

—Cable to George C. Marshall,
January 28, 1944

After Ike discovered that "there was a little bit of hurt feeling" as the result of a jurisdictional dispute between British and American officers in the process of planning Operation Overlord, he cabled General Marshall with a "personal request . . . as a matter of urgency, to help me minimize any bad effect of these [disputes] and to prevent knowledge of them getting into circulation because of the danger of hurting the war effort."

As supreme Allied commander responsible for the greatest amphibious invasion in the history of warfare, Dwight Eisenhower could have been forgiven for simply demanding that everyone involved check their feelings at the door, roll up their sleeves, and get to work. He could have been forgiven for this attitude, but, even with the stakes at their very highest and the greatest degree of self-sacrifice called for, this approach would likely have failed. Ike possessed a keen understanding that hurt feelings could trump or at least impede almost any other consideration, no matter how great the consequences. Therefore, instead of simply exerting the weight of his official authority, he constantly endeavored to maintain sensitivity to the feelings of everyone involved, even if those feelings at times seemed unjustified or childish. Ike believed this aspect of leadership so important that he enlisted the cooperation of his boss, General Marshall, in applying "salve instead of an irritant" onto what he himself described as "fancied hurts."

True, in the best of worlds, there would be no "fancied hurts," but Ike was well aware that he labored in a place far from the best of worlds. If salve would help him accomplish his vast mission, he would apply salve—and get his boss to do the same.

◆ ◆ ◆

Lesson 144

Walk the Talk

I am personally ready and proud to serve in any capacity that the two Governments may choose to assign me, under any British commander they may see fit to designate.

—Letter to John W. Burn, February 1, 1944

On January 27, Ike received a handwritten note from John W. Burn, thanking him for responding to his letter of January 17, in which Burn criticized Ike, who, as an American commander, lacked the experience of senior British commanders Burn thought better suited to overall command of the Allied forces (see Lesson 140 in this chapter). Ike replied to Burn again, assuring him that he shared his admiration for British generals Alexander and Montgomery, with whom (Ike pointed out) "I have served intimately . . . and witnessed their great qualities at first hand." Ike closed by deploring "any thought of mutual resentment among the British and American people in carrying out the great war task we have." Then he laid it on the line, proclaiming his proud willingness to serve under any *British* commander the governments of the United States and Great Britain might designate.

It is one thing to enunciate selfless principles of cooperation, but quite another, to put them into practice, even hypothetically.

◆   ◆   ◆

Lesson 145

Control Information, Ensure Security

I have discussed . . . the best means of keeping the Press securely in the dark, while at the same time not appearing to treat them as complete outsiders.

— Letter to Winston Churchill,
February 6, 1944

One of the problems of conducting a war or any other great enterprise in a democracy is controlling information and enforcing security—while still maintaining cordial and productive relations with the press. As the Allies prepared Operation Overlord, Ike could have simply clamped down, but he quite rightly feared that this would both antagonize an institution useful for disseminating productive information and encourage reporters to pry, thereby creating rather than preventing a security leak. He assured Prime Minister Churchill, therefore, that he was working to keep the press in the dark without alienating them. "Personally, I should feel disturbed if I thought that I or my Public Relations Staff were held as anything but the friends of the Press."

The control of information and even outright secrecy are necessary to the success of many enterprises, but, where information is concerned, a heavy hand is rarely the most effective means of maintaining security. Like anything else in the affairs of a complex organization, the flow of information must be managed, not simply stopped.

◆ ◆ ◆

Lesson 146

Bow to Economics

We can't close our eyes to that, no matter how much we shout "principle and agreements."

—Memorandum for diary, February 7, 1944

In planning Operation Overlord, Ike wanted to make simultaneous landings on the French Riviera (Operation Anvil) in order to draw off German defensive forces from the principal landings. In a memorandum for his diary, he noted that "At the time ANVIL-OVER-LORD was planned it was thought that no landing craft would be needed in Italy after the end of January. Now—with [Operation] SHINGLE [the Allied assault near Anzio, Italy] stalemated—there is a need there that cannot be ignored."

The great informing principle of economics is *scarcity*—the unbreakable law that says, simply, that there is never enough of anything to go around. Confronted with economic reality—a chronic shortage of landing craft (there were never enough)—Ike wrote, "We can't close our eyes to that, no matter how much we shout 'principle and agreements.' . . . With Italy requiring an allotment [of landing craft], it looks like ANVIL is doomed. I hate this—in spite of my recognition of the fact that Italian fighting will be some compensation for a strong ANVIL."

Reality trumps all anticipation, plans, principles, and agreements. As a leader, you are free to hate this fact, but you are never free to ignore it.

◆ ◆ ◆

Lesson 147

Check Your Ego at the Door

—Oh hum—

> —Memorandum for diary, February 7, 1944

Ike recorded in a memorandum for his war diary:

> Much discussion has taken place concerning our command set-up, including newspaper evaluations of personalities and abilities. Generally speaking, the British columnists . . . try to show that my contributions in the Mediterranean were administrative accomplishments and "friendliness in welding an Allied team." They dislike to believe that I had anything particularly to do with campaigns. They don't use the words "initiative" and "boldness" in talking of me—but often do in speaking of [British generals] Alex[ander] and Monty [Montgomery].
>
> The truth is that the bold British Commanders in the Med were General Andrews and Tedder. I had peremptorily to order the holding of the forward air fields in the bitter days of January—1943. I had to order the integration of an American Corps and its use on the battlelines (If I had not done that, [the capture of] Tunis would have evaded us a much longer time). I had to order the attack on Pantelleria. And finally the British ground commander (but not Sir Andrew and Tedder) wanted to put all our ground forces into the toe of Italy. They didn't like Salerno—but after days of work I got them to accept. . . . [I]t wearies me to be thought of as timid, when I've had to do things that were so risky as to be almost crazy.— Oh hum—.

Ike never published this account, and he did not protest the perception of him that was published in the British press. He reserved the right to set the historical record straight—someday—but he did not dare complain while everyone had a desperate job to do.

There would be time for whining, but, in the thick of things, the only effective course was to leave it at "Oh hum." To be an effective leader, check your ego at the door. You can reclaim it later.

◆　◆　◆

Lesson 148

The Big Picture Versus "Localitis"

. . . nor do I believe I am particularly affected by localitis.

—Cable to George C. Marshall,
February 8, 1944

When Ike received from his boss, George C. Marshall, a telegram implying that he (as Ike summarized it) "might, merely in the interests of local harmony, surrender my convictions as to operations," Ike was quick to defend himself: "In the various campaigns of this war I have occasionally had to modify slightly my own conceptions of a campaign in order to achieve a unity of purpose and effort. I think this is inescapable in Allied operations but I assure you that I have never yet failed to give you my own clear personal convictions about every project and plan in prospect." Ike denied yielding to anyone's urging him to present "any particular view," and he denied being "affected by localitis," which may be interpreted as a tendency to lose sight of the big picture by focusing too closely on the opinions, issues, demands, and difficulties that affect only you and those immediately around you.

As a leader, you must balance your own perceptions with the demands of those above you, the realities of overall strategy and the big picture, and the concerns of those immediately surrounding you. The success of the entire enterprise depends on the skill and consistency with which you achieve and maintain this balance.

◆　◆　◆

Lesson 149

It Never Hurts to Ask

I should like to make an appeal to you.

—Cable to George C. Marshall,
February 12, 1944

In the various requests I have made upon General Devers for officers with troop commands in Italy, I have accepted his refusals without question. However, in the case of Brigadier General Garrison H. Davidson, engineer of the Seventh Army, I should like to make an appeal to you.

This officer has been with General Patton since the landing at Casablanca and is not only widely experienced in the technical requirements of engineers on the battlefield, but has become a mainspring in his staff organization. In view of the fact that practically all of the U.S. battle-experienced officers on this side of the Atlantic are now in the Mediterranean theater, I strongly feel that our senior commanders are clearly entitled to a few individuals in this category.

General Patton has personally requested me to make this appeal to you, and I completely concur in his need for an engineer officer of Davidson's caliber and experience.

Ike's efforts to get General Davidson transferred from the Italian front to Operation Overlord show his determination to put the right man in the right place for the right job. Devers, in Italy, continued to resist, however, and the attempt to transfer Davidson failed. But it never hurts to ask.

◆ ◆ ◆

Lesson 150

Pick Your Fights

It seems to me this simple formula would do much to keep us out of unnecessary difficulties.

—Letter to George C. Marshall,
February 15, 1944

Noting to General Marshall that he had seen some telegrams passing back and forth "concerning so-called British and American areas or spheres of occupation in Europe after the Axis has been defeated," Ike offered a suggestion for settling (or avoiding altogether) jurisdictional squabbles. Instead of dividing up the liberated territory into administrative spheres, the United States should "refuse to take specific American responsibility for any area." Instead, Ike argued, "why should we not place ourselves on record as saying we will retain responsibility, particularly military and relief responsibility in Europe, only so long as the Allied principle of unity of Command is observed, with orders and policies issued through the Combined Chiefs of Staff?" With this declaration having been made, whenever "Great Britain should decide that she wanted to control any specific major portion of Europe strictly from London, then we should simply withdraw U.S. physical occupational facilities," including military forces and aid.

It was a simple formula, which Ike thought would "keep us out of unnecessary difficulties and would give our President a major voice in the establishing of policy."

Pick your fights. Often the best course is to let the other fellow have what he says he wants—as long as you arrange things so that he knows *he* will have to live with the consequences.

◆ ◆ ◆

Lesson 151

Instinctively Bold

I instinctively dislike ever to uphold the conservative as opposed to the bold.

—Letter to George C. Marshall,
February 19, 1944

Ike felt that the only way to "lick the Hun" was "by being ahead of him in ideas as well as in material resources." This meant bold thinking, bold planning, and bold action.

The conservative approach has its virtues, but its great drawback is the possibility of dying by inches. If boldness can bring sudden destruction, it is also the surest route to victory—especially if the competition is innovative, resourceful, and, yes, bold. Most great leaders are bold by instinct. Great leaders who are also effective leaders learn both to harness and to trust their instinct for boldness.

◆ ◆ ◆

Lesson 152

Plug Leaks

The greatest dangers . . . arise through indiscreet speculation on the part of those not officially in the know, but who have access to incomplete confidential information.

—Memorandum on security,
February 23, 1944

Secrecy and security were very much on Dwight Eisenhower's mind in the long lead-up to Operation Overlord. He thought that the most serious threats to security were the most casual: the overheard "indiscreet speculation on the part of those not officially in the know," people who had access to bits and pieces of confidential information and who used it to construct rumors, which might be harmful in themselves among friends and might also contain enough truth to be useful to enemies. Ike's solution was to advise very narrow circulation of secret documents.

Security is never casual. Those who need to know should be unambiguously admitted into the loop, but those who do not need to know should be, with equal absence of ambiguity, barred from all sensitive information. Be vigilant in searching for leaks. Plug them. Better still, prevent them by reducing "unnecessarily wide circulation of . . . documents."

◆ ◆ ◆

Lesson 153

The Power of Identity

[P]ride and esprit . . . pay big dividends on the battle field.

—Letter to George C. Marshall,
March 3, 1944

Ike was concerned when a new organizational scheme was introduced into the traditional armored division. Intended to make the division a more flexible concept, it expanded "the idea of 'separate battalion' and 'ad hoc group' organization. I think," Ike observed, "someone is forgetting the tremendous value of regimental and divisional esprit in battle." Ike believed that much of this esprit derived from identity, and although he conceded that "the German makes great use of ad hoc organizations," Ike noted that "the units making up these battle groups frequently bear permanent names. Beyond all doubt the names we find in the British Army, such as the Hampshires, the Black Watch, the Wellingtons, the Grenadier Guards, and so on, have given the organizations a pride and esprit that pay big dividends on the battle field."

Ike informed Marshall that at least for Operation Overlord, he was studying the idea with his commanders "of giving a sort of family name to groups of battalions that will ordinarily serve together. . . . My present thought is to allow the Infantry battalions . . . to select a name for themselves." Although he wanted to allow them this freedom, Ike also wanted the name selected to be appropriately inspirational; therefore, he had his staff prepare a list that included "names of past battles of the American Army and deceased American military leaders. I believe it will have a good effect."

The scheme was never put into effect, but the concept is important nevertheless. Anything that reinforces positive group identity and the individual's proud identification with the group tends to create or enhance esprit, and, as Ike observed, esprit pays dividends in performance. Effective leaders take steps to enhance affirmative group identity.

◆ ◆ ◆

Lesson 154

Bury, Don't Beat, a Dead Horse

I think it is the gravest possible mistake to allow demands for ANVIL to militate against the main effort.

—Cable to the Joint Chiefs of Staff,
March 9, 1944

As much as Ike wanted to launch Operation Anvil, an invasion of France along the Riviera, in conjunction with Operation Overlord, the invasion of Normandy, the continued manpower and landing craft demands of the stalled campaign in Italy made it impossible to conduct Anvil at an optimum level of strength without drawing resources from Operation Overlord. "This being the case," Ike wrote, "I think it is the gravest possible mistake to allow demands for ANVIL to militate against the main effort [Operation Overlord]."

Ike knew when to stop beating a dead horse, and he refused to let the corpse of Operation Anvil drag down Overlord. Effective leaders do not let go easily, but they know when to let go so that they can hang on to something more important.

◆ ◆ ◆

Lesson 155

Know Your Job, Do Your Job

I honestly feel that the American people would prefer to have me attend strictly to my own business of organizing, training, leading, and caring for the sons, brothers and countrymen they provide me for battle purposes, rather than to be concerning myself with matters properly left to my Commander in Chief and others both in and out of public life.

—Letter to Charles H. Colebaugh,
March 22, 1944

When Charles H. Colebaugh, editor of *Colliers*, asked General Eisenhower to write a Memorial Day message to be published in the magazine, Ike avoided the knee-jerk impulse to say yes. Instead, he replied that the war was "so vast and so complicated that it is especially important that each of us should strive to perform his own duties without invading the fields of responsibility of others." He told Colebaugh that writing such a message would be just such an invasion, that the task was better suited to the president, and that, furthermore, the American people would be better served by the knowledge that he was doing full-time the job for which he was chosen rather than laboring in another's vineyard.

If you know *your* job and do *your* job, everyone will benefit.

◆ ◆ ◆

Lesson 156

Discard Phantom Goals

[N]o . . . particular geographical location, including Rome, had in itself any significance from the military viewpoint.

—Cable to George C. Marshall,
March 27, 1944

Only after three full years of the Civil War did Abraham Lincoln finally find a general capable of achieving victory. Ulysses S. Grant had many fighting qualities his predecessors had lacked, but perhaps the single most important difference between him and the others was his strategic conception of the war. Whereas earlier commanders had focused on capturing cities and territories, Grant resolved to concentrate on destroying the enemy army. Having lost any number of cities, the South could nevertheless continue to fight, but without an army it would have no choice but to surrender. Grant understood that capturing cities and territories might bring glory, but it would not necessarily bring victory. As far as victory was concerned, cities and territory were phantom goals, and he rejected them.

Ike thought the same way.

He reported to General Marshall the results of a long conference with the British Chiefs of Staff, at which all had agreed (among other things) that no piece of Italian territory, including the fabled capital city itself, was worth diverting resources from operations in Italy that would directly contribute to the "maximum support [of] OVERLORD." The lure of Rome was psychologically powerful, but, so far as Operation Overlord was concerned (judged the make-or-break operation of the European war), it was a phantom goal. Ike rejected it.

Be ruthless in evaluating priorities and goals. Many goals *feel* good, but they may not directly serve your strategic purpose. These are phantoms, which must be brushed aside to enable the concentration of resources on the goals that truly matter.

◆ ◆ ◆

Lesson 157

Overcome Prejudice

[T]he fact is . . .

—Letter to George C. Marshall,
March 29, 1944

Ike was reluctant to endorse air force commander Carl Spaatz's recommendation that Major General Louis H. Brereton be promoted to lieutenant general. As he explained to General Marshall, "I have been holding [the recommendation] up for the last ten days while I have made some effort to investigate for myself the real value of Brereton as a leader and commander." Ike wrote that he had "spent all day yesterday with [Brereton's] troops and have talked to a number of British and American Officers concerning him. While I have never been able to rid myself completely of a slight feeling of uneasiness about Brereton, the fact is that all my information sustains Spaatz's recommendation, and I therefore believe that Brereton should be promoted."

Ignore gut feelings at your peril, but don't obey them uncritically. There is a fine line between what your gut tells you—against all reason and evidence—and outright, irrational prejudice. Feeling uneasy about a recommended promotion, Ike did not reject it out of hand, but instead sought the evidence and, finding that evidence, he acted on it, despite some lingering unease.

◆ ◆ ◆

Lesson 158

Make the Hard Trade-Offs

Serious considerations are involved.

—Letter to Winston Churchill,
April 5, 1944

Among the Allies, debate was intense over whether to employ heavy strategic bombing to destroy transportation centers in German-held France in preparation for the Normandy landings and invasion. Ike sent a powerful message to Prime Minister Churchill:

> The weight of the argument that has been brought against the bombing of transportation centers in occupied territories is heavy indeed. Serious considerations are involved. But I and my military advisors have become convinced that the bombing of these centers will increase our chances for success in the critical battle, and unless this could be proved to be an erroneous conclusion, I do not see how we can fail to proceed with the program. I admit that warnings will probably do very little in evacuating people from the points we intend to hit. On the other hand I personally believe that estimates of probable casualties have been grossly exaggerated.
>
> The French people are now slaves. Only a successful OVERLORD can free them. No one has a greater stake in the success of that operation than have the French.
>
> As a consequence of all these considerations I am convinced that while we must do everything possible to avoid loss of life among our friends I think it would be sheer folly to abstain from doing anything that can increase in any measure our chances for success in OVERLORD.

Trade-offs are among the hardest decisions a leader has to make, but they cannot be avoided or evaded, because they are a part of any complex enterprise. Decisions should be divorced from emotion and based instead on an analysis of the resources available, the stakes in play, and the relative interests of all stakeholders. The resulting decision will not be ideal—by definition, no trade-off ever is—but it stands a good chance of being the best *possible* decision.

◆　◆　◆

Lesson 159

Don't Invite Destructive Criticism

In any questionnaires designed to analyze mass enlisted opinion, I desire that there be no questions in which any soldier is called upon to express an opinion respecting the capabilities and character of his commander.

—Letter to J.C.H. Lee, April 6, 1944

No effective leader can afford to ignore constructive criticism and indeed should make every effort to invite and obtain it; however, criticism that undermines confidence and authority is never constructive. Ike understood this, and when General Hughes proposed formulating questionnaires to assess certain opinions of enlisted personnel in Europe, Eisenhower intervened to the extent of asking that no soldier be invited to "express an opinion respecting the capabilities and character of his commander."

Ask questions, but don't invite doubt. Walking into a buzz saw is never likely to produce a desirable result.

◆ ◆ ◆

Lesson 160

Use Human Resources Wisely

I don't want any military policemen on duty merely for show or for eyewash. I want them where they are needed and nowhere else.

—Memorandum to J.C.H. Lee,
April 28, 1944

Ike had neither the time nor the inclination to make a detailed study of personnel usage, but he did keep his eyes open, and when he saw something he didn't like, he acted: "From casual observation," he wrote to General Lee, "it appears to me that there are far too many individuals on military police duty; at least I find on many occasions two, three or four men serving in a group where it would appear that one man could do the job."

Two simple lessons here. First, if something doesn't look right, it probably isn't. Get it fixed. Second, you cannot afford to waste human resources. So don't let them be wasted.

◆ ◆ ◆

Lesson 161

Patton—Again!

I have grown so weary of the trouble he constantly causes.

—Cable to George C. Marshall,
April 29, 1944

To Dwight Eisenhower, Patton was a friend, a mentor, a major military asset, and a thorn in the side—or, as Ike once described him, his "problem child." Ike stood by him in the crisis created by the two "slapping incidents" in Sicily, and he defended him through numerous lesser outbursts, but in April 1944, he clearly approached the proverbial last straw.

Toward the end of the month, the ladies of Knutsford, the small English town that played host to Patton's Third Army, opened a Welcome Club for American GIs, a place that offered doughnuts, coffee, and conversation. Asked to participate in the club's opening ceremonies, Patton at first demurred, not wanting to tip off the Germans as to his whereabouts. Finally, however, in the interests of goodwill among allies, he agreed to appear, but not to speak. Moreover, he purposely arrived a quarter of an hour late in the hope that this would keep him out of most of the proceedings. The ladies of Knutsford, however, waited for him, and, no sooner had he arrived than he was ushered up to the podium.

Because his very brief remarks were impromptu, his own recollection is all that remains of the speech. On the surface, his remarks were entirely benign and innocuous. Clearly, before the ladies of the town, he was on his best behavior. He said that he thought "such clubs as this are a very real value, because I believe with Mr. Bernard Shaw, I think it was he, that the British and Americans are two people separated by a common language, and since it is the evident destiny of the British and Americans, and, of course, the Russians, to rule the world, the better we know each other, the better job we will do" (Martin Blumenson [ed.]. *The Patton Papers 1940–1945*. New York: Da Capo, 1996, pp. 440–441).

To Patton's horror he soon learned that army public relations officers were scrambling to effect damage control. Despite Patton's request for a total publicity blackout of the Knutsford event, several newspapers reported his remarks, some writing that he had said that the British and Americans would rule the postwar world, omitting any mention of the Russians. This did not bother the British, but U.S. newspapers, always eager to exploit sensational copy concerning Patton, ran stories denouncing his insult to "our gallant Russian allies." Very soon, senators, congressmen, and members of the American public were calling for Patton's head.

On April 29, a disgusted Eisenhower wrote to General Marshall that "Patton had broken out again." Ike understood that Patton's "exact remarks . . . were incorrectly reported and somewhat misinterpreted in the press," but "I have grown so weary of the trouble he constantly causes you and the War Department to say nothing of myself, that I am seriously contemplating the most drastic action." Eisenhower was thinking about sending George S. Patton Jr. home.

Considering the trivial nature of the incident in and of itself—and, further, the fact that Patton was apparently misquoted—the contemplated action was drastic indeed. Patton was a great fighting general, a bringer of victory. Exasperated though he was, Ike did not act immediately, but told Marshall that he was "deferring final action until I hear further from you." He wanted to know whether Marshall believed that Patton's "retention in high command [would] tend to destroy or diminish public and governmental con-

fidence in the War Department." If such was the case, "I am convinced that stern disciplinary action must be taken."

While he awaited Marshall's response, Ike wrote an uncompromising letter to Patton: "You first came into my command at my
own insistence because I believed in your fighting qualities and your
ability to lead troops in battle. At the same time I have always been
fully aware of your habit of dramatizing yourself and of committing
indiscretions for no other apparent purpose than of calling attention to yourself. I am thoroughly weary of your failure to control
your tongue and have begun to doubt your all-round judgment, so
essential in high military position." He advised Patton that he had
not made a final decision, pending word from the War Department,
but that "if you are again guilty of any indiscretion in speech or
action . . . I will relieve you instantly from command."

On April 30, Ike cabled Marshall that "on all of the evidence
now available," he planned to relieve Patton "from command and
send him home unless some new and unforeseen information
should be developed in the case." However, he also told Marshall
that he had sent for Patton "to allow him opportunity to present his
case personally to me."

Patton arrived at Eisenhower's headquarters the morning of
May 1. Patton's and Eisenhower's versions of the conference are
reported in Carlo D'Este, *Eisenhower: A Soldier's Life* (New York:
Henry Holt, 2002, p. 508). Patton recalled that Ike began the conversation by telling him, "George, you have gotten yourself into a
very serious fix" and that Patton interrupted with, "I want to say
that your job is more important than mine, so if in trying to save
me you are hurting yourself, throw me out." According to Patton,
Ike responded bluntly, telling him that there was a very serious
question about his continuing in command. Patton responded by
telling Ike that he was willing to be reduced to colonel, provided he
be allowed to command one of the assault regiments in the Normandy invasion.

Ike's own recollection of the meeting included none of this. He
recalled only that

[I]n a gesture of almost little-boy contriteness, [Patton] put his head on my shoulder. . . . This caused his helmet to fall off—a gleaming helmet I sometimes thought he wore in bed.

As it rolled across the room I had the rather odd feeling that I was in the middle of a ridiculous situation . . . his helmet bounced across the floor into a corner. I prayed that no one would come in and see the scene. . . . Without apology and without embarrassment, he walked over, picked up his helmet, adjusted it, and said: "Sir, could I now go back to my headquarters?"

Whether it was because of the interview with Patton or merely due to the passage of a few more days, Ike found himself backing away from the verge of relieving his best field commander. He cabled Marshall: "There is no question that relief of Patton would lose to us his experience as commander of an army in battle and his demonstrated ability of getting the utmost out of soldiers in offensive operations. Because [you have left] the decision exclusively in my hands, to be decided solely upon my convictions as to the effect upon OVERLORD, I have decided to retain him in command."

To Patton, Ike cabled, "I am once more taking the responsibility of retaining you in command in spite of damaging repercussions resulting from a personal indiscretion. I do this solely because of my faith in you as a battle leader and from no other motives." He followed this message by sending his public relations officer, Colonel Justus "Jock" Lawrence, to deliver, verbally, another message, strictly forbidding Patton from making any public statements until further notice.

Greatly relieved, Patton cajoled Lawrence: "Come on, Jock, what did Ike *really* say?"

Doubtless it was with some uncomfortable relish that Lawrence responded, "He said that you were not to open your goddamned mouth again publicly until he said you could!" (from D'Este, *Eisenhower*, p. 509).

The key lesson in this crisis of personnel management, a crisis that might have resulted in the loss of a great (if problematic) commander, was that Ike allowed himself to feel a full measure of out-rage, but he did not permit himself to act impulsively on his feel-ings. His measured response saved Patton's career and, far more important, it retained for the invasion of Europe a commander who would lead his Third Army in a spectacular advance across France and Germany and who would transform disaster at the siege of Bas-togne into a great American victory in the Battle of the Bulge.

◆ ◆ ◆

Lesson 162

Firing a Friend

I know of nothing that causes me more real distress than to be faced with the necessity of sitting as a judge in cases involving military offenses by officers of character and of good record, particularly when they are old and warm friends.

—Letter to Henry J. Miller, May 5, 1944

Nothing was more important during the critical run-up to the launch of Operation Overlord than secrecy and security. Major General Henry J. Miller, Ike's West Point classmate and a good friend, commanded the Ninth Air Force Service Command. While dining at Claridge's Hotel, in London, on April 18, 1944, Miller was overheard complaining about his difficulties in getting supplies from the United States, but added that these problems would be ended after D-Day, which would occur (he loudly announced) before June 15. An officer who overheard this immediately reported the security breach to Allied headquarters. Ike was stunned and acted instantly. By coincidence, Miller fell ill and was hospitalized at this time. His doctors wanted him to go back to the States for observation and further treatment. Miller wrote to his old friend: "I simply want to ask you to have me shipped home in my present grade [of major general], there to await such action as the fates have in store for me." Ike rejected his plea:

I have studied the record in your case and I am aware . . . of all the extenuating circumstances. Yet, considering the gravity of even the slightest offense in the matter of security, and in view of the character of the testimony of the two witnesses that make positive statements against you, I feel that duty prevents me from allowing the case to go unnoticed except by accomplishing your transfer to the United States to await action of the medical authorities on your physical condition. . . . I truly regret that I cannot grant your appeal, and I feel sure that you will believe this.

Eisenhower removed Miller from command, reduced him to his permanent (peacetime) rank of colonel, and sent him to the United States. A quick retirement followed. Friendship need not be incompatible with business, but the special pleading of friendship must end where the good of the enterprise begins.

◆ ◆ ◆

Lesson 163

The Future Is Teamwork

I honestly believe that much of the traditional differences in the training of combat officers of the various arms are going to disappear.

—Letter to his son, John S. D. Eisenhower, May 8, 1944

After his son, approaching graduation from West Point, finally decided on the field artillery as his combat branch of choice, Ike expressed his opinion that traditional differences in the training of combat officers for the different branches would disappear as the "necessity for team work" continued to become such that "a leader on the battle field must be rather well trained in the capabilities, powers, limitations and actual techniques of several arms."

Ike saw the future in the integration of various specialties through teamwork, and he believed that leaders could not afford to be narrow specialists.

♦ ♦ ♦

Lesson 164

Get a Troubleshooter

*I need a personal representative and trouble shooter with execu-
tive authority who can act as liaison between this superior
headquarters and the SOS [Services of Supply].*

—Letter to Brehon B. Somervell,
May 10, 1944

Ike wrote to General Somervell to secure the services of LeRoy Lutes
through the period of Operation Overlord as his "personal representative and trouble shooter [to act] as liaison between this superior
headquarters" and the Services of Supply. "While we are now entirely confident in our organization for supply," Eisenhower wrote,
"nevertheless certain weaknesses have shown up and it is inevitable
that others will develop which we can not . . . now foresee."

To troubleshoot the unforeseen, Ike wanted Lutes.

By definition, nothing can be known in advance of the unforeseen, except for its near inevitability. Prepare for it the best way you
can. Ike believed the best he could do was to put in place a person
whose sole job it would be to expedite, in any crisis, the connection
between headquarters and supply.

♦ ♦ ♦

Lesson 165

Find a Common Voice

*It has been my hope that, for the impending operation, we
would be able to institute a radio broadcasting service which
would present a program especially designed and produced for
the Allied Expeditionary Force.*

—Letter to Winston Churchill,
May 11, 1944

Eisenhower had proposed to the director general of the BBC to create a broadcast service "especially designed and produced for the Allied Expeditionary Force," the force invading Europe on D-Day, which (Ike believed) "would be of the greatest value as a factor in the maintenance of morale and would serve as a medium for disseminating 'AEF' information to the forces from time to time."

Ike understood the importance of creating a common voice for a great enterprise, and he saw radio as just the means of doing this. Unfortunately, the BBC's director general "stated that he did not consider our proposal . . . practicable . . . [and did not] believe that a combined [broadcasting] service . . . would accomplish the desired end." Stymied here, Ike appealed directly to Prime Minister Churchill, who prevailed upon the BBC director general and managed to get the "A.E.F. Radio Broadcast Service" operating immediately after the Normandy landings.

Take the trouble to create a voice that speaks not for you alone but for the enterprise, entirely, collectively, inspirationally, and authoritatively.

◆　◆　◆

Lesson 166

Get on the Same Page

Based on military considerations alone, I believe that neither the President nor the Prime Minister should make statements directly to the people of Europe before the success of the [D-Day] landing is assured.

—Cable to George C. Marshall,
May 11, 1944

After years of war, both President Roosevelt and Prime Minister Churchill were anxious to make public announcements simultaneously with Operation Overlord. Ike, however, wanted to ensure that none of these announcements would be premature and that they would convey essentially the same message: nothing more than "good wishes and encouragement to the Allied troops."

Ike was concerned that premature messages would compromise security and would needlessly endanger the forces of unorganized resistance in Europe. If they were prompted to act prematurely, Ike pointed out, the French resistance in particular would surely suffer "terribly repressive measures by the Germans before we are in a position to interfere in any way." Once the "success of the landing is assured," however, Ike was eager to have FDR and Churchill "call for the active rather than the passive assistance of the unorganized . . . people of Europe." Timing, however, was critical, and it was important that everyone be on the same page.

Much of leadership is the art of coordination and timing. This was never truer than in the case of the biggest and most complex military operation in history.

◆ ◆ ◆

Lesson 167

Rank Hath Its Privileges—Reject Them

I deplore the employment of special methods of securing any-thing for me and when this type of procedure applies to things that approach the luxury class the practice is indefensible.

—Letter to J.C.H. Lee, May 12, 1944

A position of power and prestige brings privileges as well as responsibilities. The responsibilities you must accept, but as to the privileges, it is a good idea to be more selective.

Ike was concerned that without his asking, strings had been pulled to secure for him various luxury items, including furnishings and other goods for his headquarters, and that, moreover, the delivery of these was specially expedited. "All this," he wrote, "would be bad enough if any officer other than myself were concerned but when the person who must bear the ultimate responsibility is involved I think it shows a woeful lack of judgment on the part of the officer that must have requested the purchase, and in the one that authorized it." Ike ordered a number of items returned.

A sterling reputation and a record of impeccable ethics are to be valued beyond any price and certainly should not be sold for the sake of a few creature comforts. Embrace your responsibilities without reservation or hesitation, but move cautiously where perks and privileges are concerned.

◆ ◆ ◆

Lesson 168

Inculcate an Informed Fighting Spirit

The inculcation of this fighting spirit is an essential part of the final training, and a command function.

—Letter to U.S. senior commanders,
May 14, 1944

Ike distributed this letter to all U.S. senior commanders in the United Kingdom:

Dear _____:

I feel strongly that as the day of our combined offensive approaches, it is necessary to make absolutely clear to our men the stark and elemental facts as to the character of our Nazi enemy, the absolute need for crushing him, if we are to survive, and, finally, to drive home the fact that we have defeated them before and can do it again. It is only necessary to steel ourselves to the task.

The inculcation of this fighting spirit is an essential part of the final training, and a command function. There is authorized an orientation officer for each unit of regimental level and above, and current instructions in this Theater provide for periodic orientation talks by company officers under his guidance. It is necessary, now, to direct these talks as indicated in the preceding paragraph. I desire that you instruct your subordinate commanders to take energetic action to insure the success of this aspect of our training, utilizing all available agencies for putting material at the disposal of company commanders.

Theater Headquarters will furnish commanders with "News Maps" and "Army Talks"; these will be supplemented by material to appear in *Yank*, *Stars and Stripes*, and to be broadcast over the American Forces Network.

This is not the time for long discussions on the roots and causes of the war. Our soldiers have heard this before. What is required now is to impress on them that only hard—and successful—fighting will bring victory; and that the way home is via Berlin.

Inspire your organization with information: a frank, straightforward presentation of the task at hand and its importance, together with an expression of confidence founded on the truth.

◆ ◆ ◆

Lesson 169

Issue a Badge of Distinction

I have just approved a project for placing on the uniform of commanders of actual combat units, a distinctive marking.

—Letter to George C. Marshall,
May 24, 1944

Ike notified General Marshall that he had authorized "a narrow green band around the shoulder loop of the officer's uniform, and for the enlisted man a narrow green stripe just below his chevron," to be worn by "every man who commands others in combat echelons."

Ike pointed out to Marshall that the "marking itself [is] nothing but a small, inexpensive piece of green cloth," of negligible value in and of itself, but, Ike believed, of powerful symbolic value as a badge of distinction for those who actually lead men into combat. Morale, pride, and encouragement are made (in part) of seemingly slight tokens such as these.

◆ ◆ ◆

Lesson 170

Make Values Clear

Subject: Preservation of Historical Monuments. . . . It is the responsibility of every commander to protect and respect these symbols whenever possible.

—Memorandum to Montgomery, Bradley, Ramsey, and Leigh-Mallory, May 26, 1944

Days before the Normandy invasion was launched, Eisenhower distributed a memorandum on the preservation of historical monuments. He wanted to make certain values clear, including the preservation of the "historical monuments and cultural centers which symbolize to the world all that we are fighting to preserve." Yet there was one value that transcended even this: "In some circumstances the success of the military operation may be prejudiced in our reluctance to destroy these revered objects." Ike cited Monte Cassino, during the Italian campaign, where German forces hid themselves in a great and much-loved monastery in the belief that "our emotional attachments [would] shield his defense." They did not; Allied troops did not hesitate to pulverize the monastery.

"Where military necessity dictates, commanders may order the required action even though it involves destruction of some honored site." In all other cases, where "damage and destruction are not necessary," commanders were to "exercise . . . restraint and discipline [to] preserve centers and objects of historical and cultural significance."

Define the values to which the enterprise is dedicated. If there is a hierarchy of values, make that perfectly clear as well.

◆ ◆ ◆

Lesson 171

Accept the Hazards

You are quite right in communicating to me your convictions as to the hazards involved and I must say that I agree with you as to the character of these risks.

—Letter to Trafford Leigh-Mallory,
May 30, 1944

As D-Day approached, Eisenhower's chief air officer, Trafford Leigh-Mallory, became increasingly concerned over what he projected as the massive casualties that would be incurred by airborne troops—paratroopers—in Operation Overlord. Ike replied with a remarkable letter:

Dear Leigh-Mallory:

Thank you very much for your letter of the 29th on the subject of airborne operations. You are quite right in communicating to me your convictions as to the hazards involved and I must say that I agree with you as to the character of these risks. However, a strong airborne attack in the region indicated is essential to the whole operation and it must go on. Consequently, there is nothing for it but for you, the Army Commander and the Troop Carrier Commander to work out to the last detail every single thing that may diminish these hazards.

It is particularly important that air and ground troops involved in the operation be not needlessly depressed. Like all of the rest of the soldiers, they must understand that they have a tough job to do but be fired with determination to get it done.

I am, of course, hopeful that our percentage losses will not approximate your estimates because it is quite true that I expect to need these forces very badly later in the campaign.

Leaders of all substantial enterprises accustom themselves to evaluating and taking risks. The hardest risks to evaluate and to take are those that definitely and unavoidably involve high cost or substantial losses even if they are successful. Sometimes, however, the hazards have to be accepted and the price paid. With great calm and unshaken conviction, Ike demonstrated his willingness to accept and to pay. In the end, casualties among airborne troops, though significant, were much lighter than Leigh-Mallory had feared and predicted. When it was all over, the British commander shook Ike's hand, expressed his profound pleasure at having been proved wrong, and apologized to the supreme commander for having added to his burden.

◆ ◆ ◆

Lesson 172

Managing the Unmanageable

The weather in this country is practically unpredictable.

—Memorandum, June 3, 1944

Three days before D-Day, Eisenhower prepared a memorandum on five subjects bearing on the Normandy landings. Among these was the weather, the supremely pervasive element on which the ultimate success or failure of the landings finally depended—and the one element about which nothing much could be done.

Ike faced the situation squarely, admitting that the weather across and near the Channel is "practically unpredictable." Nevertheless, "for some days our experts have been meeting almost hourly and I have been holding Commander-in-Chief meetings once or twice a day to consider the reports and tentative predictions. . . . Probably no one that does not have to bear the specific and direct responsibility of making the final decision as to what to do, can understand the intensity of these burdens."

Ike faced three tremendous problems. First, there was the unpredictability of the Channel weather. Second, he needed weather that would permit the coordinated conduct of operations in the air, in the water, and on the ground. What was acceptable in one of these environments could be disastrous in another. Third, the right weather conditions had to coincide with the proper tidal conditions, without which a Channel crossing and landing would be suicidal; high tide would conceal German mines and other lethal obstacles.

The situation, titanic in its implications, was all but unmanageable, yet Ike resolved to identify what little he could manage and then set about managing it. "My tentative thought," he concluded, "is that the desirability for getting started on the next favorable tide is so great and the uncertainty of the weather is such that we could never anticipate really perfect weather coincident with proper tidal conditions." This being the case, Ike arrived at a management decision: "we must [therefore] go unless there is a real and very serious deterioration in the weather." In effect, if the weather, miserable as it might be when the tides were right, still allowed any reasonable chance for success, Operation Overlord would proceed. It was an enormous decision, given what little Ike could do, but he knew that leadership was sometimes all about managing things that defied management.

◆ ◆ ◆

Lesson 173

Give the Order

I am quite positive we must give the order.

—Remark to officers, June 4, 1944

D-Day had been scheduled for June 5, but the stormy weather proved so bad that Ike was forced to delay the operation. On the one hand, he knew that if the Normandy invasion was not launched on the next day, June 6, the proper tidal and moonlight conditions would not occur again for another three weeks. A three-week delay would likely mean that the element of surprise would be lost. It was virtually certain that the Germans would observe the buildup of troops and materiel during this period. Moreover, with the invasion force primed and ready to go now, it would be potentially disastrous for morale to order them to step down.

On the other hand, storm and fog made air operations hazardous or even impossible. High waves could wreak havoc on shallow-draft landing craft. Facing the Germans was bad enough. The weather could be an even more formidable enemy.

As Ike reviewed weather reports, he agonized. The best his weather officer, Captain J. M. Stagg of the RAF, could offer was a narrow window of marginally acceptable weather on the morning of June 6. It was not much, and, little as it was, it was not even a sure thing.

Ike grabbed it. As Eisenhower biographer Carlo D'Este remarked (D'Este, *Eisenhower*, pp. 520–527), it "was a very slender thread on which to base the fate of the war, but it was all Eisenhower had, and he embraced it." As Walter Bedell Smith, Ike's chief of staff, observed: "Finally he looked up, and the tension was gone from his face."   "The question is," Ike said to his subordinate commanders, "just how long can you hang this operation on the end of a limb and let it hang there?"

Even if he meant it as more than a rhetorical question, no one offered an answer. The silence was broken by Ike himself: "I am quite positive we must give the order. I don't like it but there it is. . . . I don't see how we can do anything else." The time was 9:45 P.M., Sunday, June 4.

Nothing short of catastrophic weather conditions could cause the order to be rescinded. Ike's driver and confidant Kay Sommersby remarked to him: "If all goes right, dozens of people will claim the credit. But if it goes wrong, you'll be the only one to blame." Here was leadership at its knife edge: incisive, acutely painful, utterly thankless.

◆ ◆ ◆

Lesson 174

Own It All

If any blame or fault attaches to the attempt it is mine alone.

—Note written on the eve of D-Day,
June 5, 1944

During the day or evening before launching Operation Overlord, the D-Day landings on which the very fate of the world hinged, General Dwight D. Eisenhower claimed ownership of any possible failure. He scribbled a note: "Our landings in the Cherbourg-Havre area have failed to gain a satisfactory foothold and I have withdrawn the troops," it began. He next wrote, "This particular operation," but crossed out these impersonal words and instead continued with the possessive pronoun: "My decision to attack at this time and place was based upon the best information available. The troops, the air and the Navy did all that Bravery and devotion to duty could do. If any blame or fault attaches to the attempt it is mine alone."

Eisenhower then folded the note, put it in his wallet, and, as the landings successfully developed, apparently forgot about it until July 11, when he showed it to his naval aide, Harry C. Butcher. To Butcher he remarked that he had written a similar note before every amphibious operation in the war, but had torn them up once success was certain. Butcher asked to save this one for his own war diary. Without hesitation, Eisenhower handed it over.

Just about everyone who knew and worked with Ike Eisenhower identified cheerful optimism as paramount among his leadership traits. Typical was his conduct during the grave crisis presented by the Battle of the Bulge in December 1944. Gathering his top commanders for an urgent strategy conference, Ike began the session by saying, "The present situation is to be regarded as one of opportunity for us and not of disaster. There will be only cheerful faces at this conference table."

For Eisenhower, optimism wasn't blind faith, and it wasn't a religion. It was simply the only *feasible* attitude. That's the way it *must* be for those of us who accept the leadership challenge. Without optimism, the sale is lost before the prospect is approached, and the battle is lost before a shot is fired. Yet Eisenhower never allowed optimism to stand in for reality. Part of reality is the possibility of failure, and, in recognizing this, the supreme commander always made the decision to take ownership of the possibility. The point was not that he secretly thought the D-Day invasion was likely to fail, but that as the chief executive of the enterprise, he needed to own the operation in all of its dimensions: triumphant, satisfactory, disappointing, and disastrous.

Such ownership is the very substance of the leader's character. But just as important is the absence of any morbid, lingering attachment to the possibility of failure. After each successful amphibious operation before Overlord, Ike tore up the note he had written. On the occasion of D-Day, he forgot about it, but when he rediscovered the note, he unceremoniously relinquished it to his aide.

◆ ◆ ◆

Lesson 175

Create a Crusade

Soldiers, Sailors and Airmen of the Allied Expeditionary Force! You are about to embark upon the Great Crusade.

—Message to troops, D-Day, June 6, 1944

The vast majority of the wartime documents Eisenhower sent or received were stamped "Secret" or "Top Secret." The general appreciated the wisdom and necessity of disseminating information on a strictly need-to-know basis. But, in contrast to many other commanders, he also firmly believed in going outside this policy whenever possible. He understood that although discipline and a willingness to obey orders were absolutely necessary in any army, one of the great advantages the Allied forces had over the enemy was a preponderance of troops who could think for themselves. This reflected a key difference between democracy and totalitarianism, and it was vividly embodied in the armed forces of the combatant nations.

Whereas many other Allied commanders sought to "overcome" the democratic tendency toward individualism—even Patton notoriously proclaimed, "This individuality stuff is a bunch of bullshit"—Eisenhower seized on it as an advantage, what modern military tacticians would call a force multiplier, an asset that greatly increases the value of whatever an army has. He believed it was absolutely essential that each and every soldier, sailor, and airman see *for himself* the "big picture" and how he fit into it. Accordingly, Ike believed that it was up to him, as supreme commander, to paint that big picture as vividly as possible for his troops.

Anyone who was part of it knew that Operation Overlord was big: 156,000 men to be landed on the first day, supported by some 5,000 ships and 13,000 planes. But Ike made it seem much bigger. As he presented it to the soldiers, Overlord was not the most ambitious *invasion* in all history; it was nothing less than "the Great Crusade, toward which we have striven these many months." He lifted this monumental enterprise above and beyond the realm of mere military operations:

> The eyes of the world are upon you. The hopes and prayers of liberty-loving people everywhere march with you. In company with our brave Allies and brothers-in-arms on other Fronts you will bring about the destruction of the German war machine, the elimination of Nazi tyranny over the oppressed peoples of Europe, and security for ourselves in a free world.

212 EISENHOWER ON LEADERSHIP

He was leading a project of world transformation, yet his message focused not on himself, an *I*, but on *you*. It was a message not about following orders or doing one's duty but about empowerment of the individual in a great collective cause. As such, Ike's D-Day message stands as a model for any manager who needs to muster the forces of collaboration for a high-stakes purpose—in short, to create a crusade.

But you know the problem. You know that the great pitfall of any attempt to rally the troops to some "grand purpose" is that words of inspiration may come off sounding hollow. Aware of the awesome spiritual potential of an army of men and women accustomed to thinking for themselves, Eisenhower was also mindful of their uncanny faculty for piercing pretense. A boundless capacity for wisecracking cynicism was characteristic of the British Tommy as well as the American GI. Ike was therefore careful to balance inspiration with an unstinting dose of reality—

> Your task will not be an easy one. Your enemy is well trained, well equipped and battle hardened. He will fight savagely.

—a reality, however, that had *two* sides:

> But this is the year 1944! Much has happened since the Nazi triumphs of 1940–41. The United Nations have inflicted upon the Germans great defeats, in open battle, man to man. Our air offensive has seriously reduced their strength in the air and their capacity to wage war on the ground. Our Home Fronts have given us an overwhelming superiority in weapons and munitions of war, and placed at our disposal great reserves of trained fighting men.

Balancing inspiration with reality, the supreme commander was enabled to make his conclusion thoroughly convincing: "The tide has turned! The free men of the world are marching together to Victory!"

And, as a leader who required collaborative discipline *and* individual initiative, Eisenhower closed his message personally, beginning with the one and only first-person singular pronoun in the entire text, which he quickly transformed into the first-person plural: "I have full confidence in your courage and devotion to duty and skill in battle. We will accept nothing less than full Victory!"

Ike was a master of the very magic you, as a leader, must perform every day: to change *I* into *we*, your own individual will into the passion of the entire organization.

◆ ◆ ◆

Lesson 176

Down to the Individual

The enthusiasm, toughness and obvious fitness of every single man were high and the light of battle was in their eyes.

> —Cable to George C. Marshall,
> June 6, 1944

On D-Day, Eisenhower cabled Marshall to convey what hard information he could, which was little more than "All preliminary reports are satisfactory." The most solid information he had was his own perception of troops he had visited the day and the night before the landings. "The enthusiasm, toughness and obvious fitness of every single man were high and the light of battle was in their eyes," he told Marshall, knowing that as a veteran leader of men, Marshall would understand that the readiness of each individual was as important as any vast armada of ships or grand plan of attack. In the end, the greatest of endeavors comes down to the individuals who make up the enterprise. In the eyes of each there must be the light of battle.

◆ ◆ ◆

Lesson 177

Do It for the Team

You are a truly great Allied Team.

> —Message to the Allied Expeditionary
> Force, June 13, 1944

Ike issued a message of congratulations to the Allied Expeditionary Force as soon as it was clear to him that the D-Day landings had been a success. As a leader, he placed his emphasis on this force not as the greatest army ever assembled but as the greatest *team* ever put together:

> *To General Montgomery, Admiral Ramsay, Air Chief Marshal Leigh-Mallory, Air Chief Marshal Harris, Lieutenant General Spaatz and to Soldiers, Airmen, Sailors and Merchant Seamen, and All Others of the Allied Expeditionary Forces:* One week ago this morning there was established through your coordinated efforts, our first foot-hold in Northwestern Europe. High as was my pre-invasion confidence in your courage, skill and effectiveness in working together as a unit, your accomplishments in the first seven days of this Campaign have exceeded my brightest hopes.
>
> You are a truly great Allied Team; a Team in which each part gains its greatest satisfaction in rendering maximum assistance to the entire body and in which each individual member is justifiably confident in all others.
>
> No matter how prolonged or bitter the struggle that lies ahead you will do your full part toward the restoration of a free France, the liberation of all European nations under Axis domination, and the destruction of the Nazi military machine.
>
> I truly congratulate you upon a brilliantly successful beginning to this great undertaking. Liberty-loving people, everywhere, would today like to join me in saying to you "I am proud of you."

◆ ◆ ◆

Lesson 178

Run Interference

I won't have you bothered at this time by people who are not in position to help you directly in the battle effort.

> —Letter to Bernard Law Montgomery,
> June 18, 1944

As the Normandy invasion unfolded, Ike decided "to forbid, for the time being, any further visits by V.I.P.'s to the battle area." He resolved to run interference for his commanders so that they could focus all their attention on the fighting when the situation was at its most critical. This extended even to himself. On the same day that he communicated with Montgomery, Ike sent a message to Omar N. Bradley, saying that he planned "to visit you on Tuesday, June 20" but specifying that "You are not to upset any of your personal plans—anyone can meet me with a jeep, and I'll see you at your convenience during the day."

On July 12, Ike sent a cable to General Marshall to discourage him, as best he could, from allowing Henry Morgenthau Jr., secretary of the treasury, to visit France: "you will understand that there is nothing to be learned about currency problems in the little strip of France which we now possess. . . . Matters in which Mr. Morgenthau will be interested can all be discussed in London."

Effective leaders facilitate the leadership of others in every way they can, which includes blocking the occasional VIP or visiting fireman.

◆ ◆ ◆

Lesson 179

Or Else

I am tired of talking about that subject and someone had better perform or will be out of a job.

> —Letter to Omar N. Bradley, June 27, 1944

Bradley complained to Eisenhower that he was not receiving accurate lists of convoys or manifests showing the cargo they transported. He needed both in order to ensure that his vast forces were properly supplied. Ike replied that he had spoken to those in charge about making certain that the lists and manifests were delivered. To enforce his demand, Ike backed it up with the ultimate threat a leader can make: perform or be fired. It is not a threat to make lightly or idly, but should in fact be used only if you intend dismissal as the natural and inevitable consequence of failure. The message should be simple and elemental: either you are capable of doing your job or you are not—in which case, naturally, you will no longer have the job.

◆ ◆ ◆

Lesson 180

Find Out What Your People Need, Then Get It for Them

I cannot emphasize too strongly that what we must have now is effective ammunition at the earliest practicable date. We cannot wait for further experimentation.

—Letter to George C. Marshall,
July 5, 1944

Soldiers often grumble, but commanders don't always listen. Ike did.

When he heard tank troops complain that their ammunition was ineffective against the German Tiger tanks, he commissioned "actual tests against captured enemy tanks," and the results were profoundly disturbing: the 76-millimeter shell used in American tank guns would not penetrate the armor of German tanks. Worse, the "new 90-millimeter gun the War Department is placing in [U.S.] Sherman [tanks] will not be effective against [German] Tiger Panthers." Learning that the British sabot round—which featured a lightweight casing around the projectile, enabling smaller rounds to be fired by bigger guns, thereby increasing the kinetic energy of the projectile—was more effective at penetrating German armor, Ike did not hesitate in recommending that U.S. 76-millimeter shells be saboted for use in the new 90-millimeter guns as an "immediate stopgap" until a new gun, "fully capable of dealing with heavily armored tanks," could be developed.

Concerning tools and equipment, listen to those who actually use them. Find out what they need and decide how to give it to them. Then give it to them.

◆ ◆ ◆

Lesson 181

Create the Leader You Need

Could you get Vandenberg made a lieutenant general for me without too great embarrassment?

—Cable to George C. Marshall,
July 15, 1944

Ike wanted to give Major General Hoyt Vandenberg an airborne command. All agreed that he had the qualifications and the ability, but the assignment would jump him over an American major general senior to him and a British lieutenant general. The solution? Manufacture the required leadership rank for him:

> I am forced to return to consideration of Vandenberg who has every qualification except rank and, for the present, a publicized name. Could you get Vandenberg made a lieutenant general for me without too great embarrassment? He is forty-five years old and everyone here is convinced he can do the job superbly. While I agree as a policy we should require people to make good on specific jobs before giving them promotion that normally goes with it, in this particular case the rank is more than normally essential in the first instance.
>
> If you believe you can do this please notify me as I will start Vandenberg at once on the ground work of the task and

complete the organization of his command as soon as his promotion comes through.

As it turned out, after consulting with air force general Hap Arnold, Marshall recommended that Ike install another officer, Louis H. Brereton, who already had the requisite rank, in the open position. Ike complied, and Vandenberg was given another important command. Nevertheless, Ike's initial idea was a good one: it is a mistake to let titles and job descriptions stand in the way of putting the right person in the right job. If necessary, change the job title or push through a quick promotion.

◆ ◆ ◆

Lesson 182

The Measure That Matters

. . . relieved . . . for unsatisfactory performance in an attack.

—Cable to George C. Marshall,
July 27, 1944

Ike notified General Marshall that he had relieved Brigadier General John J. Bohn "as assistant division commander in the 3d Armored Division for unsatisfactory performance in an attack." Ike conceded that Bohn was "personally gallant and [had] apparently exerted himself to reach his objectives," but he nevertheless "failed to do so even though the opposition was relatively light and there should have been no great trouble in carrying out his orders."

It must have been hard for Ike to remove a "gallant" and hardworking officer from command and reduce him from brigadier general to colonel, but, in the hard arena of war, all that counted was performance. Looking at Bohn's performance—as manifested in results and the lack of results—Ike judged that Bohn, at fifty-five, was too old to summon up "the force and leadership to make his subordinate commanders do their duty." Whatever the cause, Bohn failed to produce acceptable results, and he was removed.

Humanity is inherently precious and deserves to be respected and honored; however, in war or any other competitive enterprise, performance, not humanity, is the measure of leadership. To fail in performance does not diminish a person's value as a human being, but it does reveal an unsuitability to leadership.

◆ ◆ ◆

Lesson 183

Lean Heavily, Support Totally

I am counting on you and us always will back you to the uttermost limit.

—Cable to Bernard Law Montgomery,
July 28, 1944

Tell the people you count on that you count on them, even as they can count on you. You must enable others to meet the demands you make of them.

◆ ◆ ◆

Lesson 184

Vital Time

Never was time more vital to us and we should not wait on weather or on perfection in detail of preparation.

—Cable to Bernard Law Montgomery,
July 28, 1944

With the Normandy landings accomplished and the beachheads secure, Ike worked with his generals to break out of the coastal regions and advance inland. To Montgomery, he stressed the vital importance of time: "let us not waste an hour," he urged, even if this meant beginning all-out operations in less-than-ideal weather and with preparations in an imperfect state. "The enemy must have no time for readjustment of lines, for shifting of units and for bringing up reserves."

Time is the medium in which all enterprises are developed. It is a fixed commodity, to be sure, but it is also a neutral force until you engage it and make use of it. Depending on the quality of leadership and leadership decisions, time can become an implacable enemy or a peerless ally. Ike was willing to sacrifice perfection to seize the advantages time offered his forces and to prevent those advantages from falling to the enemy.

◆ ◆ ◆

Lesson 185

Soak Up the Blame

[W]hen criticism is believed to be necessary it should be directed toward me equally at least with any of my principal subordinates.

—Cable to Alexander Day Surles,
July 30, 1944

"In a few recent articles from the United States," Eisenhower wrote to Major General Alexander Day Surles, chief army public affairs officer, "I am told there has been some sharp criticism of Montgomery." Ike was concerned about anything that might undermine the often delicate Anglo-American alliance, and American popular criticism of Bernard Law Montgomery, the most senior British general in the European theater, was especially destructive. Ike did not advocate censorship of criticism—"every writer is entitled to express his own opinions"—but he was deeply concerned that "the articles in question apparently ignore the fact that I am not only inescapably responsible for strategy and general missions . . . but they seemingly also ignore the fact that it is my responsibility to determine the efficiency of my various subordinates." He asked Surles to "please emphasize in your off the record and background conferences my definite responsibility for strategy and major activity and point out that when criticism is believed to be necessary it should be directed toward me equally at least with any of my principal subordinates."

A *good* leader never dodges criticism. A *great* leader aggressively soaks it up, knowing that by doing so he or she protects the enterprise from stain.

◆ ◆ ◆

Lesson 186

Disclose

I consider it absolutely futile and harmful to try to conceal the bitter truth.

—Cable to George C. Marshall,
August 2, 1944

On July 25, 1944, General Lesley McNair, among the most highly respected of U.S. senior officers, was killed when American bombs dropped in support of operations near Saint-Lô, Normandy, fell short. He was one of several officers and enlisted soldiers who died in this tragic instance of "friendly fire."

Ike well knew that nothing is more damaging to morale, among troops as well as the public, than death by error, yet he was anxious that the War Department make no attempt to "conceal the bitter truth." Ike wanted the full story told—albeit in the equally factual context of an account of an otherwise successful and vitally important operation in which air and ground forces worked in closely integrated collaboration. He believed that the public and the army would understand and accept the high price of success, but that they would neither understand nor accept any doubtful attempt at a cover-up. An error may result in tragedy, but deliberate deception is always a betrayal.

◆ ◆ ◆

Lesson 187

Recover

[D]o not give the incident an exaggerated place in either your mind or in your future planning.

—Letter to James H. Doolittle,
August 2, 1944

The "friendly fire" incident of July 25, 1944, in which some bombs dropped by U.S. aircraft fell short and killed American troops, including General Lesley McNair, was both tragic and shocking. What was the best response to it? Ike was quick to answer: *recover.*

He wrote to General James H. Doolittle of the U.S. Army Air Forces:

I know how badly you and your Command have felt because of the accidental bombing of some of our troops by a portion of the Eighth Air Force during your preparation for the recent jump-off of the First Army. Naturally, all of us have shared your acute distress that this should have happened. Nevertheless, it is quite important that you do not give the incident an exaggerated place either in your mind or in your future planning. It must stand as a challenge for the betterment of our technique and must under no circumstances lead us to believe in the impossibility of supporting ground troops, under proper circumstances, by elements of Strategic Air Forces.

In spite of this unfortunate occurrence, the actual benefit devolving from the great bombardment of the Eighth Air Force was extraordinary. The following quotation is from a recent letter from General Bradley:

"In the first place, the bombardment which we gave them last Tuesday was apparently highly successful even though we did suffer many casualties ourselves."

All the reports show that the great mass of the bombs from your tremendous force fell squarely on the assigned target, and I want you and your Command to know that the advantages resulting from the bombardment were of incalculable value. I am perfectly certain, also, that when the ground forces again have to call on you for help you will not only be as ready as ever to cooperate, but will in the meantime have worked out some method so as to eliminate unfortunate results from the occasional gross error on the part of a single pilot or a single group.

The work of the Eighth Air Force over many months in this Theater has been far too valuable to allow the morale of the organization to be dampened by this incident.

◆ ◆ ◆

Lesson 188

Patch Things Up, but Don't Give In

To say that I was disturbed by our conference . . . does not nearly express the depth of my distress.

—Letter to Winston Churchill,
August 11, 1944

As Ike explained in a letter to General Marshall, Prime Minister Winston Churchill was deeply distressed over the decision not to expand operations in the Mediterranean but to focus instead on augmenting operations in France. "He seems to feel that [the] United States is taking the attitude of a big, strong, and dominating partner rather than attempting to understand the viewpoint he represents," Ike explained to Marshall. "His personal hope seems to be that they can keep in Italy all the forces now operating there and with these he still has a strong hope of reaching Trieste before Fall.

. . . I am not quite able to figure out why he attaches so much importance to this particular movement, but one thing is certain—I have never seen him so obviously stirred, upset, and even despondent."

Alarmed—and, as always, seeking to preserve the Anglo-American alliance—Ike wrote to Churchill:

Dear Prime Minister:

To say that I was disturbed by our conference on Wednesday does not nearly express the depth of my distress over your interpretation of the recent decision affecting the Mediterranean Theater. I do not, for one moment, believe that there is any desire on the part of any responsible person in the American war machine to disregard British views, or cold-bloodedly to leave Britain holding an empty bag in any of our joint undertakings. I look upon these questions as strictly military in character—and I am sorry that you seem to feel we use our great actual or potential strength as a bludgeon in conference. The fact is that the British view has prevailed in the discussions of the Combined Chiefs of Staff in many of our undertakings in which I have been engaged, and I do not see why we should be considered intemperate in our long and persistent support of [Operation] ANVIL [an Allied assault in southern France, to follow up on the Normandy landings].

In two years I think we have developed such a fine spirit and machinery in our field direction that no consideration of British versus American interests ever occurs to any of the individuals comprising my staff or serving as one of my principal commanders. I would feel that much of my hard work over the past many months had been irretrievably lost if we now should lose faith in the organisms that have given higher direction to our war effort, because such lack of faith would quickly be reflected in discord in our field commands.

During all these months I have leaned on you often, and have always looked to you with complete confidence when I felt the need of additional support. This adds a sentimental [reason] to my very practical reasons for hoping, most earnestly, that in spite of disappointment, we will all adhere tenaciously to the concepts of control brought forth by the President and yourself two and one half years ago.

Ike did what a strong leader instinctively does. He expressed sensitive concern and even empathy for the feelings of a valued partner who believes he has been wronged. He also reminded him of the overwhelming success of the partnership, set the current situation in perspective, and showed profound respect, but he neither apologized nor gave in.

Letting someone have his or her way is not always the best course for the enterprise, but it does not follow that the alternative to this is trampling over that person's feelings. The strategic objective of effective leadership is to win on the *issue* in question. It is not to gain victory by defeating the *person* who holds an opposing point of view.

◆ ◆ ◆

Lesson 189

When the Need Is Special, Make a Special Appeal

I request . . .

> —Message to "Troops of the Allied
> Expeditionary Force," August 14, 1944

Through your combined skill, valor and fortitude you have created in France a fleeting but definite opportunity for a major Allied victory, one whose realization will mean notable progress toward the final downfall of our enemy. In the past, I have, in moments of unusual significance, made special appeals to the Allied Forces it has been my honor to command. Without exception the response has been unstinted and the results beyond my expectations.

Because the victory we can now achieve is infinitely greater than any it has so far been possible to accomplish in the west, and because the opportunity may be grasped only through the utmost zeal, determination and speedy action, I make my present appeal to you more urgent than ever before.

I request every airman to make it his direct responsibility that the enemy is blasted unceasingly by day and by night, and is denied safety either in fight or in flight.

I request every sailor to make sure that no part of the hostile forces can either escape or be reinforced by sea, and that our comrades on the land want for nothing that guns and ships and ships' companies can bring to them.

I request every soldier to go forward to his assigned objective with the determination that the enemy can survive only through surrender; let no foot of ground once gained be relinquished nor a single German escape through a line once established.

With all of us resolutely performing our special tasks we can make this week a momentous one in the history of this war—a brilliant and fruitful week for us, a fateful one for the ambitions of the Nazi tyrants.

When the need is special, make a special appeal. Explain the need and explain how a special effort now will satisfy the need to the benefit of all. The key is to make the appeal clear, to justify its necessity, and to predict, reasonably and fully, the effect of a successful maximum effort. As a leader, you must make demands, but you must never make them arbitrarily.

◆ ◆ ◆

Lesson 190

Get to Step Two

All of us having agreed upon this general plan, the principal thing we must now strive for is speed in execution.

—Letter to Bernard Law Montgomery,
August 24, 1944

Having successfully invaded France, the Allied military leaders next debated the best strategy for invading the German homeland itself. Eisenhower favored invasion along a broad front, whereas Montgomery wanted to make a single concentrated thrust. After much wrangling, a compromise plan was arrived at; however, Ike did not make the mistake of assuming that everyone realized that the general plan had been agreed on. He therefore sent a letter to Montgomery summarizing his understanding of their discussions and explicitly concluding that a "general plan" had indeed been agreed on. With agreement on the plan confirmed, Ike went on to outline the quality that would be key to its success: "speed in execution."

Leaders lead people, of course, but they also lead processes—and that means leading people *through* processes. Make a plan, agree on the plan, confirm the plan, define what is needed to execute the plan, then execute it. Pull the organization behind you, glancing back at each step to make sure that no one has gotten lost.

◆ ◆ ◆

Lesson 191

Why Hurry If You Have to Wait?

I cannot tell you how anxious I am to get the forces accumulated for starting the thrust eastward from Paris. I have no slightest doubt that we can quickly get to the former French-German boundary but there is no point in getting there until we are in position to do something about it.

> —Letter to George C. Marshall,
> August 24, 1944

Paris would be liberated on August 25, 1944, the day after Ike wrote this message to General Marshall. Although he understood the symbolic and psychological importance of liberating the French capital, Ike actually thought of it as a distraction from the Allied army's main job, which was to destroy the German army. Nevertheless, as ordered, he directed the liberation, then expressed impatience about regrouping for the continued drive eastward. Impatient though he was—and pressed by politicians and the public alike to advance with maximum velocity—Ike never confused haste with speed. True, he could pour everything he had into a quick thrust to the German frontier, but, having reached it, what could he do? Ike wanted to ensure that his front was broad enough and deep enough to allow him to do more than reach a spot on the map. He needed to take the time necessary to bring a strong and effective force to the enemy's doorstep, and he resisted both his urge and the urgings of others to advance for the sake of advancing.

Beware of artificial milestones. Real progress is measured in real results, not in a line scratched into a chart or a number hastily penciled into a column.

◆ ◆ ◆

Lesson 192

Push

[H]e has given the Allied Nations the opportunity of dealing a decisive blow.

> —Message to Allied commanders,
> August 29, 1944

Eisenhower was heartened by the rapid advance that followed the breakout from Normandy, but he was always wary of the negative effect of too much success achieved too quickly. Victory fever, he called it, and the only cure was to reject complacency, refuse to rest, and instead to keep pushing, push, and push harder. The enemy was collapsing? True. But that fact signaled a need for an even greater effort, not a celebration.

The German Army in the West has suffered a signal defeat in the campaign of the Seine and the Loire at the hands of the combined

Allied Forces. The enemy is being defeated in the East, in the South and in the North; he has experienced internal dissension and signs are not wanting that he is nearing collapse. His forces are scattered throughout Europe and he has given the Allied Nations the opportunity of dealing a decisive blow before he can concentrate them in the defense of his vital areas. We, in the West, must seize this opportunity by acting swiftly and relentlessly and by accepting risks in our determination to close with the German wherever met. By means of future directives the Seventh Army, rapidly advancing on Dijon from the South, will have its action coordinated with that of our other Armies.

It is my intention to complete the destruction of the enemy forces in the West and then advance against the heart of the enemy homeland.

Most races are won or lost in the stretch, the point at which both fatigue and the effort required for victory are greatest. Acknowledge the fatigue, but lead the effort.

◆ ◆ ◆

Lesson 193

Translate Your Need into Our Need

I know the anxiety at home to win this war conclusively and speedily. I assure you that that anxiety is more than shared by every soldier on the battlefront. To achieve this object I must urge that you keep flowing across the Atlantic at maximum rate all those things, including spare parts, that a modern army and air force require in battle.

—Cable to Brehon Burke Somervell,
August 30, 1944

The War Department's logistics chief, General Somervell, asked Eisenhower on August 26 to forecast his command's "needs in materiel from the United States during future phases" of the European campaign. In response, Ike cited key statistics that made the ongoing need for supplies—especially spare parts and tires—vividly clear.

Invited though he was to talk about the needs of his command, Ike closed his letter by translating *his* needs into the needs of *all*—of every American at home anxious to "win this war conclusively and speedily." Only the unstinting and uninterrupted flow of supplies would satisfy this universal need.

◆ ◆ ◆

Lesson 194

Basis of Decision

The question of losses does not arise because I would be prepared to accept a very high rate [of losses] if I thought that it would contribute to the rapid conclusion of these vital operations.

—Cable to Bernard Law Montgomery,
September 21, 1944

Determined to secure the Dutch city of Antwerp as a port to handle Allied supplies and troops, Bernard Law Montgomery proposed an airborne (paratroop) operation against the Walcheren peninsula. Ike rejected the proposal because, he explained, "terrain factors and types of targets" were not conducive to effective airborne assault. Ike made it clear that his rejection was not based on the anticipation of a high casualty rate. In the cold-blooded calculus of war, Ike was always willing to trade casualties for results—which, by shortening the war, would ultimately reduce the total casualties of war. Instead of allocating resources to an airborne assault, Ike told Montgomery that he would make saturation bombing in preparation for the ground attack a high priority.

Rejection of a request or a proposal should be accompanied by an explanation, if only to make your motives and rationale clear. Had Ike failed to explain himself, Montgomery might have assumed that the supreme Allied commander was unwilling to pay the high cost of an aggressive operation. Such an assumption would have distorted relations between the principal American and British commanders and might have caused Montgomery to base some of his own subsequent decisions on erroneous assumptions about Eisenhower's beliefs, strategy, policy, and values.

◆ ◆ ◆

Lesson 195

Stay Open

If I should ever reach the point where my old associates and my predecessors, both on the active and retired list, can no longer communicate with me freely, then in my opinion I would not be a true member of the regular Army of the United States as I like to conceive of it.

—Letter to Thomas A. Roberts,
September 25, 1944

Thomas A. Roberts, a retired army colonel, wrote a chatty, gossipy letter to Eisenhower and concluded with, "If I were still on active service, of course I would not have the nerve to write this." Ike objected to that sentence, pointing out that open communication was the very essence of the army—"as I like to conceive of it."

"No officer under whom I have ever served has attempted to make himself unavailable to me or to close his ears to my suggestions, and to that extent at least I have certainly tried to follow in their footsteps." Ike's lesson for leaders? *Stay open.*

◆ ◆ ◆

Lesson 196

Reduce Paperwork

[B]e very careful not to hound tactical commanders for a mass of detail.

—Memorandum to Walter Bedell Smith,
September 30, 1944

When officers are relieved from duty because of failure in combat or leadership, all concerned, including Reclassification Boards, will be very careful not to hound tactical commanders for a mass of detail.

A comprehensive written statement from a man's Commanding Officer, concurred in by a senior, and giving, if possible, an opinion as to the type of duty for which the officer may be considered satisfactory, should be sufficient.

I do not want to appear too arbitrary or unjust, but we cannot have combat commanders working hours at a time to prepare long lists and detailed affidavits and reports which, after all, are meaningless if the Commanding Officer has lost confidence in the subordinate who is being relieved.

Don't pull your best people out of combat for the purpose of filling out excess paperwork. Trust their judgment to the extent of streamlining activities that are not immediately and tangibly productive.

◆ ◆ ◆

Lesson 197

Block That Kick!

To the greatest possible extent I expect the senior commanders of U.S. forces to solve their common problems by coordination and cooperation.

—Memorandum to Walter Bedell "Beetle" Smith, October 3, 1944

Ike did not want lower-echelon commanders to kick upstairs to him issues and problems they themselves should resolve. Many leaders tend to micromanage. Ike was not one of them. Many other leaders assume that their subordinates crave greater authority and responsibility. Ike did not make this assumption, either. Instead, he carefully defined an upper management course that, on the one hand, refused to involve itself in micromanagement and, on the other, encouraged subordinates to solve their own problems, including those that arose between one subordinate command and another.

◆ ◆ ◆

Lesson 198

Self-Esteem

I think a man could far more easily be a hero to a whole nation, if he were lucky in his headlines, than he could to his own son. Your good opinion means a lot to me.

> —Letter to his son, John S. D. Eisenhower,
> October 20, 1944

"I wonder if you can realize how valuable to me are your congratulations," Ike wrote his son, then continued, eloquently, to define the bedrock basis of self-esteem. It is not the headline or the praise of the masses, but the admiration of the one or two or few who mean the most to you. Whatever else the example of Dwight D. Eisenhower says about heroism, management, leadership, and achievement, Ike himself always knew how finally, truly, and accurately to assess these things.

◆ ◆ ◆

Lesson 199

I Accept the Risk

I recognise part of the relief supplies will fall into German hands, but I accept the risk.

> —Cable to the Combined Chiefs of Staff,
> October 29, 1944

Having received information that "serious food shortages" in western Holland will "steadily increase until liberation takes place," Ike ordered that "on the grounds of humanity," food should be allowed into the German-occupied nation via the International Red Cross, even though part of the supplies would undoubtedly fall into enemy hands. "Any assistance to the Dutch civil population that can be provided before liberation will ease the relief problem subsequent to liberation."

Weighing risks against benefits does not reduce the weight of the risks, but it may reveal a clear preponderance on the side of benefits. The effective leader always acts in accordance with that preponderance.

◆　◆　◆

Lesson 200

The Real Secret

You sound like you were really getting to know every single man [in your platoon]; that is the real secret of leadership.

> —Letter to his son, John S. D. Eisenhower,
> November 2, 1944

"It was lots of fun hearing about your platoon," Ike wrote to his son, a brand-new second lieutenant. Proudly, the young officer's father reinforced what he perceived as John's instinctively effective approach to leadership: "If an officer can keep his position of authority, without ever losing it, and at the same time make his men feel that everything that affects them affects him also, then he will never have any trouble with discipline, training, or effective action."

Know the people you lead. Even as you assert your leadership authority, identify with them.

◆　◆　◆

Lesson 201

Train, Train, Train

The worse the weather, the more necessary it is to train.

> —Letter to his son, John S. D. Eisenhower,
> November 2, 1944

Writing to his son, a newly commissioned West Point second lieutenant, Ike asked if he "would forgive me just a little bit of technical advice on the training of a platoon." He emphasized that the "training regulations are absolutely sound," especially in their emphasis on "teamwork in the tiniest units," but Ike added that imparting the principles specified in the manual required seizing "every chance . . . for training day in and day out and in all kinds of weather. The worse the weather, the more necessary it is to train." This would not only immerse men in real-world, worst-case conditions but also toughen them up in the process.

Classroom training is valuable, but it is no substitute for experience in the real world, which means experience in a variety of less than ideal and far from ideal situations and circumstances. The difference between education and training is the difference between mere exposure and total immersion. Both are useful, but immersion is indispensable.

◆ ◆ ◆

Lesson 202

Make It Credible

I consider that the present moment is not repeat not the best for any statement.

> —Cable to George C. Marshall,
> November 27, 1944

On November 20, 1944, Eisenhower sent the Combined Chiefs of Staff a cable assessing the current state of enemy resistance. Despite

one Allied victory after another, Ike observed realistically that
"German morale on this front shows no sign of cracking at present."
He advised, in addition to continued "prolonged and bitter fighting," some "plan . . . aimed at reducing the enemy's will to resist."
In response to this recommendation, FDR and Churchill proposed
issuing a joint statement to the German army and the German people declaring that the Allied armies, which were clearly winning
the war, did not seek the destruction of Germany, but only the elimination of the Nazi party. "The choice," the statement concluded,
"lies with the German people and the German army."

Ike received a copy of the statement on November 25 and
responded to it, in a cable to Marshall, on November 27:

> I consider that the present moment is not repeat not the best
> for any statement. I believe it should follow upon some operation
> that would be universally recognized as a definite and material
> success. The enemy knows we are now having difficulty particu-
> larly with weather and that our advances are laborious and slow.
> Consequently I think that a statement at this moment would
> probably be interpreted as a sign of weakness rather than [as] an
> honest statement of intention. The conditions which would estab-
> lish perfect timing in my opinion could occur on this front or on
> the eastern front but I am quite sure that the best opportunity
> would be when we are moving forward rapidly in some important
> sector.

In any competitive enterprise, psychological warfare can be
valuable, and any good poker player knows the value of a skillful
bluff. But what happens when the other guy tells you to put your
money where your mouth is? Avoid hollow declarations and empty
threats.

◆ ◆ ◆

Lesson 203

"The Soldier Is the Army"

I get so eternally tired of the general lack of understanding of what the infantry soldier endures.

—Letter to Ernie Pyle, December 15, 1944

"The soldier is the army," George S. Patton Jr. declared more than once, meaning that, for all its officers, command structures, equipment, weapons, and vast numbers, an army ultimately comes down to the individual, how that individual feels, what that individual thinks, and how that individual performs. This is true of any organization, and the failure to understand and appreciate this truth will, sooner or later, bring any organization down.

If any single figure in World War II understood the principle behind *The soldier is the army* even more eloquently than Patton, it was the beloved war correspondent Ernie Pyle. Ike wrote him a letter, thanking him for sending him a signed copy of *G.I. Joe*, Pyle's latest account of the ordinary dogface in combat:

> I enjoyed it all. . . . But the one thing in your book that hits me most forcibly is a short sentence at the top of the fifth page where you announce yourself as a rabid, one-man, army, going full out to tell the truth about the infantry combat soldier. This sentence gives me an idea for a useful post-war job. I should like you to authorize a hundred per cent increase in your army. (I mean in size, not in quality) and let me join. I will furnish the "brass" and you, as in all other armies, would do the work. In addition, I will promise a lot of enthusiasm because I get so eternally tired of the general lack of understanding of what the infantry soldier endures that I have come to the conclusion that education along this one simple line might do a lot toward promoting future reluctance to engage in war. The difference between you and me in regard to this infantry problem is that you can express yourself eloquently

upon it; I get so fighting mad because of the general lack of appreciation of real heroism—which is the uncomplaining acceptance
of unendurable conditions—that I become completely inarticu-
late. Anyway I volunteer. If you want me you don't have to resort
to the draft.

4

FROM CRISIS TO VICTORY

The greatest hazard of the European war's closing months was created, paradoxically, by the Allies' own accumulating successes and accelerating momentum. These gave rise to a condition Eisenhower dubbed "victory fever." Ike always exuded optimism, which, in the darkest hours, was often an act, albeit a bravura performance that was thoroughly believable. Outwardly optimistic, he was always at heart a realist. In mid-December 1944, when the Germans staged a surprise counterattack in the Ardennes—the Battle of the Bulge—Eisenhower overrode Bradley, Montgomery, and others (who dismissed the massive German counterattack as a mere feint) and ordered the 101st Airborne and elements of the Tenth Armored Division to hold the village of Bastogne at all costs while most of Patton's Third Army wheeled ninety degrees from its relentless eastward advance to march north to prevent the destruction of the critically weak Allied position in the Ardennes.

In the end, Eisenhower's decision turned an Allied setback, as potentially catastrophic as it was almost impossible to believe, into a triumph that significantly hastened the total collapse of the Nazi war machine.

If victory fever was the greatest danger Eisenhower faced in the later stages of the war, he created one of the war's greatest controversies by his decision to allow the Soviet Red Army, advancing from the east, to capture Berlin. As Eisenhower saw it, this was strictly a military decision. The Soviets were much closer to Berlin than were the Western Allies, and they had more soldiers available to take it. Berlin, Eisenhower felt, was a political rather than a military objective. Moreover, General Omar N. Bradley estimated that taking the German capital would cost one hundred thousand Allied casualties, an expenditure Eisenhower was unwilling to make when so much of the German army had yet to be destroyed.

With the Western Allies advancing from the west and the Red Army from the east, Germany collapsed in a military surrender that spanned May 7–8, 1945. The lessons in this chapter focus most sharply on establishing and maintaining priorities, on necessary compromise, on addressing the sometimes conflicting interests of diverse stakeholders, on identifying the key facts in a mountain of data, and, above all, on transforming crisis into opportunity.

◆ ◆ ◆

Lesson 204

Leadership Trinity

Tactics, logistics, and morale—to these three the higher commanders and staffs devoted every minute of their time.

—*Crusade in Europe*

Naming tactics, logistics, and morale, Ike identified a leadership trinity essential in dealing with the daily tasks of war and, in fact, essential to leadership in any high-stakes enterprise.

Tactics, he said, are concerned with gaining "the best possible line from which to launch" the best possible attack. Logistics are necessary to "meet our daily needs and to build up . . . supplies and to bring in the reserve troops we would need in order to make [an] attack decisive." If tactics are about initiating an operation, logistics are about sustaining it, so that it will be effective and meaningful. "And always we were concerned in morale," which provides "*élan*," the strength, the very life force that can elevate doubtful operations to success and amplify successful operations to greatness. No leader can afford to neglect any member of this trinity.

◆ ◆ ◆

Lesson 205

Profit from It

There will be only cheerful faces at this conference table.

—To officers meeting in his Verdun
headquarters, December 19, 1944

By the end of 1944, the Allied armies were afflicted with a disease Eisenhower called victory fever. There was an almost universal belief among Allied commanders and troops that the Germans had been beaten and could offer no more serious resistance.

Then, on December 16, 1944, Adolf Hitler launched Operation Autumn Fog, a fierce and massive counteroffensive against Troy Middleton's U.S. VIII Corps, First Army, which was thinly spread across the Ardennes near the town of Bastogne, Belgium. At first, receiving dispatches in his Luxembourg headquarters, General Omar N. Bradley dismissed the assault as a mere "spoiling attack," a harassment of little consequence. By the evening, however, it had become clear that this was the unthinkable. "This is no spoiling attack," Ike said. It was a major German offensive. It quickly forced a large salient—or "bulge"—into the VIII Corps sector. Bradley picked up the phone and ordered George S. Patton Jr. to send an armored division to Middleton's aid. On December 18, Bradley summoned Patton to an emergency meeting with Eisenhower and others at Eisenhower's headquarters in Verdun.

Ike's G-2—his intelligence officer—opened the meeting solemnly by painting the situation in the Ardennes in the darkest possible shades. When he had finished, Ike quickly rose from his chair.

"The present situation is to be regarded as one of opportunity to us and not of disaster," he declared, as if to dispel the gloom created by his G-2. "There will be only cheerful faces at this conference table" (Carlo D'Este, *Eisenhower: A Soldier's Life*. New York: Henry Holt, 2002, p. 644).

Ike was not ignoring reality. The assault on Bastogne and the associated Battle of the Bulge, which had just begun, were desperately dangerous for the Allies. If the Germans could seize Bastogne, a key crossroads, they could divide the Allied forces in two and, quite possibly, penetrate all the way to Antwerp, which now served as a key port of supply for Allied forces. The battle had quickly assumed menacing proportions; major Allied losses were being inflicted by the hour; and, soon, the entire 101st Airborne and part of the Tenth Armored Division, sent to the area, would be utterly surrounded in Bastogne. But Ike saw an opportunity for an Allied counterattack, which would catch the Germans overextended, cut them off, and destroy them. If a desperate Allied defense could be converted into a strong counteroffensive, there was an opportunity to break the back of the best units remaining in the German army. In terms of the cliché, victory could indeed be snatched from the jaws of defeat.

One officer who most appreciated Ike's aggressive optimism in this situation was Patton, who promised that he could attack by December 21 with three divisions. But even Ike was skeptical about this.

"Don't be fatuous, George," he said. "If you try to go that early, you won't have all three divisions ready and you'll go piecemeal. You will start on the twenty-second and I want your initial blow to be a strong one! I'd even settle for the twenty-third if it takes that long to get three full divisions." (The meeting in Eisenhower's headquarters is reported in Martin Blumenson (ed.), *The Patton Papers 1940–1945*. New York: Da Capo, 1996, p. 599, and D'Este, *Eisenhower*, p. 680.)

But Patton insisted, and, driven in part by Eisenhower's order to convert disaster into triumph, he set about doing just that. Elements of his Third Army turned abruptly to the north, advanced on Bastogne, relieved the 101st, and went on to deal a crippling blow to the German army, which would never mount another offensive again.

A foolish leader denies danger and disaster. A great leader sees the opportunity in both, then summons the will and the skill to transform defeat into victory. It begins with an order not merely to reject pessimism, but to convert it to optimism—on the spot and in an instant. "If things go well," Ike wrote to General Brehon Burke Somervell on December 17, "we should not only stop the [German] thrust but should be able to profit from it."

◆ ◆ ◆

Lesson 206

Demand Transparency

I have always insisted upon honesty and frankness as the basis of all our dealings.

—Memorandum to J.C.H. Lee,
December 18, 1944

When Ike heard from the War Department that it "has trouble, from this Theater only, in getting clear and definite information directly from the Theater Chief of Transportation, particularly involving details of shipping," he was concerned. When it was further "intimated to me that our Chief of Transportation is not allowed to talk freely and frankly" to his counterpart in the War Department, he was furious.

Ike fired off a memorandum to the theater chief's boss, J.C.H. Lee:

> Since I have been a Theater Commander I have always insisted upon honesty and frankness as the basis of all our dealings with the War Department and with other headquarters. This applies to staffs as well as to Commanders. Consequently I can see no reason why such facts as may be in the possession of our Chief of Transportation should not be given with the utmost frankness to the proper officials in Washington.
>
> I desire that our Chief of Transportation have the greatest possible latitude and freedom in handling his difficult job and that any interference coming from inexperienced staff control be immediately eliminated, if there is any such.

Demand transparency—honesty and frankness—in all communications among members of your organization. Without it, as Ike protested, "we are not talking the same language and working from the same set of facts."

◆ ◆ ◆

Lesson 207

Hand Everyone a Rifle

This is just to remind you of the vital importance of insuring that no repeat no Meuse bridges fall into enemy hands intact. If necessary service units should be organized at once to protect them.

> —Cable to Omar N. Bradley,
> December 19, 1944

As the Battle of the Bulge developed, Ike wanted to ensure that the Germans did not reach the Meuse River, let alone cross it, enabling them to advance farther west. He authorized the use of "service units"—rear-echelon supply troops and the like—to be brought up front to guard the bridges.

When the need is great, hand everyone a rifle. That's why the army trains every soldier, regardless of his assigned specialty, to shoot and to fight. Cross-training is a good idea in any enterprise. If a customer is going without attention and there's no one from sales to help him, it's great to have someone from the back office, trained in sales, who can step in to fill the gap.

◆ ◆ ◆

Lesson 208

Get the Job Done

You now have an opportunity for a great service.

> —Message to Jean de Lattre de Tassigny,
> December 20, 1944

On December 18, 1944, General Jacob Devers wrote to Eisenhower to report that French major general Jacques-Philippe Leclerc, commanding the French Second Armored Division in the French First Army, had requested transfer from the *French* First Army to the U.S. Seventh Army. Leclerc was discouraged because French operations against the so-called Colmar pocket—a concentration of

German strength at Colmar in the Alsace—were bogged down, and he had lost confidence in General de Lattre de Tassigny.

Ike suggested to Devers that he "tell General Leclerc that you have studied sympathetically his desire to be reassigned to Seventh American Army, but that present mission of reducing pocket is one for a single army commander and he must stay on his present job until it is complete." He further suggested to Devers that he tell Leclerc that "if he will get busy and push hard to eliminate the pocket you can the more quickly consider returning his division to control of the Seventh Army."

Ike included in his cable to Devers a motivational message for Leclerc's superior, General Jean de Lattre de Tassigny, commander of the French First Army:

> You now have an opportunity for a great service to France, a service worthy of your gallant army and your brilliant reputation. You can now, by determined action, complete the operation you so energetically initiated a month ago. Quick completion of the task will save your forces in the long run, will give you splendid opportunity to refit and retrain for further great tasks and will allow other troops to concentrate more effectively. I request that you strike swiftly with your full might in the cause of France and the United Nations. With my continued respect and admiration.

Do not allow frustration to interfere with a job that must get done. Shine a light to the end of the tunnel and make it your business to persuade people to finish what they have begun.

◆ ◆ ◆

Lesson 209

No Scapegoats, Please

In no quarter is there any tendency to place any blame upon Bradley.

> —Cable to George C. Marshall,
> December 21, 1944

Even while the Battle of the Bulge raged, Ike asked General Marshall to promote Omar N. Bradley to four-star rank. While he knew that some might object that Bradley had failed to plan for a German offensive against the Ardennes and was slow to recognize it when it finally came, Ike told Marshall that "this would be a most opportune time to promote" him because a promotion "now would be interpreted by all American forces as evidence that their calm determination and courage in the face of trials and difficulties is thoroughly appreciated here and at home. It would have a fine effect generally."

Ike laid it on the line personally: "I retain all my former confidence in" Bradley, despite a "failure . . . to evaluate correctly the power that the enemy could thrust through the Ardennes." This, Ike pointed out, "astonished" not just Bradley, but all of us "without exception." Bradley, however, "has kept his head magnificently and has proceeded methodically and energetically to meet the situation."

Nothing is served by scapegoating the person in charge, especially when the organization is in the very midst of recovering from the crisis at hand. On the contrary, do what you can to reinforce confidence in the leadership of the enterprise.

◆ ◆ ◆

Lesson 210

Reciprocate

I am aware that a request of this nature would inevitably entail my giving reciprocal information to the Russians, which I am quite ready to do.

—Cable to the Combined Chiefs of Staff,
December 21, 1944

Noting a "tendency recently for German divisions formed or reforming in the east of Germany to move to the Western Front," Ike considered "it essential that we should obtain from the Russians at the earliest possible moment some indication of their strategical and tactical intentions," and he asked the Combined Chiefs for help in obtaining this information from the notoriously uncommunicative and secretive Red Army. He was, he announced, quite willing to reciprocate with full information concerning his own intentions.

Reciprocity is the engine that drives virtually all human endeavor. In urgent need of information, Ike was willing to trade value for like value. He knew he could do no less, because the principle is elementary: you cannot expect something for nothing, no matter what your job title or official authority.

◆ ◆ ◆

Lesson 211

Make the Handoff, Part 1

Now that you have been placed under the Field Marshal's [Montgomery's] operational command I know that you will respond cheerfully and efficiently to every instruction he gives.

> —Duplicate cables to William H. Simpson
> and Courtney Hodges, December 22, 1944

On December 20, at Eisenhower's direction, the U.S. First and Ninth Armies were put under the operational command of British field marshal Bernard Law Montgomery as elements of the Twenty-first Army Group. Ike had made the move because he judged that it was the most effective way to manage the Allied northern flank in the ongoing response to the Nazi offensive in the Ardennes (the Battle of the Bulge). But it was a very unpopular decision—and Montgomery did not make it any more popular by loudly voicing his attitude that he had "saved" the Americans during the Battle of the Bulge. Even if Montgomery had behaved himself, Ike knew that assigning operational command of two American armies to the senior British commander would meet with some resentment, so he prepared the handoff very carefully in cables to the two American army commanders:

> In the recent battling you and your army have performed in your usual magnificent style and your good work is helping create a situation from which we may profit materially. It is especially important now that everyone be kept on his toes and that all of us look and plan ahead with calm determination, and with optimism, to taking advantage of all opportunities. Now that you have been placed under the Field Marshal's operational command I know that you will respond cheerfully and efficiently to every instruction he gives. The slogan is "chins up." Please make sure that all your subordinate commanders exert the maximum of leadership and example in sustaining morale and convincing every man that he is in better condition than the enemy. Good luck and let us seek a real victory.

This simple message is a minor masterpiece of persuasion. Ike expressed appreciation and supreme confidence in the American commanders of the First and Ninth Armies, Hodges and Simpson, who were now subordinate to the British Montgomery, and he was almost casual in voicing his expectation that the two will "respond cheerfully and efficiently" to their new commander. Yet Ike also subtly expressed empathy for what he knew were at best their ambivalent feelings about serving under this new commander: "The slogan is 'chins up.'" Finally, Ike requested—he did not order or even direct—that Hodges and Simpson maintain high morale throughout their commands.

Sometimes you must make unpopular decisions. Ramming them down the collective throat of your organization will only amplify their unpopularity. Make your expectations clear with a calm, matter-of-fact confidence designed to produce compliance and cooperation rather than create added resistance and diminished confidence and morale.

◆ ◆ ◆

Lesson 212

Make the Handoff, Part 2

I have just dispatched messages of encouragement and appreciation to both Hodges and Simpson.

—Cable to Bernard Law Montgomery,
December 22, 1944

Just as Ike prepared the commanding generals of the U.S. First and Ninth Armies to accept their new operational commander, Bernard Law Montgomery, so he offered Montgomery a word or two to prepare him for his new command.

Dear Monty:

I have just dispatched messages of encouragement and appreciation to both Hodges and Simpson. I know you realize that Hodges is the quiet reticent type and does not appear as aggressive as he really is. Unless he becomes exhausted he will always wage a good fight. However, you will of course keep in touch with your important subordinates and inform me instantly if any change needs to be made on United States side.

I have told both Simpson and Hodges that high morale, cheerful response to your instructions and optimistic planning ahead are the slogans we must keep before us. Good luck!

Handing off responsibility can be a delicate matter. Say too much, and you telegraph your lack of confidence in the person to whom you have given the new job. Say too little, and you leave him to sink or swim—at the peril of the entire enterprise. Ike kept his handoff message brief, useful, and friendly. He informed Montgomery that he had personally requested "high morale" and "cheerful response" from Simpson and Hodges, and he also took pains to share with Montgomery important information about the personality of

Courtney Hodges—that his quiet and reticent manner were real but also deceptive, making him appear less aggressive than he really was. This was an insight Montgomery—and, consequently, the Allied effort—could not afford to be without.

◆ ◆ ◆

Lesson 213

Move from Crisis to Confidence

But we cannot be content with . . . mere repulse.

—Message to Allied Expeditionary Force
troops, December 22, 1944

Once the breakout from Normandy had been accomplished toward the end of June 1944 and Patton was put at the head of the Third Army in August, the Allied ground forces, most of the time (with the notable exception of Montgomery's ill-fated Operation Market-Garden), advanced from one triumph to the next. Like everyone else, the famously optimistic Eisenhower was heartened by this progress, but he entertained one significant fear: a dread of what he called victory fever.

Soldiers are no different from the people in your organization, people organized to undertake a collaborative enterprise. Their mood is greatly influenced by the perception of prevailing conditions. In the early days of the war, when the Nazis seemed unstoppable, that mood was typically grim and wary, but, thanks to inspired leadership, it was also resolutely determined. As Christmas 1944 approached, with the enemy defeated at practically every turn, the mood was more straightforwardly jubilant. Eisenhower feared it had become overconfident, and when, contrary to all expectation, the Germans mounted a massive surprise offensive against the thinly held Ardennes region, it was Ike who first recognized the move as something more than a mere feint. ("This is no spoiling attack," he had said.) To almost everyone else, it seemed inconceivable that the "beaten" Germans were any longer capable of such an attack.

Eisenhower gave orders to reinforce the Ardennes front, but Allied casualties nevertheless mounted rapidly. At the height of the crisis, he issued a message to the troops of the Allied Expeditionary Force. It was neither a desperate plea nor an I-told-you-so proclamation. Instead, it was an interpretation of the devastating German offensive as obvious evidence not of an Allied failure but of Allied success.

> The enemy is making his supreme effort to break out of the desperate plight into which you forced him by your brilliant victories of the summer and fall. He is fighting savagely to take back all that you have won and is using every treacherous trick to deceive and kill you. He is gambling everything, but already, in this battle, your unparalleled gallantry has done much to foil his plans. In the face of your proven bravery and fortitude, he will completely fail.

When a crisis strikes, the greatest enemy is a collective sense of powerlessness, of victimization. Eisenhower attacked this head-on by focusing on what the soldiers of his command had indisputably achieved. Characteristically, he addressed them directly, as "you," framing the first part of his message as a call to protect "all that *you* have won."

Ike would not stop, however, with this rally to the defense. In a single-sentence paragraph, he continued: "But we cannot be content with his mere repulse." It was the fulcrum on which Eisenhower raised crisis to the level of confidence, redefining threat as opportunity—a brilliant stroke of leadership:

> By rushing out from his fixed defenses the enemy has given us the chance to turn his great gamble into his worst defeat. So I call upon every man, of all the Allies, to rise now to new heights of courage, of resolution and of effort. Let everyone hold before him a single thought—to destroy the enemy on the ground, in the air,

everywhere—destroy him! United in this determination and with unshakable faith in the cause for which we fight, we will, with God's help, go forward to our greatest victory.

Never turn away from adversity. Dive into it. Dive into it, eyes wide open for opportunity, no matter how deeply submerged. The Battle of the Bulge, which began as an Allied disaster, stunningly sharp and cruel, quickly ended in the destruction of the last credible force the enemy could muster on the margins of his homeland. After this battle—because of this battle—Allied victory was assured.

◆ ◆ ◆

Lesson 214

Never Lose the "Feel" of Your Troops

[R]egardless of preoccupation with multitudinous problems of great import, [the commander] must never lose touch with the "feel"' of his troops.

—*Crusade in Europe*

Modern leaders in every field seem to fear no accusation more than that of micromanagement. Ike himself pointed out that a top-level commander "can and should delegate tactical responsibility and avoid interference in the authority of his selected subordinates." Nevertheless, he continued, the top commander "must maintain the closest kind of factual and spiritual contact with them or, in a vast and critical campaign, he will fail" (*Crusade in Europe*).

Maintaining the required contact calls for "frequent visits to the troops themselves"—personal visits, without artificial ceremony, visits that include genuine conversation, which means listening as well as talking. These take time and effort, and they are often accompanied by the miserably anxious feeling of tearing yourself away from the "big picture" work that is also critical to victory.

However, allow yourself to lose the "feel" of your troops, and you will lose the war.

◆ ◆ ◆

Lesson 215

Dealing with a Power Grab

I assure you that in this matter I can go no further.

—Letter to Bernard Law Montgomery,
December 31, 1944

Days after Eisenhower assigned command of the Twenty-first Army Group—which included the U.S. First and Ninth Armies—to him, Montgomery wrote Eisenhower a message calling on him also to assign him control (if not outright command) of Omar N. Bradley's Twelfth Army Group. He wanted, he said, to avoid another "failure"—by which he meant the initial losses suffered during the German Ardennes offensive (the Battle of the Bulge)—and he insisted that the only way to do that was to issue an order that "From now onwards full operational direction, control and co-ordination . . . is vested in C-in-C [commander-in-charge] 21 Army Group"—that is, himself.

Ike's initial reaction to this communication was sublime anger. He had already given Montgomery overall command of two American armies—and now the field marshal wanted even more. Worse, Montgomery had presented his demand for more authority as a kind of ultimatum: "I am certain that if we do not comply . . . then we will fail again." Yet instead of acting on his anger, Ike formulated a reasoned, calm, but absolutely firm reply, which unmistakably drew the lines that needed to be drawn:

> In the matter of command I do not agree that one Army Group
> Commander should fight his own battle and give orders to another

Army Group Commander. My plan places a complete U.S. Army under command of 21 Army Group, something that I consider militarily necessary, and most assuredly reflects my confidence in you personally. If these things were not true this decision could, in itself, be a most difficult one.

You know how greatly I've appreciated and depended upon your frank and friendly counsel, but in your latest letter you disturb me by predictions of "failure" unless your exact opinions in the matter of giving you command over Bradley are met in detail. I assure you that in this matter I can go no further.

Please read this document carefully and note how definitely I have planned, after eliminating the salient, to build up the 21 Army Group, give it a major task, and put that task under your command. Moreover, Bradley will be close by your hq [headquarters].

I know your loyalty as a soldier and your readiness to devote yourself to assigned tasks. For my part I would deplore the development of such an unbridgeable gulf of convictions between us that we would have to present our differences to the CC/S [Combined Chiefs of Staff—the joint Anglo-British command authority]. The confusion and debate that would follow would certainly damage the good will and devotion to a common cause that have made this Allied Force unique in history.

As ever, your friend . . .

It is quite possible—and often very necessary—to refuse a demand without alienating the person who makes it. The key is to refuse the demand and not the person. Address issues instead of personalities.

It is easier to alter the issues than it is to try to "fix" a human being. On an issue, you may be as hard as necessary. But go hard on a person, and you may provoke resentment, anger, fear, defiance, or any number of destructive emotions and attitudes.

◆ ◆ ◆

Lesson 216

Do the Right Thing

This opportunity to volunteer will be extended to all soldiers without regard to color or race.

—Draft directive, January 4, 1945

It was not until July 26, 1948, three years after World War II had ended, that President Harry S. Truman issued Executive Order 9981, mandating that "all persons in the Armed Services" were to receive "equality of treatment and opportunity . . . without regard to race." During World War II, the U.S. Army, like the other services, was strictly segregated, and black soldiers were usually relegated to service organizations and labor battalions rather than assigned to combat units. The jobs they were generally given were hard, but menial.

In the crisis created by the Battle of the Bulge, Ike needed all the combat soldiers he could get, and he therefore directed the commanders of the rear echelon, which included service and labor troops, "to survey our entire organization in an effort to produce able bodied men for the front lines."

This process of selection has been going on for some time but it is entirely possible that many men themselves, desiring to volunteer for front line service, may be able to point out methods in which they can be replaced in their present jobs. Consequently, Commanders of all grades will receive voluntary applications for transfer to the Infantry and forward them to higher authority with recommendations for appropriate type of replacement. *This opportunity to volunteer will be extended to all soldiers without regard to color or race but preference will normally be given to individuals who have had some basic training in Infantry.* Normally, also, transfers will be limited to the grade of Private and Private First Class unless a non-commissioned officer requests a reduction.

In the event that the number of suitable negro volunteers exceeds the replacement needs of negro combat units, these men will be suitably incorporated in other organizations so that their service and their fighting spirit may be efficiently utilized.

Do the right thing—for the organization and for the people who make up the organization. In the interests of both, Ike was willing to defy the social standards, norms, and expectations of his time. (Some 2,250 African American troops immediately responded to the directive, some accepting a reduction in grade to qualify for combat service. By February, 4,562 African American soldiers had volunteered for front-line service under the terms of Eisenhower's directive.)

◆ ◆ ◆

Lesson 217

Speak for Yourself

Please make certain that people in your organization responsible for dispatching telegrams do not use words purporting to express my personal opinions unless they know exactly what they are.

—Letter to J.C.H. Lee,
January 5, 1945

Someone in the office of General J.C.H. Lee, commander of the Services of Supply in the European theater, sent a cable to General Marshall over Eisenhower's signature, enthusiastically inviting representatives of the U.S. tire industry to visit the front: "It is believed that such a trip will increase the output of urgently needed tires. I agree with this proposal and would welcome such a group in the theater."

Marshall was annoyed at this waste of time and told Eisenhower as much. Ike immediately wrote to Lee. True, he had said that he would accept a visit by the tire workers, but he knew "nothing about production problems at home and the only opinion I expressed was that I was ready to cooperate, as far as we can, with people at home who bear this responsibility." Ike had better things to do than personally shepherd peripheral visitors, and he warned General Lee to make certain that, in the future, no one in his organization would "use words purporting to express my personal opinions unless they know exactly what they are."

The visit of a delegation of tire workers was no great crisis. However, Ike recognized a potentially serious problem in the release of messages that put words in his mouth. Such instances, he knew, had to be vigilantly policed, because, next time, the unauthorized ventriloquism might have much more serious consequences—not that provoking the army chief of staff to annoyance was a small matter. Let no one speak for you unless he or she truly does speak for you.

◆ ◆ ◆

Lesson 218

There's More Than One Way to Cross the Rhine

I am . . . making logistical preparations which will enable me to switch my main effort from the north to the south should this be forced upon me.

—Cable to the Combined Chiefs of Staff,
January 20, 1945

The Rhine River was one of the great strategic and symbolic objectives of the European war. To cross it would be to enter the German heartland, an unmistakable herald of the final defeat of the enemy. Eisenhower and his commanders understandably devoted a great deal of thought to the crossing, and Ike decided that providing alternatives to meet all contingencies was key:

It will be realized that a crossing of the Rhine, particularly on the narrow frontages in which such crossings are possible, will be a tactical and engineering operation of the greatest magnitude. I propose to spare no efforts in allotting such operations the maximum possible support. For this purpose I envisage the use of airborne forces and strategic air support on a large scale. In addition I foresee the necessity for the employment on a very large scale of amphibious vehicles of all types. The possibility of failure to secure bridgeheads in the north or in the south can not, however, be overlooked. I am, therefore, making logistical preparations which will enable me to switch my main effort from the north to the south should this be forced upon me.

Two clichés are indispensable to leadership: "Don't put all your eggs in one basket" and "There's more than one way to skin a cat."

◆ ◆ ◆

Lesson 219

On Censorship

In war, censorship to ensure security of information which might be of value to the enemy is obviously necessary, but following cessation of hostilities censorship must be abandoned, and a free flow of information insisted upon, so that education and public opinion may be based on truth.

—Letter to Wilbur Studley Forrest,
January 26, 1945

Ike wrote to Forrest, chairman of the Committee of the American Society of Newspaper Editors, to explain his stand on censorship. It was a necessary evil in war, but had no place in peace. All other things being equal, "a free flow of information" is the best policy for any ethical and competent organization.

◆ ◆ ◆

Lesson 220

Focus on Value, Not on Cost

I have seen press reports . . . to the effect that the Ardennes battle [Battle of the Bulge] was the costliest in American history. May I suggest it was also one of the most profitable.

> —Cable to George C. Marshall,
> February 27, 1945

In the Battle of the Bulge, American forces inflicted more than one hundred thousand casualties against an attacking force of half a million, suffering, in turn, casualties almost as heavy. It was certainly the biggest battle of the European war, and although it began as an American catastrophe, it ended as an American triumph. The last German offensive was utterly crushed, and whereas the Americans could make up their losses, the Germans could not. On this desperate battle, Hitler had spent most of his irreplaceable combat-worthy reserves, and he had exposed his Luftwaffe, already in dire extremity, to a blow that neutralized it for the last months of the war. Ike did not deny that the battle was terribly costly, but it was also enormously profitable. It broke the back of the Nazi military.

Cost is important in any endeavor, but value—the calculus of cost *and* profit—is the only meaningful measure in the end. You must never allow cost to be considered in isolation.

◆ ◆ ◆

Lesson 221

Do the Best with What You Have

From time to time I find short stories where some reporter is purportedly quoting non-commissioned officers in our tank formations to the effect that our men, in general, consider our tanks very inferior in quality to those of the Germans.

> —Letter to Maurice Rose, March 18, 1945

The Sherman tank, the main battle tank of the U.S. Army through most of World War II, was no match, going one-on-one, with the German Panther and Tiger tanks. Discouraged and fearful U.S. tank crews even took to calling their Shermans "Ronsons," a reference to the popular brand of cigarette lighter whose advertising slogan was "Lights up every time." It seemed to them that whereas American tank rounds bounced harmlessly off German armor plate, whenever a Panther or Tiger scored a hit on a Sherman, the round instantly penetrated and the tank burst into flame.

Ike investigated personally.

"My own experience in talking to our junior officers and enlisted men in armored formations is about as follows," he reported.

> Our men, in general, realize that the Sherman is not capable of standing up in a ding-dong, head-on fight with a Panther. Neither in gun power nor in armor is the present Sherman justified in undertaking such a contest. On the other hand, most of them realize that we have got a job of shipping tanks overseas and therefore do not want unwieldy monsters; that our tank has great reliability, good mobility, and that the gun in it has been vastly improved. Most of them feel also that they have developed tactics that allow them to employ their superior numbers to defeat the Panther tank as long as they are not surprised and can discover the Panther before it has gotten in three or four good shots. I think that most of them know also that we have improved models coming out which even in head-on action are not helpless in front of the Panther and the Tiger.

Ike refused to ignore the very real fact of the one-on-one inferiority of the Sherman, but he also could not ignore the fact that the Sherman, produced by the thousands, was *the* American tank of the war. He had, therefore, to motivate his officers and men to do the best they could with what they had, and he made it his business to determine just what this "best" was and could become.

Neither willful ignorance nor useless whining is an effective response to the discovery that your equipment, organization, or situation is less than optimal. The first step is to face the facts, then to figure out what can be improved and what cannot, and, finally, to determine how to do your best with what you have. This process of study complete, show everyone how to do the best they can with what they have, then persuade them to do it.

◆ ◆ ◆

Lesson 222

Be Objective About Your Objectives

May I point out that Berlin is no longer a particularly impor-tant objective.

—Cable to George C. Marshall,
March 30, 1945

No decision Dwight D. Eisenhower made as supreme Allied com-mander was more controversial than his choice to leave Berlin to the Red Army. Ike's reasons for turning south and away from the German capital included a belief that German diehard resistance was mounting in the south, that the Red Army was closer to Berlin than the armies of the Western allies, and that the cost of taking Berlin would be excessively high, with General Bradley predicting Allied casualties of over 100,000. (In fact, the Red Army suffered more than 330,000 casualties in the Battle of Berlin.)

All these considerations were important, but for Eisenhower the most critical reason for bypassing Berlin was that it distracted his armies from their principal objective, which was not to capture a city but to destroy an army. Capture a city, and the war could still grind on. Destroy an army, and the war would end.

He went on to explain to General Marshall that the usefulness of Berlin "to the German has been largely destroyed and even his government is preparing to move to another area." A day later, in a cable to Montgomery, Ike remarked that Berlin "has become, so far as I am concerned, nothing but a geographical location, and I have never been interested in these. My purpose is to destroy the enemy's forces and his powers to resist."

Ike acknowledged powerful psychological and political reasons for taking Berlin, but at this culminating stage of the war, he believed it far more important simply to destroy the enemy army. True, this was a less emotionally compelling objective than the capture of the hated German capital, but it was, in practical terms, a more efficient means of reaching the one objective that trumped all others: ending the war.

If the choice is between symbolic triumph and actual victory, sacrifice the symbol.

◆ ◆ ◆

Lesson 223

Anyone Can Have a Good Idea

[W]e cannot afford to overlook any possible chance for an improvement in our methods.

—Letter to Private First Class Paige M.
Jackson, April 1, 1945

In a handwritten letter dated March 12, 1945, and sent to Eisenhower via his company commander, Private Jackson suggested that front-line troops should sew a piece of colored signal panel cloth inside their jackets, so that they could readily identify themselves to the Allied air forces by simply reversing their jackets. This, he believed, would go far in preventing "friendly fire" incidents, such as the accidental strafing or bombing of Allied ground troops by Allied aircraft. Ike personally replied to Jackson:

I have had a number of copies made of your letter to me and am forwarding them without delay to all American Army Commanders in this Theater. These officers are constantly seeking new ideas to improve battlefield technique, and if they find your suggestion a practicable one you may be sure it will be quickly employed.

Whether or not any or all of these officers consider that your idea provides an improvement over present methods for identification of ground troops from the air, I want to assure you of my appreciation for your interest and initiative. Thank you very much for the trouble you took in committing your idea to paper, because we cannot afford to overlook any possible chance for an improvement in our methods.

Good ideas can come from anyone (even a PFC). Evaluate the idea *before* you pass judgment on the source.

◆ ◆ ◆

Lesson 224

Why We Fought

We continue to uncover German concentration camps . . . in which conditions of indescribable horror prevail.

—Cable to George C. Marshall,
April 19, 1945

As the Allied armies advanced deeper into Germany and liberated the Nazi concentration camps, Eisenhower was anxious to reveal their horrors to the world and to American political leaders. "I have visited one of these [camps] myself and I assure you that whatever has been printed on them to date has been understatement. If you would see any advantage in asking about a dozen leaders of Congress and a dozen prominent editors to make a short visit to this theater in a couple of C-54's, I will arrange to have them conducted to one of these places where the evidence of bestiality and cruelty is so overpowering as to leave no doubt in their minds about the normal practices of the Germans in these camps."

Know the stakes for which you fight or work. Know them first-hand and intimately. Then communicate them to others.

◆ ◆ ◆

Lesson 225

Psyched for the Stretch

This victory of Allied arms is a fitting prelude to the final battles to crush the ragged remnants of Hitler's armies of the west, now tottering on the threshold of defeat.

—Message to the troops, April 20, 1945

Poor performance in the stretch can still lose the race, even if you're way out ahead. Always wary of "victory fever," Ike sent a message to his troops, congratulating them on their victory in the Battle of the Ruhr, even as he took care to define it not as the end of the war, but as a "fitting prelude to the final battles":

To Every Member of the A.E.F.:
          The battle of the Ruhr has ended with complete success. Following hard upon the final destruction of the German forces west of the Rhine, the 21st Army Group thrust powerfully across that river with the U.S. Ninth Army under command. Simultaneously, rapid drives across the Rhine and from the Remagen bridgehead by 12th and 6th Army Groups provided the southern arm of a great double envelopment which completely encircled the entire German Army Group "B", and two Corps of Army Group "H", whose mobility was rendered almost zero by our magnificent and tireless air forces. Thereafter, in the pocket thus created the 12th Army Group eliminated 21 enemy divisions, including 3 panzer, 1 panzer grenadier and 3 parachute divisions. Over 317,000 prisoners of war were captured including 24 generals and 1 admiral. Many tanks and more than 750 guns were destroyed or taken.

Booty is immense and still being counted. The enemy's total losses in killed and wounded will never be accurately known.

The rapidity and determination with which this brilliant action was executed tore asunder the divisions of Field Marshal Model, and enabled all Army Groups without pause to continue their drive eastwards into the heart of Germany.

This victory of Allied arms is a fitting prelude to the final battles to crush the ragged remnants of Hitler's armies of the west, now tottering on the threshold of defeat.

Recognize and celebrate achievement not as history over and done with, but as the prelude to future achievement and ultimate victory.

◆   ◆   ◆

Lesson 226

A Leader Defined

Bradley, Spaatz, and Patton have become symbols. In the reputations of those men the mass sees its own deeds appreciated, even glorified.

—Cable to George C. Marshall,
April 27, 1945

On April 26, 1945, Eisenhower replied to a query received from General Marshall: "Would [Omar] Bradley care to go out [to the Pacific] as an army commander with present group staff, all at a later date?" Ike recommended against sending Bradley to the Pacific, saying that he would be needed in Europe after the surrender. Even more important, he felt that reducing Bradley from an army group commander to the commander of a single army, under the imperious Douglas MacArthur no less, would have the "effect of diminishing Bradley's stature in the post-war army and public opinion and

it is my conviction that we should prevent any such possibility at
all costs." Ike elaborated on this in another cable, which he sent the
following day:

> [I]t is certain that the mass feeling of the 3,000,000 American
> soldiers here is that they have done a remarkable job. The men
> remember the situation existing when we started shipping this
> Army to France three years ago, and recall the respect, if not awe,
> in which we then held the German fighting prowess. They
> regard their accomplishments with great pride. This mass feeling is
> shared by officers as well as men. For a tremendous number of
> them, names such as Bradley, [Army Air Forces general Carl]
> Spaatz, and Patton have become symbols. In the reputations of
> those men the mass sees its own deeds appreciated, even glorified.
> . . . I realize that a commander of [Bradley's] outstanding ability
> should scarcely be kept out of the battleline as long as there is
> fighting to do and except for the importance of the intangibles I
> have attempted to describe, I would readjust my own contem-
> plated organization here so as to let him go. But I believe it best he
> should stay.

As a leader, you invest in the people of your organization, even
as they invest in you, so that you become the symbolic vessel into
which they pour their collective identity, pride, and sense of
achievement. This is a leadership function quite literally incalculable in its impact on performance.

◆ ◆ ◆

Lesson 227
Dealing with de Gaulle

I must of course accept the situation.

—Letter to Charles de Gaulle,
April 28, 1945

Of all the difficult people Eisenhower had to deal with, including an assortment of American and Allied generals and political leaders, Charles de Gaulle was certainly the thorniest. From the beginning of the war, he was the courageous and bold embodiment of Free France, the nucleus around which a government in exile was built, and, for many in the French resistance movement, a leader and a symbol. De Gaulle regarded himself as the only legitimate head of the French state—and wanted to ensure that others did likewise. Anxious to help France recover its national identity and honor, he was ever wary of being forced into a subordinate role by Churchill, Roosevelt, Eisenhower, or anyone else. Haughty in the extreme, he often brought Ike to the very edge of his patience, but never quite pushed him over. Eisenhower always remained firmly anchored by his awareness that the compliance of de Gaulle was the key to securing organized and effective military and political cooperation from the French resistance, the French population, and the Free French army.

During the closing days of the war, on April 23, the French First Army captured Stuttgart. On April 24, however, U.S. forces under Lieutenant General Jacob L. Devers moved into the city. Seeking to avoid entanglement of French and American lines of communication, Devers ordered the French First Army to evacuate Stuttgart. Hearing of this, de Gaulle issued an order to General de Lattre, commanding the French First Army "to maintain a French garrison in Stuttgart and to institute immediately a military government." General de Lattre, therefore, refused to hand over the city to Devers, who, in turn, appealed to Eisenhower. Angry with de Gaulle's refusal to cooperate, Eisenhower nevertheless relented in a strongly worded letter to the him:

> I am informed that your instructions to General de Lattre were to hold Stuttgart and all other territory occupied by the First French Army until the French Zone of Occupation has been delimited. I am sure you must realize that the location of Stuttgart in connection with any French Zone of Occupation did not enter the minds

of either General Devers or myself, as this is a matter entirely outside the scope of my responsibility, which is limited to the military defeat of our common enemy, Germany.

Under the circumstances, I must of course accept the situation, as I myself am unwilling to take any action which would reduce the effectiveness of the military effort against Germany, either by withholding supplies from the First French Army or by any other measures which would affect their fighting strength. Moreover, I will never personally be a party to initiating any type of struggle or quarrel between your government and troops under my command, which could result only in weakening bonds of national friendship as well as the exemplary spirit of cooperation that has characterized the actions of French and American forces in the battle line. Accordingly, I am seeking another solution for the maintenance of the Seventh Army.

As usual, Ike acted from his conviction that nothing could be allowed to trump the supremacy of Allied amity and cooperation. But, as indicated by the italicized passage that follows, he also included in his response to de Gaulle a strong hint of the limit of such cooperation when it ceased to be mutual:

I believe that the issuance direct to the First French Army of orders based on political grounds which run counter to the operational instructions given through the military chain of command, violates the understanding with the United States Government under which French divisions, armed and equipped by the United States, were to be placed under the Combined Chiefs of Staff whose orders I am carrying out in this Theater of Operations. It was with complete faith in this understanding that I have so long and so earnestly supported French requests for armament for additional divisions.

In the present circumstances I can do nothing else than fully to inform the Combined Chiefs of Staff of this development, and to point out that I can no longer count with certainty upon the operational use

of any French forces they may contemplate equipping in the future
[italics added].

Even when you cannot give vent to your strong feelings in a
frustrating situation, it may be possible to give warning of the *natural* consequences of the action to which you object. That is what
Ike did here. His approach with difficult people was not so much to
chastise them as it was to show them how they themselves would
have to live with the consequences of their own difficult behavior.
Often—though not in this case—the approach won the concession
or cooperation he sought.

◆ ◆ ◆

Lesson 228

The Human Problems

I share your concern over the human problems.

—Cable to George C. Marshall,
April 18, 1945

With the war in Europe rapidly coming to an end, Eisenhower and
other top commanders were faced with the question of "redeployment"—deciding what troops to retain in the European theater for
occupation duty, what troops to send back to the United States (and
out of the armed forces), and what troops to dispatch to the Pacific
theater, where the war against Japan was now bloodier than ever.
    Contrary to the belief of some that top command was interested
only in troop strength—sheer numbers and the transfer of sheer
numbers—Ike wrote, "I recognize that [redeployment] problems
must be solved promptly and with human understanding if the
Army is to retain the confidence of the people at home for the con-
tinuation of the war against Japan as well as for the future. Our soldiers must be convinced that the system is fair and impartial."
Whatever solution was reached, Ike pledged that "All soldiers will

be informed fully . . . of the governing conditions in redeployment and why these conditions have been established."

Ike elaborated on the importance of "fairness and speed" the next day in a letter to General Jacob Devers:

> The fairness and speed with which redeployment is carried out will be reflected in public support of the Pacific Campaign, in the future attitude of the public to the Army, and in the confidence of the returned soldier in Army command. Failure to return all those eligible for discharge to the United States at the earliest possible date will not only result in a loss of confidence by the soldier in the Army, but will also develop an unfavorable public opinion which could well result in a loss of the good will built up by the Army in its successful campaigns.
>
> When the bell rings, we must be prepared to release the high-point men [soldiers who had accumulated the most points for time served] in each combat division who are eligible for discharge, even though it results in an immediate reduction of divisional strength below the authorized figures.
>
> We must prepare now so that we can release these men promptly when the time comes and all factors relating thereto have been announced. It is not a subject to gossip or talk about. It does require thinking ahead, determining how the approved factors can be applied so that the release of those found eligible under the system can be effected with minimum loss of efficiency to the command but with maximum dispatch.
>
> We must not follow blueprint designs rigidly, but must apply the established policies with human understanding. This requires the personal attention of the commander in all command echelons. The pattern of redeployment must be followed with utmost concern.

Making major decisions that affect the lives of members of the organization is not simply a matter of weighing the needs of the enterprise against those of the individual, but also of recognizing that in many respects, the needs of the enterprise coincide with the needs of the individual. Sound policy applied uniformly and with complete transparency throughout the organization is essential, but it is also important to exercise flexibility within policy when principles of fairness are at stake. The ethics, the human decency, of an organization are founded on the ethical judgment of *individuals* concerning *individuals* and not on blind adherence to policy, no matter how generally just that policy may be.

◆ ◆ ◆

Lesson 229

Dealing with Monty

But you have kept me on the rails in difficult and stormy times, and have taught me much.

—Letter from Bernard Law Montgomery,
after the victory

You can't just get rid of "difficult" people. In fact, some of them are the most talented and able people you've got. They may even be indispensable.

No major subordinate—Patton included—was more difficult for Ike to deal with than Bernard Law Montgomery, but none was more important to deal with effectively. Ike was proud of the letter Monty sent him shortly after the surrender of the German army. It showed how well Montgomery understood himself—and the problems he so often created for the supreme Allied commander—and it also showed how much he truly appreciated the leadership of Dwight D. Eisenhower:

Dear Ike:

Now that we have all signed in Berlin I suppose we shall soon begin to run our own affairs. I would like, before this happens, to say what a privilege and an honor it has been to serve under you. I owe much to your wise guidance and kindly forbearance. I know my own faults very well and I do not suppose I am an easy subordinate; I like to go my own way.

But you have kept me on the rails in difficult and stormy times, and have taught me much.

For all this I am very grateful. And I thank you for all you have done for me.

Your very devoted friend,
Monty

◆ ◆ ◆

Lesson 230

Surprise

[Soviet marshal Zhukov] agreed with me that destruction of enemy morale must always be the aim of the high command. To this end nothing is so useful as the attainment of strategic surprise.

—*Crusade in Europe*

When Ike met with Georgy Zhukov, marshal of the Red Army, at the end of the European war, the two discussed (among many other things) the role of morale in gaining victory. They agreed that destroying the enemy's morale was a crucial leadership goal and that the best way to do this was through "strategic surprise," which Ike understood to mean "a surprise that suddenly places our own forces in position to threaten the enemy's ability to continue the war, at least in an important area." The demoralizing effect of strategic surprise was always heightened by the addition of "tactical surprise that arouses the fear in the enemy's front-line units that they are about to be destroyed." Ike had a deep personal understanding of the potency of strategic surprise. The Battle of the Bulge had suddenly presented the possibility of a major Allied defeat on the very verge of victory, and on the tactical level, as Ike admitted, "the early effect on morale of front-line troops was noticeable."

In any competitive endeavor, surprise is a powerful force. On the largest scale—strategy—surprise is all about making the competition believe that it is impossible for them to continue to compete. On the more intimate scale of day-to-day competition, tactical surprise threatens the other fellow's latest project or his cash cow.

Achieving surprise requires the strong leadership of a highly flexible organization, which can execute bold moves quickly and with confidence. It also calls for a leader willing to do no less than destroy the competition.

◆　◆　◆

Lesson 231

The Greatest Responsibility of Leadership

At the war's beginning the average Army officer . . . placed too much faith in a surface discipline based solely upon perfection in the mechanics of training.

—Crusade in Europe

Ike's admiration for the American soldier was enormous: "The trained American possesses qualities that are almost unique. Because of his initiative and resourcefulness, his adaptability to change and his readiness to resort to expedient, he becomes, when he has attained a proficiency in all the normal techniques of battle, a most formidable soldier." But "even he has his limits," and it is the business of leadership to address and overcome them while optimizing all the soldier's best qualities. "The preservation of his individual and collective strength is one of the greatest responsibilities of leadership."

Ike was an ardent believer in discipline and training, but, by the end of the war, he had come to a realization that these, crucial as they are, were not sufficient to preserve the "individual and collective strength" of the American soldier.

> At the war's beginning the average Army officer, both regular and civilian, placed too much faith in a surface discipline based solely upon perfection in the mechanics of training. Commanders are habitually diffident where they are called upon to deal with subjects that touch the human soul—aspirations, ideals, inner beliefs, affection, hatreds. No matter how earnestly commanders may attempt to influence a soldier's habits, his training, his conduct, or extol the virtues of gallantry and fortitude, they shyly stop short of going into matters which they fear may be interpreted as "preaching."

There is no such thing as impersonal leadership. Those who try this approach may become efficient at pigeonholing and herding, but they should not deceive themselves into thinking that they are exercising leadership. All real leadership is personal and refuses to shy away from the "subjects that touch the human soul." Aspirations, ideals, inner beliefs, affection, hatreds—these subjects constitute the greatest responsibility of leadership.

◆ ◆ ◆

Lesson 232

Define the Victory

I have the rare privilege of speaking for a victorious army of almost five million fighting men.

—V-E Day speech, prepared May 4, 1945

Dwight Eisenhower's extraordinary victory speech, prepared for broadcast on V-E Day, reveals a leader who thoroughly identified with his cause and his organization. He saw his final role as defining the meaning of Allied victory for and on behalf of the forces he both led and represented:

I have the rare privilege of speaking for a victorious army of almost five million fighting men. They, and the women who have so ably assisted them, constitute the Allied Expeditionary Force that has liberated Western Europe. They have destroyed or captured enemy armies totalling more than their own strength, and swept triumphantly forward over the hundreds of miles separating Cherbourg from Lubeck, Leipzig and Munich.

More than three years ago Great Britain, China and Russia were desperately defending themselves against the onslaughts of mighty military machines, deliberately prepared to implement the Axis purpose to dominate the world. The dastardly crime of Pearl Harbor brought us suddenly and actively into that war. Our nation, always unwilling to attribute evil purposes to any people, and unready to withstand surprise attack, found itself beaten back from some of its important outposts and unable to take prompt and effective action to combat the enemy's designs. But America, fortunate in the quality of her leadership, did not become the easy prey envisaged by her self-confident assailants. Our late great President immediately met with that other indomitable spirit, Prime Minister Churchill, the man who had successfully led his country through the dark days of '40 and '41, when Great Britain stood defiantly alone as the unconquered foe of Nazism.

Even while Allied defenses in the far Pacific were still crumbling under the swift attacks of the Japanese, these great leaders, and their able lieutenants, began devising the gigantic plan of which the first two difficult parts have now reached glorious consummation.

In the very beginning the United States and Great Britain determined to combine themselves into a true partnership for the prosecution of the war. They adopted as their first objective the crushing of the European Axis. This task they undertook *first* because only here was it possible for three great powers, Russia, Great Britain and the United States, to concentrate their full might against one part of the widely separated Axis powers.

Realizing that battlefield efficiency demanded unification in action as well as in purpose, America and Great Britain decided to place their combined forces, in every theater, under single command. Out of adherence to this principle has flowed success. Air—ground—navy—supply—all have been combined into one great team without regard to national or personal considerations. Into this team have been drawn representatives of many other nations. All have absorbed the same spirit of loyalty and team-play—and their success in working effectively together under conditions of stress and strain—of difficulty and of success—is something of which every participating country can always be proud. Here the United Nations have proved the possibilities of real cooperation. And let me remind you, at home, of your own place in this team. Without your unremitting labor, your financial and moral support—without your determination, nothing could have been accomplished. We, here, clearly recognize this and are proud to feel that you and ourselves are one.

With the progress of the war in this Theater every family, every individual, is familiar. The dramatic accomplishments of G.I. Joe and his comrades of every nation—fighting in the air, on the land and on the sea—have been recorded for you daily by press and radio. . . .

Since that June day when our men first landed upon the Normandy beaches, one of the notable campaigns of all time has been carried out. Working in effective cooperation with the great Red Army and the Allied Forces fighting in Italy, the French, British, American and other Allied forces in this Theater have battled their way with ever-increasing speed and power through the most formidable defenses that Germany could devise.

The soldier, the sailor and the airman, supported by the devoted efforts of thousands laboring in the services of supply, and aided by numerous comrades in the Resistance movements, first won the battle of the beaches. They won the pursuit across France, the campaign to destroy the Germans West of the Rhine and the crossing of that historic obstacle. Then they pierced to the heart of Germany to join up there with their Russian and Allied comrades coming from the East and from the South. This has been no separate war of air, of ground, or of sea. All have been welded together into one engine of avenging power—to the dismay and destruction of our enemies.

These startling successes have not been bought without sorrow and suffering. In this Theater alone 80,000 Americans and comparable numbers among their Allies, have had their lives cut short that the rest of us might live in the sunlight of freedom. Four hundred thousand of our citizens have borne the pain of physical wounds, and additional thousands have suffered privation in Nazi prison camps. The American men and women of this Theater, constituting the mightiest military force the United States has ever committed to action, solemnly salute our own honored dead and extend to every relative, to every friend of all these, our deepest sentiments of respect and sympathy.

But, at last, *this* part of the job is done. No more will there flow from this Theater to the United States those doleful lists of death and loss that have brought so much sorrow to American homes. The sounds of battle have faded from the European scene.

Permit me now a more personal word.

It has been my great honor, and equal responsibility, to command Allied Forces in the Mediterranean, and, later, the Allied Expeditionary Force in Europe. This gives me the right to voice my lasting appreciation to numbers of people that have by their consideration, their understanding and their efficiency, made my task a bearable one.

To my own superiors in the British-American Combined Chiefs of Staff and the political heads of our two countries, I address my profound thanks. We here realize fully the immeasurable debt we owe to their wisdom, their forbearance and their staunch support. We trust that all our people have the same realization.

Merely to name my own present and former principal subordinates in this Theater is to present a picture of the utmost in loyalty, skill, selflessness and efficiency. The United Nations will gratefully remember Tedder, Bradley, Montgomery, Ramsay, Spaatz, de Lattre and countless others. But all these agree with me in the selection of the truly heroic man of this war. He is G.I. Joe, and his counterpart in the air, the navy, and the Merchant Marine of every one of the United Nations. He has surmounted the dangers of U-boat infested seas; of bitter battles in the air; of desperate charges into defended beaches; of tedious, dangerous, fighting against the ultimate in fortified zones. He has uncomplainingly endured cold, mud, fatigue; his companion has been danger, and death has trailed his footsteps. He and his platoon and company leaders have given to us a record of gallantry, loyalty, devotion to duty and patient endurance that will warm our hearts for as long as those qualities excite our admiration.

So—history's mightiest machine of conquest has been utterly destroyed. The deliberate design of brutal, world-wide rape that the German nation eagerly absorbed from the diseased brain of Hitler, has met the fate decreed for it by outraged justice. The self-styled super-race that six years ago set out on a career of pillage is now grovelling amongst the ruins of its own shattered cities as it fearfully hopes for a better fate than it inflicted upon its own helpless victims. Throughout the United Nations the rejoicing bells peal forth.

Those bells voice our happiness that the nazi scourge has been eliminated from the earth. But for the remaining enemy of humankind—Japan—those bells are sounding an imminent doom. The complete armed might of liberty and freedom is at last free to turn from the elimination of the principal criminal to the punishment of its equally despicable satellite. Already our comrades in the Pacific have made great inroads into her vitals. Japan herself must now realize her fate is sealed.

All of us here have one underlying ambition; to return speedily to our families. But we entered this war to do our duty to our country and to the cause that remains as sacred today as on that December 7th when we suddenly found ourselves at war. Wherever any man is called he will continue to do his part in assuring the completeness of victory. Some of us will stay here to police the areas and the nation that we have conquered, so that systems of justice and of order may prevail. Some will be called upon to participate in the Pacific war. But some—and I trust in ever-increasing numbers—will soon experience the joy of returning home.

I speak for the more than three million Americans in this Theater in saying that, when we are so fortunate as to come back to you, there need be no welcoming parades, no special celebrations. All we ask is to come back into the warmth of the hearts we left behind and to resume once more pursuits of peace—under our own American conceptions of liberty and of right, in which our beloved country has always dwelt.

To his own commander, army chief of staff General George C. Marshall, Ike defined the victory far more simply, in a one-sentence cable: "The mission of this Allied force was fulfilled at 0241, local time, May 7th, 1945." It was his last communication of the war.

Afterword

Lieutenant General Daniel Christman, USA (ret.)

We gathered frequently in the dining room of Quarters 100—the elegant residence for nearly two hundred years of the superintendent of the United States Military Academy at West Point—for spirited but relaxed conversation on history, politics, leadership, cadet life. As the academy superintendent in the late 1990s, I relished this give-and-take. We brought to the academy during this period some of the best thinkers and writers on leadership, strategy, and history that our nation has produced; the supper conversation reflected the energy of the participants. A frequent question proffered by many quests during these gatherings was a simple one: "General Christman, whom do you regard as West Point's most distinguished graduate?"

The "menu" of distinguished alumni was a rich one: Grant, Lee, MacArthur, Goethals, Groves, Pershing, Bradley, Patton, and Eisenhower, among others. Indeed, statues and monuments to many of these graduates literally loomed outside the window of the superintendent's quarters. Despite compelling arguments for many on the list, the consensus seemed always to focus on one graduate: Dwight D. Eisenhower, USMA Class of 1915. The reasons were varied, but one theme dominated the informal assessments: Eisenhower's brilliant command of Allied forces in the European theater during World War II. More than any other officer, Ike set the standard for successful supreme command in coalition operations; the principles he articulated and personified in the 1940s continue to guide senior military commanders in today's equally complicated geopolitical environment.

But in my view, even more profound than Ike's brilliance as a coalition commander was his influence in shaping modern leadership principles for officers in armies of a democracy. Without question, Ike had no equal in stroking, cajoling, and ultimately successfully managing such prickly alliance personalities as Churchill, Montgomery, de Gaulle, Admiral Darlan, and Italian Marshal Badoglio—to say nothing of his challenges with the irrepressible Patton. He was indeed the consummate supreme commander. Yet Ike also knew what it took to lead soldiers and build cohesive units at the tactical level; he was passionate about leadership and leader development. Through his suggestions to army leaders immediately following World War II, Eisenhower influenced not only the formal leadership program of the U.S. Military Academy but also the leadership ethic for generations of young officers who were commissioned after 1945.

In both arenas—supreme command and officer leadership—Eisenhower was a revolutionary. Before Eisenhower, no U.S. commander had been entrusted with coalition command. General Pershing fought to maintain the integrity of U.S. forces as commander of the American Expeditionary Force in World War I, but he was subordinate to the French commander in chief; Ike led Allied forces from fall 1942 and, by war's end, had over four million men from five nations under his command. His nuanced and personalized approach to combined command complemented a sophisticated coalition leadership model, a model employed by successive supreme commanders into this century.

"Unity of command" was Eisenhower's simple organizing principle, but he knew that placing a single person in charge was insufficient to ensure unity of effort. Unity of effort could only be achieved, as Eisenhower himself emphasized, through "earnest cooperation," earned in turn by a supreme commander through "patience, tolerance, frankness, and absolute honesty in all dealings, particularly with all persons of the opposite nationality." Two NATO supreme Allied commanders in the 1990s, General George Joulwan in Bosnia and General Wesley Clark in Kosovo, achieved coalition success despite numerous intra-alliance squabbles by sticking to Eisenhower's maxims. Most poignantly, during NATO's peace enforcement mission in Bosnia in 1996, General Joulwan faced the conundrum of Russian subordination to NATO command and control. Joulwan stuck to his guns in insisting on unity of command and helped broker a creative compromise with the Russians that gave the supreme commander in Europe what he needed: clear authority to direct *all* forces in his area of operation. Joulwan would never have achieved this had he not treated his Russian partner with "patience, tolerance, and absolute honesty."

Similarly, two Central Command (CENTCOM) combatant commanders, Generals Norman Schwarzkopf and John Abizaid, profited enormously from the trailblazing coalition experiences of Dwight Eisenhower. Known as "Stormin' Norman" for his occasional volcanic outbursts as a U.S. commander, General Schwarzkopf displayed a sophisticated knowledge of alliance sensitivities and alliance politics by deftly managing more than thirty coalition partners in Operation Desert Storm. He clearly personified the concept of unity of command. But he knew this could never be effectively exercised unless he had the consent of those he led, particularly his Arab partners, most visibly the Saudis. Again, Dwight Eisenhower's principles of coalition leadership proved decisive—and enduring. And they are reflected in the leadership exercised in 2005 by the coalition commander in Iraq, General John Abizaid, a student of the art of command and especially the leadership model of Dwight Eisenhower.

More than four-star generals have been the beneficiaries of Ike's focus on leadership, however. Besides revolutionizing the doctrine of combined command at the most senior levels, Eisenhower was passionate about leadership fundamentals for junior officers. What he observed in the behavior of many U.S. officers in the European theater disturbed him greatly. Too many officers, in his view, never identified with their soldiers; they operated mechanically and were too removed from the needs of their troops. Further, Ike was appalled by the behavior of junior officers who substituted screaming and, on occasion, physical abuse of subordinates for positive leadership. A quotation often attributed to Ike reflected this concern: "You don't lead by hitting people over the head; that's assault, not leadership."

Shortly after World War II, Eisenhower addressed officer leadership shortfalls as a central feature in a letter to West Point superintendent General Maxwell D. Taylor. Ike told Taylor that he felt matters of leadership should "receive the constant and anxious care of the Superintendent and his assistants on the academic board." Eisenhower thought that the curriculum should include coursework in what he termed "practical and applied psychology." He felt that it was important to "awaken the majority of cadets to the necessity of handling human problems on a human basis," and thereby to improve leadership in the army at large.

Eisenhower's suggestion was followed shortly thereafter by the establishment at the academy of the Department of Military Psychology and Leadership. It has existed for over fifty years, and although the title has been changed to Behavioral Sciences and Leadership, the department's impact in instilling in cadets the principles of small unit leadership is one of the most important developments at the academy in its two-hundred-year history. Prior to the Eisenhower-Taylor letter, West Point had no formal instruction in leadership; the subject was simply learned "on the job." Today, leader development is the core mission component of the academy. The emphasis is on values, inspiration, and imagination. Ike knew these could not be created in the intellectual equivalent of a straitjacket, with rote, mechanical instruction disconnected from the "human" problems of the individual soldier. Eisenhower shared his vision of leadership with his son, John, who was a cadet while Ike served as supreme commander; in discussion with his colleagues, Ike also shared his frustration with the leadership he observed in theater; and he imparted his vision of twenty-first-century leadership to Maxwell Taylor, who had the wisdom to act on Ike's vision. The result of the Eisenhower revolution in leader development is a U.S. officer corps universally recognized as the most professional cohort in the world.

Ike returned to West Point in 1965 for the fiftieth reunion of his class. It was also the graduation week for my own West Point class, and I had the chance to meet and chat with Eisenhower prior to lunch. It was a moment I cherish to this day. The supreme commander who "connected" with his troops and who shaped the leadership ethic of my generation was an engaging conversationalist. It was the Ike I admired from film and history: the supreme commander who took the time to write to parents of his soldiers, to talk to 101st Airborne Division paratroopers prior to their D-Day jump, to prescribe leadership doctrine while he commanded millions. He was, in short, inspirational. And he personified the essential bond—trust!—that ties leader to led in armies of a democracy. His soldiers trusted him because he exuded the essential values of integrity and respect, values that remain the core of our army's leadership doctrine.

The most moving memory I have of Eisenhower's passing is a Bill Mauldin cartoon published in 1969, shortly after Eisenhower's death. It was a drawing of a U.S. military cemetery, with hundreds of crosses and stars of David sketched in the background. In the foreground were the simple words, "It's Ike himself. Pass the Word!" From an artist who popularized the GIs "Willie and Joe" during World War II, it was a tribute that spoke volumes—about leadership, about greatness, and about West Point's most distinguished graduate.

The Author

Alan Axelrod is the author of many business and management books, including the *BusinessWeek* best-sellers *Patton on Leadership* and *Elizabeth I, CEO*, as well as books on military history, U.S. history, and general history. He has served as consultant to Siemens AG, Earl Swensson and Associates Architects, Richard E. Steele Jr. and Associates, and Saint Joseph's Hospital of Atlanta, and to numerous museums and cultural institutions, including The Henry Ford, the Metropolitan Museum of Art, the Margaret Woodbury Strong Museum, the Airman Memorial Museum, and the Henry Francis du Pont Winterthur Museum. A sought-after speaker, Axelrod has been featured at the Conference on Excellence in Government; the Leadership Institute of Columbia College; the annual conference of the Goizueta School of Business, Emory University; and elsewhere. He has been a creative consultant (and on-camera personality) for *The Wild West* television documentary series (Warner Bros., 1993), *Civil War Journal* (A&E Network, 1994), and the Discovery Channel, and has appeared on MSNBC, CNN, CNNfn, CNBC, and the major broadcast networks as well as many radio news and talk programs, including National Public Radio. He and his work have been featured in such magazines as *BusinessWeek, Fortune, TV Guide, Men's Health, Cosmopolitan, Inc.*, and *Atlanta Business Chronicle*.

After receiving his Ph.D. in English (specializing in early American literature and culture) from the University of Iowa in 1979, Axelrod taught American literature and culture at Lake Forest College (Lake Forest, Illinois) and at Furman University (Greenville,

South Carolina). He then entered scholarly publishing in 1982 as associate editor and scholar with the Henry Francis du Pont Winterthur Museum (Winterthur, Delaware), an institution specializing in the history and material culture of America prior to 1832. His first book, *Charles Brockden Brown: An American Tale*, a groundbreaking study of the first professional novelist in the United States, was published by the University of Texas Press in 1983, and his second book, *The Colonial Revival in America*, published by W. W. Norton in 1985, chronicled the nineteenth- and twentieth-century popular passion for all things colonial.

Following a stint as associate editor at Van Nostrand Reinhold in 1984, he became senior editor at Abbeville Press from 1984 to 1991 and then vice president of Zenda, a consulting firm to museums and cultural institutions. In 1994, he left Zenda to become director of development for Turner Publishing, a subsidiary of Turner Broadcasting System, and in 1997, he founded the Ian Samuel Group, a creative services and book-packaging firm.

Axelrod's most recent books include *Patton: A Biography* (Palgrave Macmillan, 2006), *Lincoln's Last Night* (Chamberlain Brothers/Penguin, 2005), and *Office Superman: Make Yourself Indispensable in the Workplace* (Running Press, 2004).

Index

North Atlantic Treaty Organization
(NATO), 13, 14, 281–282

O

Occupation: jurisdictional squabbles and,
184; military priorities and, 13, 130,
227–228, 261–262; redeployment for,
227–228, 269–271
Offenses: easing, 159, 177–178; not
holding a grudge about, 110–111
On-the-job training, 72
Openness, 231, 263–264
Operation Anvil-Dragoon, 169, 180,
187–188, 223–225
Operation Autumn Fog, 241–242.
See also Battle of the Bulge (Ardennes)
Operation Avalanche, 72, 132–134, 143,
145–146, 181
Operation Desert Storm, 283
Operation Husky. See Sicily invasion
Operation Market-Garden, 250
Operation Overlord: conduct of, 215–238;
launch of, 207–214; overview of,
11–12, 129–130; planning and
preparations for, 166–207. See also D-
Day
Operation Shingle, 163, 180
Operation Sledgehammer proposal, 45–46
Operation Torch: alternative plan for,
59–60; Churchill's plan for, 11, 15–16,
46; Eisenhower's command of, 11,
15–16, 71; focus on, 51–52; launch of,
72–79; mobilization and planning for,
37–69; Patton and, 65; personnel
conflicts in, 52–53; success of, 71
Opportunism, 61–62
Opportunity: turning apology into,
175–177; turning crisis into, 209–210,
241–242, 250–252
Optimism: mandating, 42; realism and,
209–210, 239; seeing opportunity and,
242; wishful thinking and, 145–146
Overconfidence. See Victory fever
Ownership, 209–210

P

Pacific theater, 275, 278; deployment
decisions and, 269–271
Palermo conquest, 72
Panama Canal Zone, 6
Panic, 49
Panther tanks, 216–217, 260
Papers of Dwight David Eisenhower: The War
Years (Chandler), 14
Paperwork reduction, 231–232

Paris, liberation of, 13, 130, 227–228
Partners, securing, 80–81
Passing the buck, 20, 93–94, 232–233
Patriotism, 151–152
Patton, General G. S., Jr., 183, 281;
appointment of, to II Corps command,
107, 108; in Battle of the Bulge, 239,
241, 242, 250; dog of, 170; Eisenhower's
early friendship with, 5–7, 101–102;
Eisenhower's support for, 65, 75,
109–110, 126–127, 155–159, 196–197;
on foxholes, 142; on leadership, 120;
leadership qualities of, 126–127,
265–266; Mediterranean and Italy
conquests by, 72; military pedigree of, 3;
naming of, as Deputy Commander for
Ground Forces, 98–99; 1942 messages
to, 66, 74–75, 85; 1943 messages to,
101–103, 109–110, 112; in Operation
Torch, 75; on perfection, 48; problems
with, 65, 92, 101–102, 109–110, 126,
129, 155–159, 171, 193–197, 281;
slapping incidents of, 109, 126,
155–159; on soldiers, 237
Patton Papers, The (Blumenson), 194,
242
Pearl Harbor, 9, 15, 17, 27–28, 275
People: allocation of, 91, 192–193; getting
to know, 234; importance of things
versus, 95; investment in, 31–32, 266;
redeployment of, 227–228, 269–271;
requirements for, 39; retention of good,
66, 90–91, 109–110, 183, 193–197; as
solution, 64. See also Personnel
management
People skills, 126, 127, 146–147
Perfection, attitude about in war and
business, 48–49
Performance: dismissal for poor, 105,
137–138, 215–216, 218–219;
evaluation of, 69, 125–127; as measure
of individual's value, 68–69; setting
high standards for, 67, 79–80, 99–100;
unsatisfactory, 218–219; waiting for, 93
Pershing, General J. J., 7, 281, 282
Personal time, 29. See also Life-work
balance
Personality: command presence and, 36;
conflicts of, 12, 44, 52–53, 131,
172–174, 177–178, 266–269, 271–272;
fears of cult of, 36; individual
responsibility and, 37–38
Personnel management, 109–110,
192–193. See also Dismissal; People;
Promotion; Retention